W9-CMM-886

Civility and Disobedience

TO SALLY

CIVILITY
AND
DISOBEDIENCE

BURTON ZWIEBACH

Queens College, City University of New York

CAMBRIDGE UNIVERSITY PRESS

CAMBRIDGE

LONDON • NEW YORK • MELBOURNE

FERNALD LIBRARY
COLBY-SAWYER COLLEGE
NEW LONDON, N. H. 03257

Published by the Syndics of the Cambridge University Press
The Pitt Building, Trumpington Street, Cambridge CB2 1RP
Bentley House, 200 Euston Road, London NW1 2DB
32 East 57th Street, New York, NY 10022, USA
296 Beaconsfield Parade, Middle Park, Melbourne 3206,
Australia

© Cambridge University Press 1975

Library of Congress Catalogue Card Number: 74-12977

ISBN: 0 521 20711 8

First published 1975

Printed in USA

Typeset by Radnor Graphic Arts, 320 King of Prussia Road,
Radnor, Pennsylvania; printed and bound by Halliday Litho-
graph Corporation, Hanover, Massachussets.

JC
328.3
Z85

67950

Contents

Preface

A preface to an essay on disobedience can serve many purposes, but one of them must be to justify the existence of the book itself. In a word, this book seeks to criticize and refute the conventional view of disobedience, to indicate the relation of disobedience to the fundamental political question of obligation, and to create a justification of obligation which may perhaps stand up – as the others, in my opinion, do not – to critical inspection. I do not claim, as justification for this book, that I have succeeded. I do claim to have attempted to do what most writers on disobedience do not do: to make a strong case for disobedience and to show that, in order to discuss the problem soundly and realistically, it must be treated as part of a larger and more fundamental set of issues.

I did not always see the problem this way. When I first thought of writing a book on disobedience, I conceived of it in fairly narrow terms: it was to be an essay on the meaning of legality. The conventional defense of disobedience is that one may justifiably disobey a law thought to be unjust but that, in order to affirm one's commitment to lawfulness in principle, one must be prepared to accept the penalties imposed by law. This argument appeared to me to be especially vulnerable for its narrow view of legality. The commitment to legality imposes obligations on public authority as well as on the individual: the need of the individual to *cooperate* with public authority (by accepting punishment for his disobedience) is clearly dependent upon the extent to which public authority acts to uphold or further the principle of legality. Where public authority acts to subvert legality (as in a political trial), obedience to authority is participation in this subversion. Furthermore, the conventional view entails a narrowly positivistic definition of legality. It is possible to argue that legality refers to norms of right or justice – that is, to the integrity of the legal system conceived not merely as a set of authoritative rules, but also as a set of moral norms. Certainly, it is necessary to refer to moral norms outside of the law in order to justify the worth or need of legality – to discover *why* laws deserve obedience and why legality is itself valuable. Hence, the

vii

contention that one ought to avow loyalty to law itself is the beginning rather than the conclusion of argument.

I was also interested in attacking two other theories: the one which holds that we have a *prima facie* obligation to obey the law, and the second which holds that disobedience is rarely or never justified in a democracy where lawful means exist to change unjust laws. These theories were based, I believed, upon contradictory or ambiguous notions of legality, or else were vastly overstated and made to carry a weight of theory they could not bear.

My initial assumption that one could deal adequately with disobedience by expanding the usually narrow concept of legality proved unsatisfactory. As I began to examine the question, I became convinced that disobedience raises problems which cannot be resolved by discussion of legality alone, but which go to the heart of many of our most fundamental political dilemmas.

One of these problems involves the meaning of the concept of rights. If this concept has any validity, it must mean that public authority cannot impose on us a duty violative of a right. That is, when we have a right, we can have no duty to obey a law which violates it. This carries us far beyond the notion that disobedience is merely protest against injustice, and can be used to justify a new theory of disobedience as – in appropriate circumstances – a right itself. More important, it raises one of the most formidable questions in political theory: the question of obligation. Why and under what conditions ought we to obey public authority and the laws it makes? This is a problem central not merely to disobedience, but to fundamental matters like freedom, human rights, participation, and democracy.

Nearly all works on disobedience ignore the question of obligation. (The works of Rawls and Wolff are exceptions but, for reasons which appear in chapters 2 and 4, their arguments seem to me to be unsatisfactory.) Generally, writers treat disobedience as a discrete problem, abstracted from larger issues in political life. The results are unredeemingly superficial. Discourse on disobedience becomes an exercise in the logic of legality or worse, as in the case of Justice Fortas, a homily in behalf of judicial authority. But disobedience raises questions about themes like the meaning and extent of freedom, the limits of law, the nature of citizenship in a free society. More than this, all arguments about disobedience with which I am familiar *necessarily presuppose* views on obligation and the failure to articulate and examine these views results in discussion in which unstated assumptions ultimately determine the theoretical conclusions. To paraphrase Nietzsche, such arguments do not pervert political thinking; they merely pass over it in silence.

I encountered several difficulties in attempting to deal with obligation, but the most significant was the failure of the traditional approaches to provide adequate accounts of it. Having rejected natural rights, utility, and religion, I turned to the theory of consent, that grand and persistent accompaniment to liberalism and democracy. A study of consent theory, however, convinced me that it was incoherent and incapable of justifying obligation or providing an adequate basis for freedom. I was, then, compelled to raise the question anew and arrived at a theory which held obligation to be justified, and at the same time limited, by the need to create civil society – or, as I phrase it, a culture of civility. The concept of civil society was a brilliant invention of the seventeenth century; but as social conditions have radically changed since then, I believed it obviously necessary to redefine it, to develop a newer vision. This I attempt to do in chapter 1. The problem is, how is civility to be attained? If, as I argue, the mechanisms of classical liberalism have proved insufficient, what may be put in their place?

The answer to these questions is contained, I suggest, in the concept of the common life. Civility can be attained and obligation justified only by the creation of a common life, which is nothing less than the translation of civility into concrete political terms. The common life is the theoretical foundation for judging the rightness of the obligations imposed by public authority. It is the source of human rights. Most of chapter 3 is devoted to an examination of its meaning and texture. This concept, which has its genesis in the work of Rousseau, Marx, and Lindsay, has, I believe, another significant virtue. It is a corrective to the artificial and unsatisfactory atomistic individualism which characterized classical liberalism and whose effects can be seen in the centrifugal and anomic patterns of life in contemporary western society.

In considering the rights implicated in the concept of the common life, I was struck by the lack of systematic concern in modern political theory with a general theory of rights. Most discussions of rights are, in practice, little more than arguments *ad hoc* for the inclusion of this or that value in a theoretical bill of rights. But do the conditions of modern life not warrant a re-thinking of the bases of human rights? Believing that they do, I sought to examine my notions of civility and common life to see which values implicated in them might serve as a foundation for the articulation of rights. Ultimately, I define and justify four basic categories of rights – or conditions of obligation – grouped under the headings of citizenship, freedom, equality, and accountability.

The theory that disobedience is at times a right required, I thought, some elaboration. Clearly disobedience may take many forms: to which of them was my theory relevant? To answer this question, I endeavored to make a systematic examination of the types of disobedience which might be done of right. I did not intend to create a formal typology, but merely to consider the basic varieties of disobedience and their implications. I also wished to consider the relation of disobedience to political stability and violence – largely to dispel the common charge that disobedience leads inevitably to instability or anarchy, and to attack the connection between disobedience and violence drawn by opponents of disobedience.

A final question remained. Disobedience presents practical as well as theoretical problems. When people disobey the law and are arrested, they must (hopefully) defend themselves before and be judged by courts. Now as it is unlikely that the members of these courts will share the disobedients' view of justice or right, we are entitled to ask what relevance a justification of disobedience has in the hard world of busy lawyers and harried judges. The answer to this question is, I hope, contained in chapter 8, where I argue for the permissive treatment of disobedience in the courts. Chapter 8 thus has a very limited, but crucial, function. It is not an attempt to back away from the implications of the rest of the book: it is an attempt to meet a problem which arises in a context where the declaration that the state is illegitimate or a law viciously unjust may have no effect. In that case, unless we are prepared to abandon those who practice disobedience in order to maintain the purity of the theory upon which they act, we must fashion a more modest, and perhaps dishonorable, alternative.

Part One

CIVILITY

1. *The setting*

Liberalism, civility, and disobedience

The decade of the Sixties in America revealed a profound tension in liberalism. We are accustomed to think of this tension in terms of the dramatic realignment of forces which took place over the issues of race, poverty, and war. But equally important – perhaps more important – was the response of liberals to the protest movements and acts of disobedience which arose over these issues. Briefly, many liberals found themselves opposing the protest movements and supporting the claims of order and legality.

The reasons given to justify this response were various. Clearly, liberals have to do more than cite the virtues of order and legality which, though numerous, cannot be dominant in a philosophy which seeks to promote the claims of freedom. Liberalism, after all is a philosophy which holds political authority to be conditional and limited and which, therefore, must leave some room for various forms of resistance to authority wrongfully or excessively exercised. Recognizing this, some liberals – Kristol and Hook for example – justified their opposition to the protests and acts of disobedience by citing a different value: civility.[1]

Civility can mean many things and much of the third and fourth chapters of this book will be devoted to defining and analyzing it. In much recent liberal writing it seems to be related to a vision of society in which social conflicts are resolved through a process of non-violent accommodation – a process inconsistent with uncompromisable attachment to passionately-held ideas. A free society, in this view, is largely built upon the virtues of tolerance and the willingness to compromise demands. Further, in a democratic society, where lawful means exist to remedy injustices, the assertion and resolution of demands must take place within the law rather than against it. Civility, in this view, presupposes commitment to lawfulness and to the stability of democratic institutions.

On the face of it, this argument does not appear to be inconsistent with a commitment to freedom. But doubts arise once we reflect on the changing character of the institutions upon which the

3

liberal notion of civility is based. The institutionalization of compromise has taken the form of a politics of pluralism; while the protection of the individual against the compulsions of public authority has been pursued by giving to the individual rights against authority and by stressing the security of his property. But as pluralism has developed, it has legitimized an ever-increasing concern with stability and has tended to convert rights into interests, defined as preferences or claims subject to compromise. Moreover, the character of property has changed dramatically: the critical property in contemporary society is not the private property of the individual, but corporate property. These developments result, I shall argue, in a loss of the mechanisms which the individual may rely on to protect himself against the demands of public authority and, hence, in a diminution of individual freedom.

The changing character of civility is a result, in other words, of the changing character of the institutions of civil society. If these changes are of the nature I have suggested, it is doubtful whether civility, as it is currently understood, can be consistent with the commitments we associate with liberalism at its best. Or so I shall argue shortly. What is needed is a new conception of civility; and from this new conception, a different approach to disobedience may follow.

The changing character of authority and civility

The central thesis of this book is that disobedience is justified when it is a rightful denial of the obligation imposed by a law or other communication of authority: when, in other words, we are not obligated to do what the law or public authority commands. The justification of political obligation, I argue, depends upon the creation of public authority based upon a new concept of civility; hence, disobedience is rightfully undertaken only in the name of this new concept. I shall explicate the new concept of civility in chapters 3 and 4. For the present, it may be taken to mean the conquest of violence and barbarism in social affairs and the creation of alternative modes of conflict resolution. It is, I argue further, the condition precedent for the attainment of moral life.

This conception of civility is derived from the seventeenth-century contract theorists, and more particularly from Hobbes and

Locke. Their invention of the concept of civil society was a major theoretical development, giving to political association a moral dimension missing since the demise of Christendom while at the same time carrying forward the secularization of politics. Moreover, they characterized civility in ways keenly related to the factors threatening social disintegration at the time.

Two problems especially stood out. One – perhaps most clearly identified with Hobbes – was the instability created by vast social and economic changes and religious conflict. The second – about which Locke was especially concerned – involved the constitutional limits placed upon the ownership and use of property. As Europe shifted away from a feudal and toward a capitalist economy, the need to protect the interests of a rising and vital class, holding a new type of property, became imperative. For Locke, the entire enterprise of civil society derives from the need to protect property which exists, even as a social institution, in a state of nature.[2] It is not too much to say that, with Locke, civility comes to be identified with a stable market economy and with the freedom necessary to make such a society possible. Such a concept of civility was neither gratuitous nor unfairly narrow. The market economy could be looked upon as an important mode of limiting the arbitrary power of the state, as creating institutional protection for the individual – a wall of safety behind which he could develop his liberty.

The need in the seventeenth century was not to maintain civility but to create it. To do this, social contract thinkers – and most especially Locke, but certainly Hobbes as well although he was more circumspect about it – were willing to contemplate the institution of vast social changes, even revolutions. They thought of these not as mass revolutions, but as revolutions led and directed by elite spokesmen for the new civility and, therefore, once successful, the ground of a new and more profound stability. It is no wonder, then, that Locke refused to recognize the legitimacy of disobedience. Disobedience is an everpresent destabilizing possibility which could be indulged in by Monarchists and Catholics as well as by whiggish Protestants. But Locke knew that revolutions are rare. And if, after the Whig revolution, Monarchists and Catholics can be denied toleration – as Locke, in his *First Letter on Toleration*, argued they should be – they can be denied the security of political organization and hence some of the wherewithal to make a counter-revolution. But the same degree of organization needed to make a revolution is not required for disobedience. Revolution on Lockean terms is, hence, comparatively safe and ultimately stabilizing, while disobedience posits a continuing danger.

The fact that we have established civility (as Hobbes and Locke understood it) in the West is by no means irrelevant to my argument. Indeed, it is in certain ways critical to it. For the very attainment of the stability and protection of property which Hobbes and Locke sought raises threats of great magnitude today. Twentieth-century western society has pursued civility by developing organizational and technological arrangements which do not merely support stability, but which elevate stability into the highest of political virtues. The very institutional arrangements which Locke saw as protecting the individual from arbitrary public authority have been transformed into elements of public authority. Property organized as corporate property has developed into a form of political power indistinguishable from the power of the state, except that it is less accountable. New dimensions have been added to the notion of public authority and those dimensions now pose grave threats to the values which make authority rightful. The discussions of obligation and disobedience in this book are written in the light of these new dimensions. It is now time to explore some of them as a prelude to the discussion which follows.

The dangers of stability. I have suggested that contemporary politics makes stability the highest of political values. This is not due to the triumph of authoritarian conservatism over liberalism. It is due to the reconstruction of liberalism itself. The politics of contemporary liberalism – the public philosophy which guides the actual political behavior of men of affairs – is group politics, which reduces the goal of policymaking to the resolution and management of conflict rather than the attainment of justice and social good. In the process of doing this, group politics also restricts individuality and diversity and, necessarily, the scope of freedom itself. Let us see how this is so.

The norms of group politics are built upon a presumption of the legitimacy of political bargaining and upon an opinion that bargaining is, in normal circumstances, the preferable mode of policymaking. But bargaining, when institutionalized as a fundamental political process, has questionable consequences. If it is an exaggeration to say that the legitimization of political bargaining implies that right equals might,[3] it is no exaggeration to say that the possession of political power, of the capabilities and resources needed to form effective coalitions, are prerequisites to having one's claims considered. A bargaining system tends to exclude or dilute the claim of the disinherited, the powerless, the poor. When it considers their claims, it tends to fashion inadequate or symbolic remedies. For what impels you to bargain seriously with me? I must possess something you want or be able to do something you do not want. If I have no critical resources and can mobilize no sanctions which make ignoring my claims costly or unpleasant, there is simply no motive other than charity which requires you to consider them. Little wonder then that the powerless have been able to secure a hearing in those two antithetical forums most resistant to group politics – the courts and the streets. But, for different reasons, neither of these forums is satisfactory, however useful they may be in encouraging the system to consider the claims of the powerless.

Group politics reduces all moral claims to interests – that is, to preferences having no value other than being preferred. This is wholly consistent with the moral vision of group politics. During the formative years of liberalism, public policymaking was conceived to involve the examination of alternatives followed by the choice of an assumed right one, which was then embodied in a rule. These rules, it was hoped, would reflect the public interest or the common good. This hope appeared sensible, since the principal value systems of liberals – natural rights first, utility afterward – were thought to be simple systems whose basic principles allowed rational men to deduce right rules. Consequently, even though the majority might be excluded from formal participation in the political process, they were supposedly included in the benefits that enlightened social rules created. This supposition was strengthened by liberalism's growing attachment to democracy and progressive extension of suffrage.

Toward the end of the nineteenth century, however, doubts about the legitimacy of this process began to grow. The loss of belief in clear standards of right derivable from natural law or utility encouraged the belief that the older view of policymaking was arbitrary, that there were no easily discoverable rules of right to be applied. This loss of belief was later reinforced by the pluralist contention that concepts such as public interest and common good were ambiguous and perhaps meaningless. At best, it was argued, these were standards relevant to very few policy decisions: in the great majority of cases there simply is no interest or good common to all of society. There are only preferences of different groups. These preferences are often in conflict and groups strive to get their preferences accepted by identifying them with a public interest or common good. These phrases, then, are merely rhetorical devices. If there is a public interest, it must be interpreted as the sum of group preferences.

But in the large majority of cases, the argument continues, group preferences conflict. And in the absence of cognitively derived moral standards, the demands of different groups have no intrinsic value other than being preferred by or beneficial to those groups. In the consequent absence of an overriding, discernible public interest, how may public policy justly be made? There are, apparently, only two alternatives: the arbitrary imposition of policies by public authority or the creation of a process whereby the conflicting groups themselves reach, through a process of bargaining, a compromise acceptable to a majority. This majority is, in fact, nothing but a temporary coalition of minorities. Thus, the process creates safeguards against the tyranny of a majority as well as against that of an elite minority. The government acts as a broker, sets up some of the ground rules of the bargaining relationship, imposes certain limits to the terms of the eventual compromise, and occasionally presses for its version of right policy. It is thus, in its own right, an interest group.

Such a policy process is seen as the inevitable outcome of an open society containing powerful interest groups. But it is also held to be just because it reflects a majority assent and works toward the elimination of coercion. For if policies are the products of a system of bargain and compromise, they are in a real sense voluntary. A non-bargaining process would require obedience to rules whose rightness cannot cognitively be proven and which are therefore arbitrary. Obedience to such rules is tantamount to coercion and tyranny. By a remarkable coincidence, therefore, the realistic solution is also the preferable one, given the concerns for freedom and absence of coercion.[4]

But the reduction of political claims to interests is ultimately harmful. The protection of individual goods and individual aspirations is, at least in part, a function of the extent to which those goods and aspirations are thought to lay an authentic claim for realization upon society. But this requires a belief that these claims and aspirations are in some real sense principled *and* uncompromisable. This has often been confused with a theory of absolute rights and caricatured as a belief held only by naive rationalists or simple-minded fanatics. It need not be so, as I hope to show in chapters 3 and 4. It need only mean that, in those cases where individual goods, rights, and aspirations are seen to be crucial – where protection of things like individuality, self-assertion, diversity is in principle defensible – no significant inroad be made upon them which is not the result of a principled decision.

This notion is not so difficult to grasp. All I mean is that a restriction on a legitimate individual right ought not to be the result of a bargain struck either for the sake of convenience or stability. In the same way, the decision that something is a legitimate right cannot be made by compromising opposing interest claims. For this would violate the very meaning and significance of the concept of rights and would make rights indistinguishable from other and less imperative social norms.

Take, as an example, the notion of public support or welfare. If it is supposed that I have a right to a decent standard of living, the decision as to what the standard of public support may be is not incontestable. It may be set too low in the opinion of some and too high in the opinion of others. But the principle justifying public support in the first place demands that it be set by some means other than compromise among opposing groups, especially where the recipients are not or are inadequately represented. It is not enough for the advocates of a high standard to settle for a low one in order to effect a compromise with those who want no assistance at all. Such a procedure, however realistic, debases the society, the recipient, and the process by treating the recipient as a commodity and the issue of public support as a matter of no greater political importance than the cataloguing of mice. It is no doubt possible to entertain a theory that no one has a right to public support. In that case, the provision of welfare may be opposed or held justifiable on other grounds. It may be that there are other factors than the standard of living which are relevant. But whatever the theory, the dilemma cannot satisfactorily be resolved by escaping from principled argument and embracing a solution which is reached by avoiding the central questions. In our courts, it is common enough for juries – and judges – to resolve a case of doubtful liability by granting the plaintiff the verdict but reducing his recovery. Such a process is often a way of avoiding another principled decision: what should social policy be where one person is injured but where no one is legally or sufficiently at fault? But who can deny that it debases justice and makes law into just another ordinary business technique? Consider the justice of the plea made by Peter Townsend a decade ago:

> Why is the new increase in the rate for the single person to be 6*s*? Because, the Minister of Pensions told us last Monday, there was a 4*s* increase last September and this puts the total increase on a par with the increase in national insurance. Why should the full rate for a single person now be 63*s* 6*d* rather than, say, 70*s* or 80*s*? This is no doubt the exact amount that the Government thinks it can afford and get away with, but can a political democracy do no better than that? Is there nowhere a rational explanation, nowhere a principle?[5]

The protection of individual goods calls for legislative and judicial action which is principled – which is, at least, based on standards. No one need deny that, in the legislature, bargaining and compromise will always play a crucial role. But in some important way, if the good of individuals is to be protected, there must be limits to what bargaining may achieve and, hence, to what may be bargained over. And today these limits are being eroded by the norms of group politics; they are being eroded not only in legislatures, but even in those forums where we commonly suppose them to best protected: in the courts.

Increasingly, the impact of group politics on the courts has resulted in the conversion of ideals like free speech, fair legal process, and so forth, into ideals which more nearly approximate the norms of group politics. Increasingly, the courts have come to accept the premise that these ideals are to be considered not fundamental rights which act as firm barriers to state action, but interests —claims which can be bargained over and which express preferences rather than demonstrable values. The putting forth of a fair procedure claim entitles the judges to balance it against competing claims and, hence, to reach a satisfactory compromise between the claimants. Now clearly constitutional ideals possess no absolutely true, logical, and unique meanings and courts must be allowed to consider what things are to be weighed when deciding whether a particular legal procedure is fair. But saying this is far from saying that the interests of the state in proceeding in a certain way are to be balanced against the interests of the individual in not having it do so. The former belief is a simple outcome of the ambiguity of legal concepts and the complexity of social conditions. The latter belief is an outcome of the conviction that constitutional ideals are merely interests asserted in behalf of individuals which must be weighed against competing interests asserted in behalf of other individuals or of the state. The difference between these two beliefs is hardly negligible. Among other things, it encourages the defense of an individual person's right on the grounds that the invasion of one person's rights could lead to the invasion of everyone's rights. Lost in this argument are the crucial questions whether rights are valuable in themselves and stand for the principle of human dignity; and hence deserve protection even if the rights of only one are threatened. More important, perhaps, the conversion of rights into interests encourages individuals to frame their rights in terms of group or associative rights, in order to create an interest powerful enough to meet the social interests (in stability, efficiency, fulfillment of social preferences, and so forth) asserted in behalf of society by the government.

The conversion of rights into interests strips them of legal status as well as of traditional authority; and it legitimizes the opportunistic or partisan redefinition of these rights. For the meaning of a right can be no more stringent or principled than its capacity to bind our thinking. Both are affected by the bargaining process. The juridical reduction of rights to interests need not necessarily result in the crude replacement of the formal judicial process by an overt bargaining one. It can result in legitimizing the contraction of the notion of rights itself. Consequently, while the balancing of interests may have a serious enough effect on the judicial protection of rights, it may have an even more serious effect if it teaches us that it is right to consider the meaning of positive rights, the fulfillment of aspirations, the legitimacy of newly claimed rights not as principles to be justified by reason, but as interests to be defined and attained by bargains.

If goods, aspirations, and rights are translated into interests, and if the conflict of interests is to be resolved primarily through bargaining, it follows that the goods most likely to be protected are the goods put forward by groups – that is, the goods which can be achieved through the influence or power of coalitions. This means that the individual goods most likely to be systematically protected are those implicated in the preferences of groups. But this means that we are engaged in a profound alteration of the meaning of individuality. The conversion of rights and goods into interests will inevitably encourage those who seek to attain these things to identify them with the claims of groups, for that way at least some of their goods may be realized. Thus, individuality may come to be seen in terms of a harmony between individual and group goods – a process which must end with the individual perceiving his rights wholly in terms of group interests and being encouraged to identify his legitimate aspirations with those of groups. But this development, familiar enough in political literature, is the very antithesis of individuality. Commitment to a community may be the condition of civil life, but the total identification of one's aspirations with those of the community is the death of liberty. For the diversity which is the life of liberty, the capacity to identify and demand recognition of developing aspirations must necessarily be restricted. The individual's rights may be protected, but they will be recognized as rights only as they conform with and are implicated in norms advanced by groups.

Except for violence, a thoroughgoing group politics thus offers no mechanism for the systematic expression and political recognition of individual goods, especially those of the powerless. Where the goods of individuals are not implicated in the claims put forward by groups, they increasingly cannot be considered in the political and judicial processes. But thirty centuries of thought and experience have, it seems to me, borne out the obvious truth that all individual goods are not implicated in group or communal goods. The diversity of human wants and needs has falsified or trivialized every claim of an ultimate harmony between individual and group goods and the whole modern development of the concept of liberty owes its significance to that perception. A politics which is devoted primarily to the consideration of group claims may develop a rudimentary notion of liberty: it may create or perpetuate a society in which governmental persecution or dictatorship are minimized. But it cannot create a society where the *promotion* of individuality and the diversity of goods is a condition of that society's existence. As I have noted, where the whole emphasis is upon the interests of groups, individuals seeking to realize their goods are encouraged to identify them with group claims. But this creates pressures to conform one's ideals to those of the groups most likely to support them – in other words, to conform to standards different from those one might otherwise choose. But rigorous constitutional protection to choose what one might conform to is not what we mean by liberty. Because of the ordinary pressures to conform in society, liberty requires a politics which not merely tolerates, but promotes diversity and individual commitment to personal goals. Wider opportunities for voluntary action, consideration of legal ideals as legal ideals, broad and permissive boundaries for dissenting behavior and life styles are critical. Moreover, mechanisms must exist for the political protection of this diversity and not merely for the realization of values put forward by groups. This might mean a reintroduction of a view of social ideals as more nearly absolutes than interests. The things relevant to liberty are entitled to greater *prima facie* validity, to a degree of protection which might even seem arbitrary. The widest possible latitude ought to be given to those things implicated in free expression, privacy, and so forth, whether or not that latitude is bound to result in a greater degree of social instability than we are used to.

Taken at face value, then, group theory demands that the only moral claims with which politics may be concerned are interests: claims which can be bargained over because they express nothing more than the preferential demands of groups. Their claim on the attention of public authority exists only as they are supported by sanctions of one sort or another. Even in the unlikely situation of an equality of bargaining power among all groups and the willing identification by individuals of their claims with those of relevant groups, such a process cannot attain justice; for justice demands that claims be judged by their moral worth rather than by the bargaining power of those who put them forward. Moreover, the evasion of moral argument, on the grounds that moral ideals are merely preferences incapable of being shown to be true or obligatory, merely allows the more powerful to impose their moral preferences on the less powerful without having to defend their position or justify their preferences. Self-deceit is the occupational hazard of relativists. Shaw once noted that 'the Master of Arts, by proving that no man has any natural rights, compels himself to take his own for granted'. In a bargaining system, we might substitute 'others' for 'himself'.

What can the political good in a bargaining system refer to? Clearly, it can refer to no concrete social ends presumed to be desirable in themselves. Liberty, political participation, equality, tradition, leadership, are desirable because they are the conditions necessary to the proper functioning of the system. It is the bargaining process itself that is the highest good. If it were otherwise, the group process would have to be considered subservient to all or some of those ideals. But group theorists do not admit that this can ever be the case. Because they conceive political goods to be statable only as interests, only that system which gives the freest play to interests can be called good. 'Only the give-and-take of a free society's internal struggles', writes Seymour Lipset, 'offers some guarantee that the products of the society will not accumulate in the hands of a few powerholders, and that men may develop and bring up their children without fear of persecution.'[6] And, according to the group theorists, a free society is one in which groups may freely form and press for recognition of their interests. Now, if this is what makes the system desirable, the virtue of group politics lies less in the concrete benefits it attains than in the procedures which are presumed to permit their attainment. Commitment to a set of bargaining procedures rather than commitment to ends becomes the highest social good.

It is at least questionable whether the analysis of empirical evidence supports this claim. The optimistic predictions at the end of *Political Man* appear, today, too optimistic; the democracy defined in *Who Governs?* appears to exist only within boundaries of acceptable policymaking laid down by elites. The freedom which exists in western society may reasonably be attributed to social and political traditions which antedate group politics. Furthermore, if one questions the propriety of reducing moral claims to interests, one may rightly see the relation of group politics to liberty as highly ambivalent. On the one hand, in satisfying certain material demands, it has unquestionably produced conditions which aid in the development of liberty. On the other hand, the liberty it aids is reduced by the translation of moral goods to interests. For in doing this, group politics tends to restrict the realization of newly-emerging individual aspirations to those one can share with a group and to those which may develop from improved conditions. But surely the tradition of liberty means more than that. It means, at the least, protection of – indeed celebration of – individual diversity and personal moral claims. Further, if the preservation of the group system is the highest social good, views which challenge the legitimacy of the group as the chief actor in politics are themselves illegitimate *a priori*. This is surely a reduction in freedom.

Let me summarize. In the process of creating civility based upon an open, pluralistic society, we have debased the ideals which make such a society desirable. We have begun to reduce the legitimacy of individual claims, to translate moral ideals and rights into interests, to rely upon a bargaining procedure to protect them, and to set the highest store upon the stability of that procedure. A continuation of these tendencies must lead to grave restrictions on diversity and individuality, and to a denigration of the concept of rights itself. To put it simply, it tends to reduce the meaning of civility to order. But such a reduction of the notion of civility is inconsistent with the liberal vision. The task of liberal theory is to recreate and redefine civility so that it may once more be consistent with those things which make liberalism valuable.

The new public authority. A new vision of civility must be developed in a context of public authority different from the one we have inherited and are used to.

The concepts of politics and public life arise from the confrontation of our uniquely intimate spheres of action with activities which largely determine the boundaries and qualities of those personal spheres. The recognition that there is such a thing as politics – whatever we choose to call it – follows from the commonsense perception that there are conflicts, threats, and activities which seriously affect us and which transcend the limits of our persons to involve us willy-nilly in relations with others with whom we have no personal relations. The public realm is a product of the need to impose order on and to formalize these a-personal relationships – to regularize them. The public realm exists not merely by reason of the fact of plurality, but because of the need to regularize the conditions of plurality.

It is characteristic of private realms of action that the things done there, and the obligations incurred, are voluntary. Private relations involve relations with others which are governed not by formal rules, but by agreements. But the need to order things by regulation is a general characteristic of public behavior. Where we are involved in enterprises with others whom we do not know, we lose the condition of intimacy. Agreement becomes impossible as a mode of procedure and is replaced by a formal ordering of obligations. Public behavior is behavior governed by formal rules which derive not from our personal commitments, but from the supposed needs of the enterprise itself. However we might approve of these rules or participate in the making of them, or willingly obey them, they become, once made, impersonal standards existing independently of our approval.

In general, we may say that the rules which govern the public realm are the products of authority. I wish to characterize authority in a familiar way. By the word 'authority' I refer to a type of communication which elicits compliance primarily because compliance is considered due the author of the communication. (For the sake of convenience, 'authority' may also be used to refer to the author of such communications.) Force need not be used, although its threatened use is helpful in gaining compliance. In other words, when I speak of authority I refer to communications acted upon because those to whom the communications are addressed are willing or eager to carry them out. They may be willing because they fear the consequences of disobedience, or eager because they believe the author to be right or entitled to command by reason of status, etc. Whatever their reason, they comply in the absence of immediate and overt force. Authority so conceived is defined by social norms. X complies with Y's communication because he sees it as legitimate, or because he sees Y as deserving of obedience, or because he is fearful of disobedience.

But not all authority is public. The public, like the political, has always been thought of in terms of actions which affect society in general, which concern the life-chances of all or many members.

Public authority thus possesses a profound potential for redirecting the personal lives of all members of society, although it need not always be used to do this. Hence, it may be differentiated from the authority of families, churches, and similar institutions, sometimes called 'parapolitical' institutions. This differentiation frequently leads to confusions. It would be wrong to assume that the activities of parapolitical institutions are never public or political *ex hypothesi*. They are not public or political where they concern the internal arrangements of such institutions (although here they may be political-like or, as Plato might say, the image of the political). That is, decisions made by a parapolitical institution for its members *qua* members may rightly be distinguished from decisions made for society by public authority. But it does not follow that decisions made by that institution *which affect society at large* are not public. Similarly, where a parapolitical institution (such as a church) is composed of most members of society, its decisions concerning its internal arrangements are decisions which fit the characteristics of public activity.

Generally, public authority that attaches to actors in a complex society attaches not merely to their persons, but to the roles they fill. This attribution springs from the demands involved in preserving the social-political tie itself. Without the attribution of authority to roles rather than persons, there can be no guarantee of the persistence and regularity that are at the root of political relationships; for in political relationships some means must exist for evaluating and anticipating communications as authoritative, and normative conclusions as to who is to be obeyed and which communications call for obedience must be based on some general notions concerning future as well as present actions.

I take the concept of the public, then, to stand for that realm of action in which behavior is governed not by voluntary assumptions of obligation, but by rules created by authorities whose actions affect society in general.

This definition has not exactly surprising implications for the modern world. Primarily, it forces us to widen our concept of public authority to include nominally private actors, such as corporations – to recognize the desuetude of 'private' economic enterprise.

Laissez-faire theorists viewed economic activity as private. In part, this was due to the presumably private nature of property and the fact that, in a laissez-faire system, economic activity reflected that nature. For this reason, among others, Smith believed that the corporation was an improper form of business organization. Business organization should reflect the personalism associated with property and should retain the element of privacy conveyed by such notions as that of the 'company' (whose very name means 'those who share bread'). But corporate property is defined precisely by the absence of this personalism and corporate organization deprives the economy of its private nature. In addition, under laissez-faire, economic decision-making was supposedly based on the essentially private techniques of assertion of interests and bargaining over values. Where prices and wages reflected the interests of individual participants and were set by competitive bargaining, where economic decisions were made only by a collision of personal interests, where societal economic policy was not a product of authority, but was a residual by-product of private negotiation and voluntary agreement, the belief that economics was chiefly a private activity seemed coherent.

But this, as it turned out, was not to be the case. A corporate economy increased the extent to which economic power involved, as Morris Cohen put it, '*imperium* over our fellow human beings'[7]. Moreover, as the corporate economy grew, the power of major economic actors and institutions became indistinguishable from government power.

The private nature of laissez-faire economics was altered almost immediately when it was realized that conscious social planning was needed to make it effective. The creation of a labor pool, the encouragement of employer aggregations and the discouragement of employee aggregations, the prevention of monopolies which formed in defiance of economic laws, the reform of poor relief, the extension of the suffrage to the bourgeoisie, the use of protectionism to aid domestic industry, the governmental stabilization of currency and direct aid to industry all became parts of the corporate economic system. Moreover, as the corporate economy developed, it became further involved in the process of social control. Corporations made fundamental decisions concerning wages, prices, economic development, investment, and location of industry that affected the lives of hundreds of millions. This function continues to the present day. Today, as in the past, corporations play the leading role in the development of transportation and communication networks, exercise immense influence on governmental policy, run a parallel judicial system, and exercise predominant influence in decisions concerning land-use patterns and exploitation of natural resources. They have stepped into newly-developing spheres of social activity, sometimes in partnership with government, sometimes alone. Investment in developing areas of the Third World; creation and maintenance of common markets; involvement in urban planning; support, and in some cases control of, technological research and development, are leading examples.

The modern corporation is not merely engaged in enterprises which, by reason of their scope and consequences, may be associated with politics in its most basic sense: the corporation is a rule-making body as well. Perhaps the most dramatic example of its rule-making power is the administered price. When prices are determined not by a complex process of competitive bargaining between innumerable independent buyers and sellers, but by corporate decision based upon projections of costs and sales and geared to produce a pre-determined level of profit, we are faced with a process indistinguishable from classical governmental rule-making. Moreover, this rule-making does more than rationalize the process of production within the individual corporation. It serves to systematize and impose order upon the corporate economy in general. It is an integral part of the process by which the resources of a society are allocated and distributed.

In addition to the administered price, the rule-making role of the corporation may be seen in the way in which investment and development decisions are made, in its ability to discipline its shareholders and employees, in its role in urban and technological development, in its forceful impact upon educational goals and ideals.

Concentration on the corporation – the pre-eminent example of the private institution become public – obviously ought not to blind us to the fact that the trade union and, to a lesser extent, the professional association, have undergone similar transformations. The rights of these organizations to determine many options for their members, to discipline dissenting members, to set self-interested standards for admission to membership, are frequently combined with a right or power to control crucial aspects of a member's life.

For example, if membership in a trade union or professional association is a prerequisite for working in a trade for which one is trained, the ability of that organization to discipline its members is closer to the ability of a government to discipline than of a truly voluntary association. The dependence of the member makes his membership more compulsory than voluntary and converts the sanction possessed by the organization into something that more closely resembles government sanction than private. Again, the role of the trade union in wage-setting, or of the professional association in the setting of professional standards, is in effect a form of participation in regulation.[8]

Now the persistent carrying on of such functions, sanctioned by law, confers, little by little, a genuine legitimacy upon the actors. The assumption that liberty and self-fulfillment are the products of group politics, the identification of democracy and justice with the procedures of group politics, the attention paid to the wholly instrumental 'rules of the game', have created together an overwhelming legitimization of the bargaining system. Naturally enough, the legitimization of the bargaining system has turned into a legitimization of the institutions which play the leading roles in that system – that is, of the chief groups which compose it. It does not matter that this legitimization is originally a legitimization of certain procedures. Persistent participation in a legitimate procedure encourages an identification of participant and process: the participant comes to share in the process's legitimacy. The participants' rules become in themselves binding upon the whole of society. In the normal course of affairs, society is powerless to contest price policies, wage agreements, investment decisions, plant relocations, and so forth. Where they are contested, it is in a context not of public authority against private actor, but of one level of public authority against another. Laws favorable to and protecting the rule-making prerogatives of such actors abound; in many cases, these laws do not *grant* such prerogatives, but merely *recognize* those already claimed and exercised. Restrictions created by private actors on public interference with their work (as in the case of the governance of corporations) are enforced just as the decisions of a governmental bureaucracy are. These actors, whatever their conventional status, share the same conceptual space as governments. They are, in every sense but the conventional, part of the new public authority. It is true that they are, in certain respects, lower in the hierarchy of public authority than the government. But because of their legitimized power profoundly to affect contemporary life, this hierarchical differentiation is irrelevant to their status as public authorities.

Conclusions

Let me summarize the conclusions of this chapter and indicate the next development in my argument.

I suggest that the political and social institutions created by liberalism now threaten to subvert and restrict liberty. This is partly the result of an insensitivity to the notion of individuality developed by pluralism and partly the result of the conversion of rights to interests. In addition, the problem of the individual's relation to public authority is given a new dimension because many of the institutions presumed in the past to support the individual against public authority have now become part of public authority itself and exercise legitimized power over the individual.

This changing character of civility means that, if we wish to preserve the goods traditionally associated with liberalism at its best, we must develop a new civility. Now the analysis of the relationship of individual to authority – and hence the analysis of disobedience – can take place only within the context of a theory of obligation. I shall argue in chapter 3 that political obligation may be justified by the need to create civility. The contours and meanings of civility thus determine the nature of our political obligations and prescribe the limits of rightful disobedience. The creation of a new civility is tantamount to the justification of political obligation.

The argument now turns to the problem of political obligation.

2. *Traditional justifications of obligation: a critique*

There are clearly two senses in which the word 'obligation' may be used with respect to politics. The first sense is the descriptive: I may be said to be obligated to do something when I have no choice but to do it or suffer unpleasant consequences. The second sense is the prescriptive sense: I may be said to be obligated to do something when, for one reason or other, I ought to do it, irrespective of the consequences. I shall be concerned with obligation only in this latter or prescriptive sense: I should like to know why it is that people ought to obey political rules.

I raise this question not without serious apologies. It is after all one of the more frequently discussed topics of political theory. But it is, all the same, an unsettled question – one which many philosophers have found confusing and difficult. The different accounts that have been given of obligation – natural law, utility, consent, and so forth – are satisfactory in some ways but unsatisfactory in many other important ways and sometimes generate contradictions which are resolvable only by appealing – however covertly – to other standards. Is it possible, reflecting upon the deficiencies of most traditional accounts of obligation, to set out an account that is both coherent and convincing? To answer this, it is necessary first to consider some common approaches to political obligation. I shall discuss the inadequacies of these quite briefly, because my objections are either clear or common enough not to require extended discussion. I shall reserve consideration of the theory of consent for a following section because I believe it deserves more extended treatment.

Some common accounts of obligation

Religious accounts. Some writers ground the obligation to obey the rules of a regime or state in religious traditions. They might argue, for instance, that God is the source of moral norms and that the norms laid down by God entail or imply obedience to public authority within stated limits. Some have argued in favor of divine right, or have based the duty to submit to authority on the ground that political authority in general comes from God, and so forth.

The primary difficulty with justifying obligation by referring to a religious tradition – apart from the obvious problem of convincing non-believers – is that the implications of religious traditions are usually ambiguous or conflicting. This is a serious drawback where the tradition is held to be not a record of related philosophical speculations which can be varied and modified, but the authoritative record of God's word which is persuasive and binding solely because of that authority. Take Christianity, for example. In the past two centuries, Jesus' message has been convincingly shown to be rational-humanistic (Voltaire), romantic (Schliermacher), utilitarian (Mill), liberal (Harnack), socialist (Shaw), and existentialist (Maritain). These views imply, and have been taken to imply, very different views on subjects such as political obligation. The moral and theological views of these men, and of others such as Barth, Bultmann, Gilson, Niebuhr, Tillich, are frequently at war with each other and at times present radically different interpretations of Christianity. To which version or what segment of the Christian tradition are we entitled to refer in seeking to ground obligation? It may be that one of these various interpretations is true, but as they are all well argued and as the historical record is exceptionally scanty, it requires something like divine guidance to choose between them. Further, it is not exactly eccentric to suggest that the works of most theologians are less interpretations of a tradition than articulations of personal religious commitments made more compelling by appeals to what they conceive to be the essence of that tradition. But where reasonable arguments can be advanced to support many and conflicting interpretations, the most likely explanation for this conflict lies in the unresolvable ambiguities of the tradition being interpreted.

The problems endemic to the Christian political tradition are legendary. Consider Paul's advice to obey political power because it comes from God. This injunction, taken literally, gives us no way to differentiate the obedience owed to legitimate authority from that owed to wielders of raw force. On one view, this may not be unreasonable. Augustine recalls with evident approval a pirate's defense of his behavior before Alexander the Great: I rob with one ship and am called pirate, he remarks, while you rob with many and are called Emperor. But such an argument, however pointed, resolves nothing. It merely invites us to ask what the real differences between a pirate and ruler ought to be. Yet it is precisely on this question, on the question of the resolution of the problem of justifiable authority which so troubles the modern world, that Paul's injunction offers no assistance. Indeed, it was not meant to.

Again, Paul's injunction is clearly related to the more general New Testament premise that politics was unimportant because Judgment was near. If that is seen not to be the case, Paul's injunction appears less compelling and, on its face, quite arbitrary. Jesus only recommended that we render unto Caesar the things which are Caesar's and seems frequently to imply that far less is Caesar's than is popularly imagined. Certainly, he reserved the right to decide what exactly was Caesar's. If he recommended the payment of taxes, he also recommended that some people leave off following the productive trades upon which nations and people depend for sustenance and follow him into a life of pure spirituality. He refused to recognize the authority of the high priests. He encouraged, by his actions if not his words, a conflict of loyalties which necessarily had political repercussions.

In general, early Christianity appears, like early Stoicism, to be quite apolitical. If there is a political theory, it is rooted in the emphasis on personal righteousness over public right and if there is a theory of obligation it is largely a prudential one, based on the need to prove to Rome that Christians were not political subversives. Prior to the late medieval period, there is little discussion of obligation. Beginning in the twelfth century, the disputes engendered by Papal claims of political authority produce discussions of Paul's injunction which carve out so many exceptions to it as to render it doctrinally useless. As many revolutionaries as conservatives have since been able to base their views on Christian philosophy. The grounds on which Luther differentiated resistance to Papal authority – which was at least partly political – from resistance to secular authority are at best as unclear as the justifications offered by Calvinists for their different behavior in Geneva, France, and England.

What is true of Christianity is true of other religions. The obligation of the citizen is not an open question in the Old Testament, nor is it possible to derive guidance by studying the implications of Old Testament doctrine. Of course we know that God or one of his prophets occasionally deposed an heretical king, but this offers little guidance to the citizen confronted with, say, racially discriminatory laws. In truth, the question of disobedience is not raised. The Old Testament assumes that the subject will and should obey. Yet what are we to make of prophetic resistance to prescribed rituals, or of Elijah's tragic veto of the policies of Ahab? Is such behavior only the prerogative of prophets? What, then, is the status of those who follow the prophet into disobedience? Of what significance is the still, small voice of conscience? Considered in its entirety, I think it is fair to say that the Old Testament is, on this issue, at least as confusing and indecisive as the New.

Some religious traditions may be more definite, but their antiquity works against them, for the considerations they give to the problem are frequently irrelevant to the concerns which move us. The Hindu concept of kingship as fatherhood tells us what a king ought to do, but it offers little guidance on how to cope with a bad one and none on the responsibilities of republican governments whose goal is supposed to be liberty rather than paternalism. The political dilemmas of the modern world are vastly different from those which existed during the formative years of the world's major religions. It is folly to try to solve the profound and often little-understood political dilemmas of the modern world with the ambiguous weapons of a confused and superstitious antiquity. We are still left to develop a theory of obligation by ourselves.

Natural law and natural rights. In the preface to his *Discourse on the Origins of Inequality*, Rousseau remarks that the many conflicting interpretations of natural law agree on at least one point: that it is impossible to understand – and hence to obey – natural law without being 'a very profound thinker and a very great metaphysician'. The theory Rousseau was attacking was the Enlightenment theory of self-evident moral truths. Rousseau correctly perceived that if the maxims of natural law were indeed self-evident, there ought not to be so much controversy about them. The conflicting recommendations of natural law thinkers, the subtle distinctions they drew, were if anything evidence that the traditional theory of natural law was inadequate and that the true function of the phrase 'natural law' was to dignify the conclusions of a particular philosopher's ethical theory.

A century later, the British philosopher David Ritchie pointed out the remarkable resemblance between traditional theories of natural law and Burkean prescriptiveness. He argued, in *Natural Rights*, that the 'natural', the obviously true, is in practice most likely to mean the customary – the things we are used to. It takes no especially brilliant analysis to show that the identification of the natural and the right with the expectations of a society is not only the reverse of what most natural law thinkers wished, but is an unlikely candidate for moral honors. 'Do what you are used to doing' is not, as Tussman has pointed out, the highest ethical advice. But even if the right is not taken to mean the customary, if it is true that men overvalue the things which promote their personal goods and tend to interpret moral maxims self-interestedly, a moral theory based upon self-evidence tends merely to ratify personal preferences.

Equally persuasive is another well-known argument concerning the meaning of the phrase 'self-evident'. Obviously, a moral rule such as 'Do not kill', or 'Killing is wrong', is not self-evident in the sense that 'Blue is a color' is self-evident. Indeed, it is hard to see how moral rules may be self-evident at all, since the validity of moral rules always rests on something other than the logic of the words comprising them. What we normally mean by saying that a moral rule is self-evident is that it is compelling, easily justified, deducible from almost any reasonable hypothesis, etc. – that, to use a well-known formulation, we cannot bring ourselves to doubt it. These things may mean that some moral rules are more appealing or easier to justify than others, just as $1+1 = 2$ is easier to prove than a complicated equation. But they do not make those rules self-evident.

Since Hume, it has become common to believe that the process of reflection by which we derive ultimately untestable moral conclusions, erroneously said to be self-evident, is not reason but intuition. Reason involves the giving of reasons, analysis, the troublesome and continuing attempt to find justifications. But the nerve center of a natural law based on self-evidence is the denial of the possibility of finding reasons to justify a certain order of commitment which we are nonetheless entitled to call true. If we omit divine revelation as an authoritative source of these commitments, and if we believe that they are more than emotive reflections or arbitrary affirmations, what but intuition are we left with? How better to account for the conflicting opinions of undoubtedly rational men, each convinced of the self-evidence of those opinions?

To the extent that natural law is an intuitive theory, based upon supposedly self-evident truths, or to the extent that it merely sanctifies conventional expectations and values, it is arbitrary as a basis for obligation. There is no compelling reason to suggest that what has been done in the past ought to bind us in the present or that the expectations of a community are immune from basic challenge. On the other hand, obligation grounded upon intuited rules of right is obligation grounded upon rules which by their terms are beyond rational argument. But it is precisely to rational argument that dissenters must appeal. It is precisely because the rules of a social order are felt to be *not* self-evidently valid that principled dissent occurs in the first place. If a dissenter is able to do no more than pit his intuitions against those of the community, his bare conviction of validity against its, what confidence, if any, may be placed in the eventual resolution of the conflict? Indeed, who can doubt the shape of the outcome? It is only too likely in any event that the resolution of a particular social conflict will be primarily a function of power. But the reduction of moral argument to argument over intuitions merely underwrites that unpleasant outcome rather than doing whatever little can be done to attenuate it. A rule which is beyond rational argument is, in the end, a rule whose defense rests upon the passions or convictions it may awaken. What sane man would be willing to submit his dissent to a judge to whom truth is a matter of intuition and every opinion concerning it supported chiefly by the passion with which it is affirmed?

The intuitive theory also suffers from the defect, already mentioned, that all persons' intuitions are not the same. How, then, can intuition serve as a source of standards? In the past 100 years, scholars have produced enormous amounts of evidence to show how far ostensibly intuitive moral rules are shaped by cultural experience and traditions. Once we consider problems less limiting than murder or anarchy, there is a wide divergence in intuitions which either should not exist or which render an intuitive theory practically worthless. Besides, where intuitions differ, there must come a point where we decide that some are right or are to be preferred to others. On what conceivable intuitive basis can we do this?

Finally, it is painfully obvious that, even if intuitive natural law does allow an individual to understand his own moral outlook, it is not adequate to enable him to *communicate* that outlook to others. That is, while he can communicate the results of his moral deliberations, he cannot subject those deliberations to public scrutiny to determine whether they are arbitrary, incoherent, and so forth. An intuitive theory of natural law renders fruitful public discussion of political rights impossible. But what is more germane to inquiry into obligation than such a discussion? What prevents us from creating a satisfactory basis for judging obligations more than its absence?

In the modern world, the resurgence of interest in natural law has been accompanied by a conscious effort to subject it to rational analysis. Most modern natural law thinkers seek to appeal to norms implicit, in one way or another, in the terms of moral discourse or the survival of the social enterprise. They see things like human survival, the keeping of agreements, the mutual applicability of claims as things necessary to any social enterprise and which may serve as bases for various inferences. In addition, the inferred rules themselves must be universal, in the sense that their applicability is not limited to particular times and places, that they are compelling, not easily changed, etc. What emerges from such considerations is, as Hart has pointed out in *The Concept of Law*, a natural law considerably reduced in scope but still valid.

Joseph Tussman has suggested that the validity of natural law rules is a function not of their truth, but of the inappropriateness of their denial.[1] Right and truth are not the same things, but we arrive at the conclusion that *a* is right by a process of reasoning parallel to that used to show that *b* is true. We suspect arbitrariness, distinguish between the subjective and the objective, guard against the effect of impulse, attempt to outface skepticism and relativism, and so forth. In affirming a moral rule, we ask whether it can be universalized without absurdity. We find that certain rules (e.g., one need not keep one's agreements, one can treat oneself as

an exception to moral rules) become absurd if universalized, while
the universalization of others is the condition of viable social life.

This approach allows us to avoid many of the traditional pitfalls
and shortcomings of natural law. We need not commit ourselves to
a teleological interpretation of nature or to an intuitive discovery of
moral laws immanent in the universe. Nor need we resort to the
common subterfuge of pretending to derive a system of norms from
a model of human nature in which those norms are already, and
arbitrarily, encased. Yet it is unclear why we are entitled to call
such a construction *natural* law. There is no compelling reason to
identify a universal moral rule with natural law. What entitles us to
call a law natural is its relation to or derivation from the needs of
human nature. Thus, Hart contends that we are committed by the
terms of political discussion to the survival of the social enterprise.
He considers how the needs and attributes of human nature inter-
act with that commitment and finds that certain norms are entailed
by that interaction. Yet he finds that only five norms are so entailed – five and no more.[2]

Yet Hart's construction, while interesting, cannot answer the
problem of obligation. It is pointless to speak of obligation as
required by the survival of society. If it is undeniable, it is also not
very helpful. For the question is not whether *some* form of obligation is necessary, but *what form* it might be. If the only thing relevant to obligation is the necessity for social survival, then any form
of obligation, however oppressive, is justified so long as it reasonably guarantees survival. No discriminatory apparatus exists to
enable us to distinguish between tyrannical obligations and non-
tyrannical ones. Indeed, there is no way to classify obligations as
tyrannical or non-tyrannical in the first place.

One might argue that such a theory demands a minimal degree
of obligation: the limits of obligation are the requirements for survival. But that means that we cannot distinguish between obligations necessary for the survival of society and obligations necessary
for the survival of a decent and civilized society. Surely, we are
entitled to demand of a theory of obligation that it maximize the
opportunities for decency and civility as well as survival. Certainly,
we cannot assume that decency and civility follow inevitably from
mere survival. The Leviathan state guarantees no more than that
these things are possible in orderly society. Surveying our experi-

ences in the twentieth century, might we not wish to frame our obligations that they become probable?

In traditional natural law theory the substance and limits of obligation were related to the norms of natural law. A justifiable obligation was one which was consistent with these norms, an unjustifiable obligation one which was inconsistent. But if Hart is correct there are very few norms of natural law and these are insufficient to serve as adequate bases for the protection of liberty against tyrannical invasion. The protection of life and property, the keeping of agreements, the reliance on forbearance and compromise, the preservation of order, while all justifiable, do not necessarily describe what we should call a legitimate social order. Certainly, these things do not, without more, invalidate repression of speech or religion for reasons of stability, inequality of condition or opportunity, oppressively severe legal sanctions, dedication of the state to conquest or war, invidious group discriminations, subversion of human dignity, manipulation of personality, and other similar actions which might justify a challenge to legitimacy.

Perhaps Tussman's injunction against treating oneself as an exception might carry us further – if we knew what it was we ought not to be an exception to. If Tussman has in mind the equalization of formal rules of society – such as laws – we might wish to ask whether formal equality is enough and whether massive economic inequality need not be confronted. If he has in mind informal rules – such as customs, economic rewards, etc. – we might consider the extent to which inequality of condition or opportunity need not entail anyone treating himself as an exception to any rule. The rich and the poor are equally entitled to inherit as they are equally forbidden to steal bread or sleep under bridges. Equality is produced by having equalizing rules to obey rather than being equally obliged to obey inegalitarian ones. If Tussman means to recommend equality *per se*, how does he derive it from his approach to natural law – from such things as keeping agreements and not treating oneself as an exception?

Moreover, it is clear that certain kinds of norms – such as the promotion of forbearance and compromise – are counsels of perfection rather than norms convertible into legal rules and relatively clear restrictions. We are entitled to doubt whether they can ever be used as standards except in limiting cases.

The point I am trying to make – perhaps at too great a length – is simply this: we still have to give a reasoned account of obligation after exhausting all that modern natural law can tell us. There is no doubt that this account can be consistent with natural law, but it is not entailed or implied by it. Natural law cannot, by itself, provide an adequate account of obligation if we are determined to relate obligation to things like liberty, dignity, equality, or civility. However, as I shall argue in chapter 3, Hart's version of natural law, building as it does upon the perceptions of Hobbes and Hume, provides the most persuasive starting point for the discussion of obligation.

Utility. Of the many criticisms of utilitarianism, one of the most common and most justifiable is that it is conceptually ambiguous: that the maximization of happiness is an empty and often confusing goal and is based on an irretrievably naive psychology. In recognition of this, some writers have suggested that it is possible to import some clarity into utilitarianism by seeing it as concerned not so much with the positive goal of attaining happiness as with the negative goal of reducing unhappiness. 'The elimination or mitigation of misery, suffering and pain is surely a task sufficiently definite whatever may be thought of the difficulty of defining positive good. It has indeed been suggested that instead of the general happiness of the greatest number it would be more practicable to aim at the least pain of the smallest number.'[3]

But, although utilitarianism may be more coherent when viewed this way, it is still inadequate as a basis for political obligation. Unless pain and unhappiness are given the widest possible meanings (as entailing, for example, such things as the inability to contribute to social life), we are forced to admit that there are many things men may wish to attain cooperatively besides absence of misery. The failure to attain those things frequently identified with the highest human aspirations need not cause unhappiness, even though it might be true that that attainment would produce a more profound type of happiness. Whether this is in fact the case is at best unclear. Bentham would not have thought so. He argued that pushpin is as good as poetry if it produces an equal measure of happiness and believed that we had no warrant to assume that universal devotion to poetry would produce greater happiness. Nor would he have agreed that it was legitimate to consider the question of the profundity of happiness, to ask with Mill whether it was better to be Socrates dissatisfied or a fool satisfied. Once the question of the profundity or comparative worth of pleasures is introduced, the real standard of value becomes the way we judge or compare the profundity or worth of pleasures and not the attainment of happiness.

I believe it was for this reason that Mill sought to give the widest possible interpretation to the term 'happiness'. In that famous third chapter of *On Liberty* where he tacitly discards utilitarian arguments altogether, he identifies happiness or well-being with self-fulfillment. He claims that the development of the individual human personality to the fullest extent possible, the realization of individual potential, the reduction of crippling psychological restraints, ought to be our true aim. But this is nothing else than an abandonment of utility, for the question now is not what promotes happiness but what promotes self-fulfillment and it is by no means obvious that they are the same. Indeed, it is obvious that the fullest realization of my potential may make me less happy or may force me to pay the price of psychological distress. Think of the pain engendered in a man who has realized his potential when he views the state of his fellow men or the world. Swift is said to have laughed twice in his life and Ruskin was wracked with guilt over his good fortune. The intellectual and moral development of Augustine made him progressively less happy. May it not be that the happiness generated by self-fulfillment turns inevitably to guilt or sorrow? The ultimate development of the human potential is the transcending of the limits of the human condition. But the Greek tragedians, Shakespeare, and Nietzsche show us how incompatible that transcendence may be with happiness.

A route sometimes taken to escape from this conclusion is to argue that happiness does not refer to pleasure in its ordinary sense, but refers to the ultimate and profound satisfactions to be derived from self-knowledge. But if utilitarianism has any meaning, it must mean that individual pleasures and pains are irreducible and are to be defined in the way we ordinarily define pleasures and pains. For this reason, I consider this interpretation to be either wholly arbitrary or a pointless verbal quibble.

Self-fulfillment may not, in any case, be a wholly admirable or coherent concept. Dostoevski's Grand Inquisitor may be right in arguing that man's fulfillment entails political subservience and escape from the burden of moral responsibility. But the question of political obligation is predicated upon the assumption of moral responsibility, for it is only with morally responsible persons that we can raise the question of justifying obligations.

On the other hand, the Grand Inquisitor may be wrong. While the evidence that men are happiest when they embrace rather than avoid moral responsibility is not exactly overwhelming, neither is it non-existent, and those of us who value things like liberty are committed to it at least as a possibility. But it is clear that what people have in mind when they speak of self-fulfillment is some such conception. They have in mind not the fulfillment of man's natural goals, nor even of the moral goals men actually have, but of the highest and best goals men may aspire to. Rather than things like benign subservience, conflict, accumulation, death, they have in mind the development of moral responsibility, courage, health, talent, taste – in short, of the things we may not find in men but wish to. Self-fulfillment means the fulfilling of what is good in man, of that portion of his potential which is valuable. As such, however powerful or dramatic or compelling it may be, its value is based upon the value of the goods it chooses to fulfill. But this must be established by arguments none of which can be utilitarian. Self-fulfillment, in other words, is a moral hypothesis to be explored rather than an end to be defended.

There are other critical ambiguities or contradictions in utilitarianism which render it inadequate as a basis for obligation. Utilitarianism justifies obedience because it leads to and is a necessary component of social welfare, defined in terms of pleasures and pains. But this notion of social welfare, of the general happiness, is confusing. It is not clear *how* we ought to evaluate the consequences of the relevant behavior – whether we ought to consult the pleasures of individual persons or of society in general. On the question of obedience, most utilitarians do not suppose that I am obligated where the consequences of obedience are personally best for me, but when they are best for society as a whole. On other questions, however, they do not apply the same test. Bentham claimed that pushpin was as good as poetry if each gave equal pleasure. Now it is possible to argue that poetry advances the happi-

FERNALD LIBRARY
COLBY-SAWYER COLLEGE
NEW LONDON, N. H. 03257

67950

ness of society more than pushpin because it raises society's cultural level, increases civility, sensitizes individuals to human aspirations, and so forth. If the consequences of valuing poetry are on the whole better for society at large than the consequences of valuing pushpin, may we not say that poetry is better? The answer depends on how we are to evaluate pushpin and poetry: are we to consider the consequences to individuals or to society in general? We cannot say. On this question, as on others, utilitarianism gives us no way to determine in what cases and under what conditions the pleasures to be consulted are those of society or of the individual. But in the absence of a principle which helps us to make such a determination, the assumption that obedience must be justified by its consequences for society rather than for the personal pleasure of individuals is quite arbitrary. It is possible to argue that there is an ultimate harmony between individual and social happiness, but the evidence does not support such an argument. Furthermore, on the issue of obedience, the assumption of harmony is all too frequently invalid on its face, defensible only where we import some notion of the *true* will or *true* pleasure of individuals and oppose it to their immediately perceivable will or pleasure. Such a notion is, however, quite arbitrary and certainly inconsistent with the whole thrust of utilitarianism.

Two further problems are presented by the need to weigh the consequences of obedience and disobedience. First, suppose we live under a regime which is minimally satisfactory: which promotes the well being of members of society but does so in a barely satisfactory way. Suppose also that it is challenged by a revolutionary group whose program proposes changes designed to maximize well being. How are we to decide whether to support the regime or its revolutionary rival? If we must decide by evaluating the consequences of obedience and revolution, we must balance known consequences against hypothetical ones. It is often difficult enough to assess the effects on well being of the acts of an existing regime. Assuming we can do this, can we, with confidence, assess the possible effects on well being of a regime not yet in existence? If the consequences are to determine our obligation to obey a particular law, we are also asked to balance hypotheticals. If the law has been in operation for a while, we may know something of the consequences of obedience. But the consequences of a new law or of disobedience are largely hypothetical. They are inferred from considering, as fully as we can, relevant historical and sociological evidence. Assuming that there is relevant evidence, which we may agree on as relevant, the conclusions we may reach will in any event be tenuous. The history of modern government is replete with political acts and laws whose consequences belied expectations. To make a utilitarian point, social well being is unlikely to result from exclusive reliance on such a procedure. The evaluation of possible consequences is a necessary and inevitable component of social decision making: we all wish to consider at least the range of possible consequences our acts may have. But it would be foolhardy to base a decision on something as critical as obligation solely upon the evaluation of consequences: so long as these conclusions are necessarily tenuous, we must seek some other kind of principle to guide us.

The second problem presented by the need to weigh pleasures concerns the limits it imposes on our moral vision. We can weigh pleasures only if – and to the extent that – these pleasures are measurable. Some of them are no doubt measurable. Health, housing, literacy are measurable indices of social well being just as production statistics and employment levels are measures of economic well being. There are many critical pleasures which cannot be measured. Utilitarians, for example, might surely wish to know something about the guilt, alienation, frustration, and misery caused by unemployment – yet these are things which resist measurement. Measuring student–teacher ratios and reading levels may give us some help in assessing education but, as we have discovered, they are inadequate by themselves: we might, for example, wish to assess the quality of what is being taught, the relationships developed between students and teachers, and similar things. In our communal life, the respect for human dignity, the promotion of privacy, the creation of satisfying and fulfilling work, the development of a sense of community are things which depend in part on evaluations aided only imperfectly by measurement. In short, as H. B. Acton has argued,[4] there are many pleasures which are part of happiness and yet which cannot, or can imperfectly, be measured. Some of these are things which help to make social life valuable and worthwhile and which may reasonably be considered indispensable to any decision concerning obligation. On what basis, then, is

it right *a priori* to restrict consideration of obligation to consequences which are measurable? The implications of such a restriction are frightening, for it seems likely to encourage an identification between the constituents of political obligation and the ideal of
statistical uniformity. A society in which most people are literate,
employed, and adequately housed may still be a society in which
education is a mode of manipulation, work is deadening and housing morally depressing. There is nothing in principle which prevents
any statistical achievement from being trivialized or rendered
hollow in practice. And there is much which indicates that a definition of well being in terms of things which can be measured
excludes from its compass some of those values or pleasures that
make life fit for human beings to live. In any event, even if all of
this is trivial, even if the restriction of well being to measurable
things is justifiable, it cannot be justified on utilitarian grounds but
by appeal to moral arguments concerned with the just categorization of pleasures.

I have dealt in this section only with the inadequacy of utility as
a basis for obligation and I have not felt it necessary to recapitulate
the traditional criticisms which emphasize its psychological naivete,
or the philosophical poverty and ambiguity of the standard of happiness, or the implicit and questionable assumption of an ultimate
harmony of pleasures. I confess that what troubles me about utility
is less its faulty logic or limited applicability (both of which may
have been exaggerated) than its reduction of all vexing moral
dilemmas to deceptively simple calculations regarding pleasures
and pains. For this prevents us from seeing that, even if the psychology of such a view were not tragically naive, the origin of
moral dilemmas often lies precisely in our inability to assess the
pleasures and pains involved. Even more important is the tendency
of utility as a world view to reduce the value in all things to the satisfactions of man's wants. The rejection out of hand of the possibility
of things being valued for their own sakes encourages a vulgar
egoism which sees nature and other men as instrumentalities for the
satisfaction of wants and the production of pleasures. The sustaining
of life becomes useful and to the extent that it is useful it loses its
imperative. Human dignity becomes not an axiom of just political
existence but a device. The mixture of illusion and reality which we
know as the tradition of civility, the permanence we assign to art,

the notion of human aspiration, all come to be redefined as useful – to what? Lessing wanted to know what was the use of use; why it was that the commonsense notion that certain things are prized because they are useful or help us to attain other things must be transmuted into a religion. Utilitarian philosophers seem not to have appreciated the extent to which their philosophy encourages the vulgarization of nature or the caricature of moral aspiration. They see, quite rightly, that there is no logical reason for it to be interpreted that way and believe that such a construction is arbitrary. But is it? It is certainly legitimate to ask not merely what a philosophy means, but what it is likely to be taken to mean. The historical associations of utilitarianism with egoism and self-interest, with history purged of its richness and complexity in the guise of progress, with naked economic exploitation, are not merely accidents of the times. They are perfectly sensible conclusions to be drawn from the self-assured science of instrumentalism. Where everything becomes a thing for use, where social life is a tissue of measured values and productive actions, the capacity to search for something which stands above our desires is lost. But that capacity is the condition of morality as well as sanity. Mill realized this and repented. The necessity of his repentance is the most convincing reason why utility cannot determine the question of obligation.

Consent

The logic of consent: the social contract. I come now to the most common justification of political obligation: consent. It is hard to overemphasize the force of this concept on the public mind. Whatever critical assaults have been made upon it, it has become so popularly identified with democracy and with the western liberal tradition that its rejection often seems tantamount to the rejection of liberal democracy itself. It is a fixed point of orthodoxy in modern politics, a moral referent, an aid and comfort to argument. The fact that it is neither essential to nor dictated by the theory of liberal democracy appears at best to be irrelevant. This might not really matter if the notion of consent were viable or coherent. But it is not.

On the surface, there is a strong commonsense basis for consent theory. Since men are forced to do things by governments and since the things they are forced to do are not always immediately perceivable as good or beneficial, it seems reasonable to suggest that governments may rightly require those things only when those who must obey authorize it. Again, we often seek a community bound together voluntarily and sharing a common purpose or well being: this smacks strongly of consent. Moreover, most of us are convinced that in a free society concerned with the well being of its members most of the members would consent. Evidence of consent is thus taken to be evidence of the existence of freedom and well being. Consent is seen in the loyalty people display, in their continuous legitimation of government by free voting, and so forth.

The problem is, very few people actually consent, even if by consent we mean something besides deliberately affixing one's signature to a social contract. Only by resorting to Locke's fiction of tacit consent – whereby I am presumed to have consented while I continue to reside in a society, own property, or take advantage of the benefits that the society offers – can we speak about consent at all. And Hume was restating the obvious when he suggested that, as most people have no choice in the matter, to impute consent to their continued residence, etc., was to make of consent something less significant than was intended.

Now, everyone knows he never signed a social contract and never had his philosophical preferences consulted. He also knows that many of the things often interpreted as outward signs of consent – oaths of loyalty, pledges of allegiance, frequent voting – are in reality nothing of the sort: that if he has made a pledge he has thought no more about it than he has of prayers in church; that it is likely that his pledge is a product of habit, convention, social pressure, legal coercion and similar things; that he has no more control over the structure of the social order than he has over the position of Ursa Minor and attaches a proportionate significance to his pledge to it; that he has probably not thought for ten minutes about the questions to which consent is ostensibly related and would not know where to begin if he wished to; that he is not even certain of what or who it is he must consent to (state, society, constitution, government, administration, national ideals?); and that his pledge is in part a result of the state's attempt, in a process unaccountably named education, to convince him that what he finds around him is really quite natural and pleasant and that only a scoundrel would suggest otherwise. If by consent we mean a conscious and rational decision, made after weighing the situation and the alternatives, of the rightness of our political system or the government's moral fitness to impose its will upon us, I think we must all agree with Joseph Tussman that few people consent at all. If, furthermore, we assume that consent is meaningful only where there are acceptable alternatives to it, fewer still can be seen freely to consent.

Perceptions such as these, however ordinary, must force us to reconsider the aptness of consent as a political concept. Let us ask, first, how consent may do the things it is supposed to do: justify our obligation and legitimize the state. On the surface, this appears to pose no problem. My obligation depends on my promise to obey and a government is legitimate when enough of its citizens voluntarily agree to obey its commands. Just how many 'enough' is is hard to say and surely the fact that, in practice, a liberal democracy may be approved of by a great majority of its members does not resolve the question. In fact, the question of who must consent and the possible implications of majority consent show us the difficulties of accounting for both obligation and legitimacy by consent. If we maintain that every individual must consent, we may certainly account for obligation, but then legitimacy would require a utopian unanimity. If a majority (or a plurality or a two-thirds majority or whatever) must consent, then we can account for legitimacy more easily (if not more justly), but we are in difficulty when we turn to obligation. If I am in the minority and do not consent, is it right to say that I have no obligation? In that case, we are in the odd position of saying that I have no obligation to obey a legitimate government. If it is right to say that I do have an obligation, then that obligation proceeds from something other than my consent: namely, the acts of others. Can a consent theorist justify basing my obligation on something other than my consent? Suppose seventy-five percent of a population consents to a government which enslaves the rest. We are now faced with the argument that not only is the government legitimate, but the minority is obligated to assent to their enslavement. The notion of legitimizing a regime by the consent of the governed may appeal to our democratic impulses, but we cannot be so foolish as to believe that such consent is unambiguously justifiable. Majoritarianism may result, as we all know, in tyranny and the repression of rights. Moreover, the involvement of mass movements and mass support with the totalitarianism of our time should caution us to regard the consent of the majority as something less than a necessary foundation of liberty. Even if consent is otherwise a coherent theory, its validity must depend on the way consent theorists can resolve the problem of who need consent.

When and why do I consent? Consent is not a once-for-all sort of thing. When I promise to obey, I do so on the condition that the regime will continue to act as it acted at the time of my consent. Consent is not so much a promise as a free and continuous process of assent and I am bound by the terms of my consent only where I can evaluate the regime as substantially the same as or better than it was when I initially consented. When the question of legitimacy is raised, it is precisely because I believe that the terms of my consent have been or may have been violated. How does consent theory help me to understand my obligation in these circumstances? If I am in doubt as to whether I should obey a regime, it is no answer to say, 'You have consented to it' – that is just the question I am trying to decide. The real question is, 'Ought I to consent to it?' What I must reflect on are the grounds of my consent, the reasons for it – in other words, the things I would wish to know to resolve my doubt. Hence, it is not the fact of consent, but the conditions which justify consent which I must consult to resolve the problem of obligation.

Consent may be nothing more than a commitment for which no reasons need be given: in that case, it is arbitrary to say that such commitments by a majority can legitimize a government or bind non-consenters. On the other hand, consent may be a commitment for which justifying reasons must be given: in that case, *it is not consent but the reasons which justify it which obligate and confer legitimacy.* That is, consent may legitimize a regime, but if the reasons which justify consent are present, it may be said that I ought to consent, that my obligation is not one which I rightly may refuse. In that case, my obligation is not really voluntary. If I have no justifiable choice but to consent, then the reasons limiting my choice and mandating my consent – and not my consent itself – are the true sources of legitimacy and obligation.

We can see this clearly in the classical doctrine of consent offered by Locke. Locke knew, as we all know, that consent is rarely if ever explicit and, like the consent theorists who followed him, he saw most consent as tacit. Tacit consent is an inference from certain behavior which amounts, in the end, to the enjoyment of certain benefits. According to Locke, things like the acceptance of protection against criminals, or ownership of property, constitute tacit consent. Taken literally, such a notion renders consent meaningless. It might mean, for instance, that one who accepts the protection of a tyrannical government against criminals tacitly consents to the tyranny and makes it legitimate. I cannot help but enjoy certain benefits: even revolutionaries travel on public roads, enjoy – whether they like it or not – protection against foreign enemies, use publicly supplied facilities, etc. If one reads Locke literally, the mere decision not to emigrate is the equivalent of consent and the revolt against James II involved a breach of political obligation. Since Locke wished to justify that revolt and since, whatever we think of Locke, we must agree that he was not an imbecile, the conclusion is inescapable that he had something else in mind.

While Locke ostensibly makes consent the source of political obligation and legitimacy, what has consistently interested students of Locke are the extraordinary limits he places on the functioning of consent. The purpose of civil society is to secure certain natural rights and the process by which civil society is defined or deduced is heavily influenced by the moral obligations imposed on us by natural law. For this reason, it quickly becomes clear that there are certain things I cannot consent to: 'a man, not having the power of his own life, cannot by compact or his own consent enslave himself to anyone, nor put himself under the absolute, arbitrary power of another to take away his life when he pleases'[5]. Throughout the *Second Treatise* Locke stands by this type of assertion: the law of nature imposes clear limits on what men may do, both as legislators and as consenting individuals. The natural law is composed of a limited number of invariable and self-evident truths. Consequently, the boundary of consent, the permissible ambit of consent, is limited. The natural law commits men to certain things not variable by choice. Consent is not a product of desires or wants, but is, in effect, the means by which the natural law is translated into the law of a social order. If men must carry out the law of nature, and if that law commits them to certain things, it follows that, even if they have no duty to consent to civil society, they are certainly bound once they desire to create such a society or live within its borders to consent only to a certain version of it (i.e., one which is consistent with the law of nature and so protects natural rights, is not an absolute monarchy, etc.). 'The power of the society or legislative constituted by them can never be supposed to extend farther than the common good, but is obliged to secure everyone's property by providing against those three defects . . . that made the state of nature so unsafe and uneasy.'[6] It is hard to get around the conclusion that natural law describes what men ought to consent to and that man has no choice but to consent to a state based on it.

If we ask what occurs where consent conflicts with natural law, we get a similar answer. If there is one thing Locke is clear about it is the inability of human desire to vary the command of the law of nature. Now of course Locke presumes that all men, if given a free chance, would frame their consent in accordance with natural law. But if Locke were forced to admit that this is in fact untrue, he would have to say that, in case of conflict between them, the natural law would govern and invalidate consent inconsistent with it. Locke recognizes this by speaking about inalienable rights – rights no reasonable man would voluntarily give up and could not even if he wished to.

Now if I cannot alienate my rights explicitly, I cannot do it by indirection either. I can waive nothing tacitly which I could not waive explicitly. The conclusion seems inescapable that Locke meant the enjoyment of benefits to amount to tacit consent only where consent was justifiable in the first place – that is, where the regime operates in accordance with natural law. Hence, by remaining in a tyranny, accepting protection of my estate, etc., I cannot be supposed to have tacitly consented to that tyranny.

These considerations make it very difficult to see consent as a legitimating factor, for consent can legitimate only those governments faithful to the law of nature – those governments to which I could not deny my consent, if I chose to live in society at all, without denying the validity of the natural law. A consent whose terms are inconsistent with natural law can have no legitimizing function, nor can consent obligate us to do things prohibited by natural law. On the other hand, if a government does abide by the natural law and exercises its trusteeship in accordance with the terms of the social contract, then our mere enjoyment of its benefits is a tacit consent which does obligate us. Moreover, if we consciously desire to refuse our consent to it, we should be at a loss to account rationally for our refusal and hence could not justify it. But this is hardly what we mean by consent – at least freely given consent. For with the relatively insignificant exception of emigration, there seems to be no way we can avoid consenting to a government legitimized by natural law. In this case, it is hard to see what role consent really plays in the determination of legitimacy or the justification of obligation. *Both seem to be justified, in the overwhelming majority of cases, by the nature of the government rather than by any act of commitment on the part of persons.* Consent seems to be little more than a sign or recognition of the validity of an obligation and the legitimacy of a government, for that obligation and legitimacy cannot be justified by reference to consent but to the reasons which determine whether consent can rightly be given.

This can also be seen if we examine the basic mechanism for deducing consent: the social contract. The social contract is an attempt to account for the moral norms upon which our evaluation of politics and political authority is based – an attempt to account for the principles we rely on (or ought to rely on) to give our consent. Yet the one thing which must strike us immediately in Locke is the extent to which he believes that contract to be inflexible, the extent to which its terms are invariable and binding, leaving no room for the exercise of choice. There can be no absolute monarchy; there are relatively strict rules governing legislation and the relation of legislature and executive; the rights men give up to civil society are strictly limited to those necessary to make government possible; the rights government is explicitly required to protect are universal and identifiable. In other words, the rights protected and the obligations secured by the social contract are not the products of a freely-made agreement, but are the mandates of a universally binding natural law. 'In truth, the original contract could not have read any otherwise than it did, and the powers it gave and limits it placed can be logically deduced from the laws of nature and conditions in the state of nature.'[7] To the extent that the terms of our consent reflect the terms of the original contract, consent is irrelevant because choice is prohibited. The terms of the original contract reflect self-evident natural laws and, as such, present *the only possible terms of agreement* (except for minor matters, such as the organization of the government or the manner of choosing the legislature, where choice is possible).

The terms of consent are thus wholly contained in the invariable contract. If you choose to remain in a society faithful to the contract, you are obligated. If you choose to emigrate, you are obligated to the society you move to under the same conditions. If you choose to remain in a society which violates the contract, neither that act nor any explicit commitment can rightly obligate you or make that society legitimate. If you are a revolutionary and cast away, so far as you are able, the benefits a society offers, you cannot argue more than that the society has violated the terms of the one valid contract. You cannot rebel on the grounds of a new social vision but only on the grounds of the unfaithfulness of the government to the one valid vision. But a society unfaithful to the contract is illegitimate whether or not anyone rebels. Your consent or dissent cannot alter either this or your obligation, both of which are derived from natural law.

The extent to which actual agreement to the social contract is functionally irrelevant to social contract theorists, or is arbitrarily produced by the terms of their discussion, is one of the more remarkable and paradoxical elements of social contract theory. Nor does this crucial flaw appear only in the work of early contract theorists. Consider the argument of John Rawls in his recent and widely-acclaimed work, *A Theory of Justice*.[8] Rawls argues that the principles of justice – 'the first virtue of social institutions' (3) – are those that would be agreed to by free, equal, rational men in the state of nature, which Rawls calls the original position. It is crucial that the covenantors operate behind a 'veil of ignorance'. That is, while they know 'the general facts about human society' and that 'their society is subject to the circumstances of justice', they know no particular facts about themselves or their society (137). They understand, in general, 'political affairs and the principles of economic theory; they know the basis of social organization and the laws of human psychology'. But 'no one knows his place in society, his class position or social status; nor does he know his fortune in the distribution of natural assets and abilities, his intelligence and strength, and the like. Nor again, does anyone know his conception of the good, the particulars of his rational plan of life, . . . the special features of his psychology', or to which generation he belongs. As for social knowledge, 'the parties do not know the particular circumstances of their own society . . . its economic or political situation, or the level of civilization and culture it has been able to achieve' (137). In such a situation, Rawls believes, two principles of justice would be chosen: first, 'each person is to have an equal right to the most extensive basic liberty compatible with a similar liberty for others'; and, second, 'social and economic inequalities are to be arranged so that they are both (*a*) reasonably expected to be to everyone's advantage, and (*b*) attached to positions and offices open to all' (60).

Now one problem, although admittedly a minor one, is that the veil of ignorance is pierced on occasion by what appear to be arbitrary exceptions. For example, in seventeenth-century contract theory it was not supposed that the parties were ignorant of the particulars of their society – indeed, it was the very knowledge of the burdens of the state of nature that motivated them to agree in the first place. Rawls seems to ignore this. The original position is not supposed to reproduce an actual or fictitious event: he argues that it is designed as an abstract setting for rational deliberation (138) and, hence, he seems to believe that we can dispense with the problem of motivation. That would be an acceptable position if consistently held. But it is not. He introduces motivational arguments at various points. For instance, the parties are held to possess good will toward the next generation – they are, in essence, heads of families – and 'desire to further the welfare of their nearest descendents' (128). Again, he assumes that, as rational persons, they do not suffer from envy (143). If motivational assumptions such as these are necessary for the argument (as they are) can we dispense with a motivational assumption that explains the need to enter into a contract in the first place?

In truth, Rawls does not dispense with such an assumption, but he arbitrarily pierces the veil of ignorance just enough to provide it. The parties must know that they are 'roughly similar in physical and mental powers . . . and vulnerable to attack' (127). They understand that they exist in 'the condition of moderate scarcity' (127). They know that they are disinterested in one another's interests (except for the interests of the next succeeding generation) and that they 'put forward conflicting claims to the division of social advantages under conditions of moderate scarcity' (128). In other words, the parties know a great deal and much of what they know supplies a motive for the agreement. But why is this knowledge permissible and not other? Surely not because it is required *ad hoc* to justify certain arguments. Yet much of this knowledge cannot rightly be called general: scarcity is an empirical conclusion or an assumption upon which a particular economic theory is based. Even if we presume that it, like the knowledge that people will put forward conflicting claims, can be deduced from general political knowledge, that deduction can only be made if we believe our society to be like all or most others. In that case, we should be *assuming* particular facts to be true: and our operations will be motivated by that particular assumption. We learn about politics through our experience of politics. If Rawls wishes, for analytical purposes, to discard such learning, he must do so in entirety: he must leave us with the barest of political intuitions. He cannot leave us with sophisticated knowledge of some particular aspects of politics and ignorance of others, where both can be learned only in the same way.

This is, as I have said, a minor problem which could not by itself vitiate Rawls' argument. I should now like to turn to some major problems which I believe do seriously compromise his theory.

Rawls' social contract theory is an attempt to account for political obligation as well as for abstract conceptions of justice. This is made clear from the start. We are told that 'laws and institutions no matter how efficient and well-arranged must be reformed or abolished if they are unjust' and that 'everyone possesses an inviolability founded on justice that even the welfare of society as a whole cannot override' (3). The principles of justice not only 'specify the kinds of social cooperation that can be entered into and the forms of government that can be established', but they regulate the claims we may make upon each other, 'assign basic rights and duties and . . . determine the division of social benefits' (11). This point is explicitly maintained and extensively analyzed in Rawls' discussion of obligation and disobedience (Chapter VI, pp. 333–91).

The basic argument of social contract theory is that obligation is justified by agreement. I am obligated *because* I have agreed to the principles which regulate my conduct. Since the good is not, without more, reducible to the right, obligation cannot derive simply from the worth of certain principles. Something else is needed to import obligation and in this theory that something else is supplied by my promise, my voluntary undertaking, my agreement to abide by those principles. This means that, in order to justify obligation, it must be shown that I *have* promised: it is not enough to argue that I *ought* to promise or that I *would* promise given the proper circumstances.

Now, initially, Rawls does not try to show that I *have* promised. He derives his principles of justice and his theory of obligation by asking what kind of agreement would be made by rational, free, equal persons in the hypothetical original position. But the agreement that can be constructed out of the original position is not an agreement I *have* made. It is the agreement I *would* have made – or, better, *might* have made – *if* I were in the original position and *if* I were the representative rational person and *if* I conceived of the problem of justice as Rawls does – in other words, if I were not me, but someone else. But if obligation can derive only from my promises, then the fact that someone other than me has promised cannot impose obligations upon me, even if that someone else is not a real person but a constructive rational person. The only way to create obligation is to show that I agree to the terms of the social contract. Rawls makes such an argument, but it is, I believe, quite arbitrary. Let me suggest why this is so.

Other philosophers before Rawls have tried to combine a particular and substantive vision of political right with a commitment to agreement as a fundamental postulate of legitimation and they have faced similar problems. For our experience tells us that, if men were really left free to choose, most of their choices would be made self-interestedly. Now we must make a clear distinction between the effects of self-interested calculation in a hypothetical situation – such as the original position – where the parties may be presumed to be capable of reaching a harmonious conclusion, and the effects of self-interested calculation in an empirical situation where the veil of ignorance is non-existent and where agreement on the terms of justice will very much be affected by each person's opinion of the impact of the agreement on his existing life style. In the empirical situation, one cannot argue, e.g., that a wealthy person, consulting *his* interests, would agree to the difference principle. Indeed, it is Rawls' recognition of this that makes the veil of ignorance necessary. But this means that, if the self-interestedness hypothesis is true, the terms I would actually agree to are not the same, or need not be the same, as the terms of the agreement created in the original position.

To obviate this, we can deny the self-interestedness hypothesis and assume that, given proper social circumstances, men are beneficent and altruistic. But the creation of such circumstances cannot be imagined without the initial presence of a good deal of the beneficence that the circumstances themselves are supposed to create. Alternatively, we can accept the self-interestedness hypothesis and postulate a situation, like the laissez-faire market, in which pursuit of self-interested goals produces the common good. The problem here is that it has never been shown that such a postulate can apply to more than a segment of human society such as a distributive economic marketplace, if even to that. A third alternative is to assume that agreement to the terms of the original contract can be sought not in what men actually will, but in what they would will if they were rational. But the distinction between my rational and irrational selves – between my autonomous and heteronomous selves as the advocates of positive freedom often put it – is (as I shall argue in greater detail in chapter 4) psychologically arbitrary. I cannot divide myself up in such a way that I recognize as real or legitimate only those decisions which emanate from my rational self. For to do so would be to deal with a person who is an analytical construct – that is, who is not me but is another's interpretation of me; or, to put it another way, who is merely a model of me and hence an abstraction of me. Now the promise of such a construct or model is not my promise at all; and if political obligation can be produced only by agreement, it is fair to say that, whatever legal and philosophical fictions may be introduced, *my* agreement has not been given.

There are two ways out of this dilemma. One of them (which suffers from being quite narrow) is to assume that the restriction to the promises made by my rational self is legitimate where the analytical construct which is called my rational self is a product of my own interpretation of myself, and is not the interpretation of another. The problem here is immediately obvious. In the absence of discussion with and education by others, I cannot know what is rational. Consequently the construct called my rational self is always, and to what extent I cannot say, the product of others. Again, in order to imagine a social agreement based on such a theory, we would have to imagine a populace which agreed on the rational-irrational distinction, interpreted what is rational in the same way, and sought to act upon the maxims of the rational self, at least at all crucial times. But as such populace is clearly an imaginary one, *its* hypothetical conclusions cannot be used as a model of my own.

Rawls chooses a second way out of this dilemma. He presumes that we shall be able to reach the situation where the principles chosen in the original position match our 'considered convictions of justice' (19). By contrasting the principles thought to be chosen in the original position with our intuitive judgments, and by going back and forth between the two and making adjustments in each where there are discrepancies, we can eventually 'find a description of the initial situation that both expresses reasonable conditions and yields principles that match our considered judgments duly pruned and adjusted' (20). This state of affairs is known as 'reflective equilibrium'. It means that I do in fact accept, or can be persuaded by reflection to accept, the principles chosen in the original position (21). Hence, reflective equilibrium plays a role in Rawls' theory similar to the role that tacit consent plays in Locke's: if the concept is valid, then, even if the original position is wholly hypothetical, I may be fairly said to have assented.

In other words, I may be said to have consented (and thereby have incurred obligation) where the conclusions arrived at by the hypothetical rational man in the original position mirror the conclusions I would arrive at in the state of reflective equilibrium. If that is true, then consent must be interpreted to derive from the conclusions of all persons in a state of reflective equilibrium. But Rawls offers no evidence that all people in that circumstance would choose his conclusions. Indeed, there seems to be no way to show this: the overwhelming weight of empirical evidence is against it. The only argument he offers is what rational men would choose in the original position. At the very least he must show how and why our considered judgments would be the same. This, I believe, he cannot do. But if he could do it, then the social contract would be irrelevant. The existence of obligation could be justified by the fact that men actually choose Rawls' conclusions. It is not even clear that the social contract would be needed to serve as a model of the agreement. If it is not, and, if our considered judgments match the conclusions of the social contract, we can only wonder why it is necessary to postulate the veil of ignorance since we reach the same conclusions with or without it. But even if Rawls is correct in assuming that the social contract would be needed as a model or as an initial source for discussion, it is clear that obligation must derive from our actual – or considered – judgments and not from the hypothetical contract.

The conclusions I would arrive at in a state of reflective equilibrium are conclusions of reason. Both the original contract and my considered conception of justice reflect rational thinking. What I should now like to argue is that Rawls' conception of rationality is – for lack of a better word – ideological and that his conclusions, far from being the necessary conclusions of rational men, reflect principles that liberal market-oriented covenantors would be likely to think of. In a word, the terms of Rawls' covenant are arbitrary. (I shall deal with Rawls' approach to rationality as it is reflected in his theory of the original contract although the criticisms would be applicable to his notion of reflective equilibrium as well.)

The charge that Rawls' theory is arbitrary should not be surprising, given the history of contract theory and the conflicting variety of agreements and principles that contract theorists have deduced from starting points similar to Rawls'. The point is that the conclusions of social contract theory largely depend upon the knowledge and motivations with which the original covenantors are endowed. But we do not *know* what knowledge or motivation they may be endowed with. Each theorist is free to create his own conditions and we can guard against only the most obvious forms of arbitrariness. Indeed, contract theorists do not discuss whether we *can* know what the original covenantors might be said to know or how we can avoid endowing these hypothetical constructs with a knowledge which necessarily reflects the theorist's experience and commitments.

Rawls' arbitrariness rests on his peculiar concept of rationality, a concept which reflects current and traditional market economics. The rational means 'taking the most effective means to given ends'

and little else. Above all, since 'the initial situation must be characterized by stipulations that are widely accepted', the concept of
rationality necessarily excludes 'any controversial ethical elements'
(14). Let us put aside the question whether the initial situation as
presented by Rawls *is* characterized by stipulations that are widely
accepted (a dubious proposition, I believe, yet one about which
Rawls characteristically offers no evidence). Is not this 'narrow
sense' of rationality, however 'standard in economic theory', controversial? Or are we to believe that the definition of a concept in
terms of efficiency is not an ethical definition?

Rawls' concept of rationality is one that may be held by modern
economic man; but it is by no means the only, or the most persuasive version of rationality. Its persuasiveness clearly depends upon
our ability to share Rawls' economic and methodological orienta-
tions.

Why should the original covenantors not assume that rationality demands a belief in natural law or that no rational person could
doubt the existence of a divinely ordained order of the universe?
Such views of rationality have been advanced and have captured
men's imaginations. They certainly do not represent modern concepts of rationality, but a restriction of rationality to its modern
economic meaning is clearly forbidden by the veil of ignorance.
The point is that what is held to be rational changes from era to
era: there is no single timeless concept of rationality. If Rawls
believes that there is, he is obliged to show why: but he does not
do it. He merely assumes that the rational has a single meaning,
that being the one he attaches to it.

But what would the original position look like if painted by a
man of 1400? Would he not vary the picture painted by Rawls radically? Would the social contract be made by men equally free and
rational or by representatives of the different orders of society so as
to reflect the divine ordering? Would his conception of what it
would be rational to choose be the same? Would the veil of ignorance be a presumption or would it reflect man's faulted nature and
hence yield radically different interpretations of what man in the
original position can know and not know? And is this not a valid
conception of rationality, however objectionable or inadequate it
might be on other grounds?

Rawls' conception of the rational reflects the market-liberal conception of the rational: Rawls' original covenantors, far from being only hypothetical rational men, are liberal market men. The absence of dogmatic beliefs, of overriding concerns for order, of the conviction of the need to reproduce a divine plan, are marks not of the absence of a defined ethical philosophy, but of the presence of one. Indeed, Rawls' whole theory of rational action is based upon presuppositions that have grown out of market-liberal social science, such as the notion that rationality requires that men will be moved to maximize advantages and minimize or hedge against risks. Typically market-liberal conclusions emerge from the original position because the very conception of the original position is laden with market-liberal presumptions.

An example of this is the conclusion Rawls feels would be drawn concerning equality. Rawls suggests that men in the original position would agree to inequalities so long as those inequalities were necessary to make everyone better off. But this is clearly not the only view of equality which rational men might take. Might the men in the original position not value most a sense of community and mutual respect of each other's worth, believe that only perfect equality would create this, and hence opt for perfect equality even conscious of the possible economic costs involved? Sophocles believed that equality was valuable because it stabilized human social relations. Nicholas Heming believed equality reflected the equality of souls before God. There is no reason why rational men must choose Rawls' difference principle. Indeed, there is no reason why the issue of equality must be seen to concern only the distribution of economic goods. This position, like the difference principle, reflects views which might be held not by all men, but by market-liberal men, by persons schooled in an approach to rationality which stresses some things over others.

There are other evidences of Rawls' market-liberal construction of the original position. Consider his concept of the veil of ignorance. The assumption that parties could arrive at a fair and rational agreement only by being ignorant of their own social positions and values presumes that justice can only result from agreements made by atomized individuals. This is reflected in the essentially individualistic conception of justice that ensues. But it is possible that rational men could believe that justice is possible only in a society conscious of the bonds of community that make it possible for people to wish to do justice to others. They may believe that societies can regularly pursue justice where just rules are supported by a shared passion for justice, by a common desire to do justice and that this can occur only where the concept of justice itself reflects a sense of community. In another context, Rawls seems to accept at least part of this notion. In his discussion of majority rule, he suggests that the coherence of majority rule depends upon a common conception of justice and the fact that the different sectors of society have confidence in one another (231). But the construction of the original position is such that justice derives from agreements made by individuals consulting only their own interests and ignoring the possible demands of community. Although we should not push the point overmuch, especially in view of Rawls' limited egalitarian conclusions, Rawls' original position uncomfortably resembles a marketplace in which the rules that emerge reflect only the agreements made by individual self-interested participants.

There are other features of the original position which reflect a market-liberal orientation. For example, while the parties are not presumed to take an interest in one another's interests, they are presumed to take an interest in the interests of the next succeeding generation: 'we may think of the parties as heads of families . . .' (128). Now the concerns that heads of families might have for their descendants' well being can be imagined to be various, but characteristically Rawls articulates this concern in a special economic context. The parties in the original position are to be aware of the importance of saving – that is, they understand that in each generation an amount of capital must be put aside for succeeding generations. But is it likely that, in a non-market society, the concern of heads of families with the well being of the succeeding generation would be primarily articulated in such a way? Is the extensive concern with capital savings a universal concern or does it reflect a view likely to occur to covenantors in a market society, whether liberal or not?

Other examples exist,[9] but I believe I have given enough to make my point: Rawls deduces principles from an original position in which these principles are already encased. The original position is characterized by something besides fairness: it is characterized by liberal-market values disguised as rationality which create and determine the outcome.

The conclusion we are driven to, I believe, is that, if the principles of Rawls' contract are valid, they are valid not because anyone agreed to them in fact, but because they are morally compelling – that is because Rawls presents convincing reasons why we *ought* to agree to them. Why, then, speak about them in terms of consent? If we speak about a hypothetical agreement, actually produced by moral argument, we speak about a set of norms I am not free to dissent from unless I can produce a better argument. But the virtue of consent is precisely that it depends on freely made choices. The reason we value consent is that we value the concept of a social order based on voluntarism whose goals are determined by and whose acts reflect the values and wishes of its members. Neither Locke nor modern contract theorists such as Rawls create such a mechanism. What they create instead is a conception of legitimacy and obligation justified by rational argument and supposed to be not consensual but true or valid. Such a procedure is, I think, the best available, but it is not what we think of when we speak of consent.

It is possible to argue that, even if we cannot derive the standards which justify obligation by consent, we should refer to consent to decide whether the regime fulfills those standards. In other words, consent is employed to answer the question, Who decides? If consent does not determine the conditions a regime must fulfill to be legitimate, it may be used to decide whether those conditions are satisfied.

Apart from the objections one might have to this particular mode of evaluating a regime (e.g., that the will of the majority is not necessarily the rule of right or a reliable guide to the evaluation of regimes), one other objection recommends itself. It is hard to see why such a decision should be called consent at all. For, by definition, the people have no control over the standards which they must apply and no say in how those standards are to be interpreted. They can only say whether they are, as given, being reasonably fulfilled. But to have no control over the terms and conditions of the exercise of authority, the determination of social goals, the very definition of the moral texture of a social order, is hardly consent. It differs in no important way from ordinary democratic procedures which concern the rightness of regime policies. If that is what is meant by consent, then it does little harm to call legitimate regimes consensual. But it still leaves us with the crucial problem of determining what the standards of legitimacy should be.

Consent as fact: civic religion, social contentment, egoism. Suppose we were faced with a theorist who claimed that, whatever the defects of social contract theory, a legitimate regime is one which has, *in fact,* the approval of a majority of its citizens: that consent is important and that it is, in principle, possible to discover whether a majority has consented. We might ask such a theorist to reflect upon the nature of that consent – upon its sources and motives. The strange fact is that consent theorists, in failing adequately to consider this question, have overlooked some of the commonest facts of human social life. No one needs to be told that societies do not invite their members to make free, objective choices about their allegiance. Hume long ago noted that even in relatively free societies the refusal of allegiance is often the subject of sanctions. In some states, I have no choice but to obey; in others, my choice is limited by my awareness of the extremely unpleasant results that likely will follow from an avowal of disloyalty or a rejection of the state's legitimacy. Moreover, the traditional option offered to dissenters – emigration – is usually a chimera, for even if I am allowed to emigrate there must be a legitimate society willing to take me in if that option is to be meaningful. More important, emigration is so drastic a step that few people are willing to risk it. For many people – the poor, the disinherited, the ignorant, the aged, the unskilled – emigration is now not only a practical impossibility but is unlikely to result in any real improvement in their lives. Hume rightly compared their option to the situation of a person unwillingly taken aboard a ship and given a choice between conforming to the ship's discipline or swimming across the sea to shore. On one level, then, consent may only be evidence of the fear of dissent. There are, however, other levels of argument.

Every society creates a civic mythology or civic religion which it attempts to inculcate in its members. Its educational process, its civic rituals, its sports, its professed values, its manipulation of its history, its control over or influence on public information, its suppression or cooptation of dissidents, are all designed to influence its members' choices. We are assaulted by manipulative forces on every side. Whether the manipulation is crude – as in the American schools' perversion of the history of the westward expansion or as in our learning to evaluate other cultures by considering what they have given to us – or subtle – as in the identification of religious teachings with conventionalist moral exhortation, or the willingness seriously to entertain such discussions as whether economic equality is subversive of freedom – the result is consistent: it is to condition our perceptions of social reality in such a way that the political and cultural traditions we are used to appear both natural and reasonable. What Shaw said of Englishmen is true, more or less, of most of us: we are free to believe whatever the government and public opinion permit. There are some, it is true, who escape such control, but they are few. For the rest, consent is likely to represent not the conclusions of free rational men, but the opinion of people whose understanding of the world has been manipulated to produce approval.

It is also true – and obvious – that the acts usually taken to indicate tacit consent (continued residence in a society, obedience to its laws, acceptance of its authority, etc.) have by no means as unambiguously political connotations as they are assumed to have. They frequently indicate only that we are at home in a particular cultural milieu and that our willingness to accept the authority of a regime may reflect less our opinion of that regime than our reluctance to uproot ourselves from the pattern of social traditions and personal ties which help to define our personalities. It is precisely this fact that has escaped most consent theorists. My dissatisfaction with a government may be overwhelmed by the perceived consequences to my social or personal life of emigrating or otherwise rejecting it. I am, after all, educated and socialized within a particular culture, know its language, am comfortable with its customs. My choice of an appropriate life style, my expectations concerning social behavior, my resolution of personal and sexual tensions, even my tastes in food and the way I organize my daily routine, are factors which tie me to a society which helped to form them. These things, together with my family life, friendships, social or economic status, may be powerful inducements to remain in place if the political price I must pay for them is not too great. I shall summarize all of these inducements in the phrase, 'social contentment'.

On the whole, consent theorists have been unable to specify the role social contentment plays in consent. Clearly, it is a strong motive for obedience and, in a society like our own which focuses enormous attention on the importance of the private life and treats public institutions as necessary nuisances, in which a satisfactory private life is the *summum bonum*, it may become the chief consideration. But a regime ought not to be legitimated by opinions related to everything but its worth. Joseph Tussman, in a different context, has shown how acts of even tacit consent must be done consciously and knowingly, with awareness of their meaning, if they are to function as acts of consent.[10] Consent is an act of affirmation. It has meaning when those who consent understand that they are doing more than approving of the nature of their private and social lives. They must realize that they are authorizing a regime to act for them in a certain way and that that authorization is to be the source of the regime's right to act authoritatively. The acts which constitute evidence of tacit consent must therefore be acts whose intended consequence is the legitimation of the regime.

When we consider the fact, as Tussman later argues, that few people act with such awareness, we cannot avoid concluding with him that few can really be said to consent. But even among those who can be said to consent, we cannot know how many are moved to do so by the press of social contentment and how many are aware of the ambiguities of their consent.

It is true that the worth of a regime can in some part be inferred from the quality of the private lives of its citizens. But such an inference must refer to the private lives of all of its citizens, not just of those who constitute a sufficient majority or a favored class. Hence, factors of fairness, equality, and justice must be introduced into any discussion of the quality of private lives. This then involves judging the worth of a regime not by referring to *our* private satisfactions, but to the way the private satisfactions of *all* are advanced or not – hence, by referring to standards normally thought of as public standards. Such judgment requires a disinterested evaluation of the private lives lived by all the members of a society and of the quality of justice in a society: it cautions us to ignore our own social contentments or at least judge them equally with the contentments of all. But the burden of my argument is that that is precisely what most people do not do and that this thus constitutes one of the grave weaknesses of consent theory. The standards by which one ought to judge the regime are standards consulted by very few. For the most part, consenting members consult the quality of their own lives.

Now something like this must be what we mean by egoism. The traditional notion of tacit consent holds that my consent may be inferred from my voluntary enjoyment of the benefits offered me by society. A society which offers real benefits to two-thirds of its members is thus entitled to their consent and the consequent presumption of legitimacy so long as they enjoy these benefits. Now suppose that I am one of those old-fashioned romantics who has a genuine concern for the well being of my fellow men, who is disturbed by the thought of starving children, or who believes that I am not free where a sizeable number of my fellows is chained. It is entirely plausible that I should conclude that a regime under which such things take place is not entitled to be called legitimate. Yet at this point I discover that while I continue to enjoy benefits I cannot withdraw my allegiance from a regime which denies them to others, that I cannot be my brother's keeper. To do so I should have to renounce my own enjoyment of benefits and take my place among the victims – an act we think of as saintly and hence rare. We have known for centuries that it is at best difficult to be both a good Christian and a good citizen. But should we value a theory of legitimacy which makes it nearly impossible to be both? The notion of tacit consent – unsupported by any groundwork of rational good or natural law – makes altruism illegitimate in the absence of a sacrifice few are brave enough to make. There may be nothing incoherent or illogical in this, but there is not much good in it either.

The notion of tacit consent, tied as it is to social contentment, encourages me to look inward to judge the public realm and to regard my obligation as based on the good I derive from a regime rather than the good shared by all citizens. It encourages me to dissent only where I am harmed or threatened and to divorce my political commitments from consideration of harm or threat to others. Sometimes such a procedure is satisfactory. In certain cases, consulting my own interests really involves protecting the interests of others. Your freedom to speak or your enjoyment of fair legal processes are clearly threatened by their denial to me. But there are many other rights or options which are not so limited. The denial of the franchise to blacks did not prevent whites from voting; the unavailability of higher education to the poor did not make it harder for the rich to pay tuition; the existence of a restricted officer class did not make cannon fodder out of gentlemen. And there are many social privileges whose significance is enhanced by their not being universal. Governments participate in a thousand informal ways in supporting – directly or indirectly – social repressions and discriminations. By glorifying certain segments of the community rather than others, by desultory enforcement of egalitarian ideals to which they are nominally committed, by inadequate provision for health, housing, or education, they are able to perpetuate noxious or discriminatory social practices which overtly affect only a portion of the community. But ought such practices not be the concern of those who are unaffected by them? Ought we assume that they cannot form the basis for my refusal of consent if I am one of the privileged? Ought tacit consent to underwrite brute self-interest and make it impossible to justify a somewhat nobler motive? If consent is indeed a coherent theory, it can be a just one only where the process of giving one's consent can be insulated against the temptations of self-interested social contentment. Since this seems improbable, one can only conclude that those who value things like human liberty, dignity, equality, must look for some other standard on which to base political obligation.

It is necessary to say one final word about the function of social contentment in the legitimating process. Sensible men understand the full and terrible meaning of the extraordinary value the West has placed on the private realm and its consequent denigration of the public one. The sum of human value is not comprehended by private satisfactions. Public life is critical also and the creation of an authentic and just public life is part of what human life entails and modern western society lacks. Participation and involvement in public affairs may not be desired by all, but we have a right to expect that a government worthy of men will not only permit but will encourage such participation. The notion of an overriding common good may be a chimera, but no decent and free society can proceed without some commitment to goods which can be shared by all and a determination to consult standards more universal than the satisfaction of private interests. A theory which identifies public good with private satisfactions and which encourages men to turn inward and cultivate only their own gardens creates a standard of public good fit for idiots rather than men. Two centuries of experience with the philosophy of self-interest should be enough to disabuse all but the most stubborn and incompetent of the awesome horrors implicit in it. Consent, as it turns out, is a theory of self-interest – at least as it is most commonly put forward. But legitimacy and obligation must be made to depend on an assessment of the quality of social life and the universalization of social benefits rather than on inferences to be drawn from social contentment and self-interest. I have argued earlier that consent is incoherent and will argue shortly that obligation and legitimacy may be justified only be appealing to standards derived by rational argument. We now see that even if consent were not incoherent the practical result of invoking consent in the modern world would be to record the satisfactions of a favored majority. This objection certainly does not destroy the logic of consent; but the consequence of retaining it would be that, for the sake of doctrinal consistency, we should lower the moral worth and meaning of legitimacy and obligation.

Protection of liberty against consent. The problems of basing obligation on consent are compounded where, as is frequently the case, the mechanism of consultation excludes a significant part of the population. Consider, for example, Locke's exclusion of servants from the consent process. In *The Political Theory of Possessive Individualism*, MacPherson points out that, in the seventeenth century, the word 'servant' referred to anyone who worked for another for wages.[11] This comprehended over half of the population of England at the time – hence, Locke actually excluded the majority from the consent process altogether. In practice, even the most liberal societies have not consulted all the people or universalized free choice in the matter.

The very exclusivity of the concept 'people' in traditional consent theory was quite dramatically, if inadvertently, demonstrated by that most famous of all social contracts – the Mayflower Compact. The historical significance of the Mayflower Compact has been questioned by critics of social contract theory on the grounds that it was not an independent confirmation of that theory but a product of men who already believed in it and acted on their convictions. But more important, the Mayflower Compact excluded from the consensual process the very people whose land and property were being appropriated. Far from being a social contract which founded a society, the Mayflower Compact was an agreement among conquerors setting out the conditions for sharing spoils. The social order so created in effect set the pattern for future interpretations of consensual legitimacy: in accepting the Mayflower Compact as a legitimate instance of a social contract, Locke and his followers ratified the rightness of limiting consent to an exclusive segment of the community. In practice, this has always meant the more favored segment – that segment of the community more likely to consent. Women, the young, the rootless, the alienated, the illiterate, the poor, were excluded from the population consulted. Often, they were joined by the foreigner, the stateless person, the slave, the member of a despised race. Today they include millions who, while theoretically members of the community, are in fact excluded from participation in it by informally imposed disabilities – imposed often with the tacit consent of the government. We can now see that, far from being an arbitrary modification of consent theory, this shrinkage of the concept of the people is inherent in the very viability of consent, for it eliminated the need to seek agreement among all interests and classes in the creation of social institutions. It is the real meaning of Locke's assumption that while unanimity may be required in the decision to create a society, only a majority assent is needed to validate the institutions – particularly the political ones – of that society. For if the unanimous consent of the people is utopian, the consent of substantial portions of all classes in society is not. It is a perfectly plausible outcome under conditions of approximate equality. Such a condition seemed both out of the question and wrong in principle to Locke and has never been widely accepted with regard to social and economic conditions in any liberal society. The legitimation of such a society through consent was possible only where at least the most radically deprived interests and classes could be excluded from the consultative process. But if this shrinkage is a condition of the viability of consent, it is also its chief embarrassment. For it becomes a reason to suspect the obligations created and the legitimacy conferred. We are now faced with a notion of obligation which, however intentional and conscious, however rooted in promise or commitment, may itself be unjustifiable on moral grounds. The translation of an exclusive consent into legality and legitimacy almost always places the dissenting behavior of the non-favored or excluded people into the category of revolutionary criminality and thus subjects it to ostensibly justifiable punishment. In practice, political obligation is justified by legitimacy. We have seen that even consent theorists reach this conclusion. But if obligation is to be based on a legitimacy conferred by consent and that consent is solicited only among a portion of the population, then what is the obligation of the rest except sheer servitude? And what name can we give to such a legitimacy but domination?

We tend to be misled by the evocative language of consent theorists, by the rhetorical appeal of slogans like 'the consent of the governed'. We are still captivated by Fortescue's vision of a *dominium politicum et regale*, in which the 'kynge may not rule his peple bi other lawes than such as thai assenten unto'; or by Locke's spirited defense of the right of a people to remove the tyrant – so captivated indeed that we tend to see the problem in the simplistic framework in which they put it: as a struggle between two parties (king and people) in which the authority of the one is based upon the assent of the other. But of course there are not two parties to such an agreement but millions, and 'the people' is not a group but a diffuse amalgam of persons with conflicting interests, ideals, wants, and needs whose consent is ambiguous; is based upon differing and often conflicting judgments of personal advantage, public good, and practical necessity; and is frequently given without thought. Once we realize this, and realize also that wholly different views of political right issuing by accident in consent may still not speak to the legitimacy of the government consented to, we can begin to understand the horrible absurdity of binding an ignored or dissenting minority to a legitimation granted by a majority. Understanding this requires us to frame obligation and legitimacy in such a way that the things necessary to liberty and human dignity are preserved inviolate against consensual invasion.

3. *Civility and obligation*

Right and good

At least since Sidgwick's *Methods of Ethics*, we have known that the predicates 'right' and 'good' are not reducible to each other. But too much may be made to depend on this idea. Like the notion that moral conclusions cannot validly be drawn from factual premises, the distinction between right and good does not end discussion but impels us to carry it forward. In the one case we are told merely that we must introduce other (moral) premises; in the other that we must specify the connection between right and good – that is, introduce premises of action or choice.

My belief that it is better to suffer evil than to do it does not, by itself, impose an obligation upon me. But where I am faced with a choice of suffering evil or doing it, my choice is incoherent if I choose to do it. It may be that the statement '*a* is good' is not further reducible to the statement '*a* ought to be done'. But if any action may be predicated upon premises of which *a* is one, and if *a* gives the best account of the goodness of the action, I am obliged to do *a*. In the absence of such an assumption moral evaluation becomes pointless or trivial, for the purpose of moral evaluation is not merely to compare ideals but to guide action. Obligation is in part a conclusion about the worth of a particular choice. In every case, the ascription of obligation must refer to a moral standard or value which can be justified in terms of goodness. Equally, a judgment of worth – a value or ideal – entails an obligation to act in accordance with it where we are faced with a choice of actions one of which embodies that value or ideal. Where ideals conflict, moral evaluation may create a serial order of worth, in which case we are obligated to act in accordance with what is evaluated as best. If 'ought' is not reducible to 'good', the question, 'What ought we to do?' can be answered only by referring to something evaluated as good; while the evaluation of something as good creates, in appropriate circumstances, an obligation independent of any other commitment on our part.

It thus may be possible to arrive at a theory of obligation by considering the moral ideals relevant to a defensible social order. If it is necessary for men to form and live in social groups outfitted with adequate political authority, if we can show that human life and moral action itself are in general impossible on any other supposition, we may be able to account for the political obligations of men without resorting to consent or requiring any explicit commitment to create obligation.

Civility

Political obligation arises from the perception that some mechanism is needed to meet common threats – threats which involve whole groups and societies. At the same time, any mechanism decided upon must have a serious effect on the moral lives of the people concerned with it: on their capacities to make moral decisions, on their freedom, needs, and aspirations. We are consequently always faced with choosing ways to meet common threats that are consistent with the legitimate demands of the moral life. For this reason we would be wrong to make obligation depend solely on commitment or to divorce our account of obligation from standards of goodness. Whatever may be true of other types of obligation, political obligation is inseparable from a judgment of the worth of political institutions and practices and their relation to things like moral decisionmaking, freedom, needs, and aspirations. In addition to this, questions of political obligation do not arise in the abstract, but are always located in a context of choice. If it may be said that we have no choice but to engage in politics, it is also true that we must choose what political acts we ought to do, what groups and institutions we ought to recognize or accept as authoritative, what laws we ought to obey, and so forth. Political obligation can only be defined and understood in terms of choices like these or in terms of choices concerning types and boundaries of authoritative behavior. The resolution of these choices involves us in assessing the worth of competing options.

This assessment is the chief factor in deciding on the rightness of obligation. For obligation itself is not difficult to justify. The commitment which many philosophers believe is essential to the existence of obligation – that commitment which converts judgments of worth into moral oughts – is, I think, an unarguable presumption inseparable from the very existence of human association and life. Without it, human society could not survive and the discussion of moral norms would be pointless.

I do not wish to labor one of the commonest and most obvious points in political literature and would not if it were not the case that many contemporary theorists tend to ignore it completely. But as Hobbes and Hume – and lately Hart – have argued, the threat to survival is what gives politics its importance and makes things like obedience to laws and keeping one's promises compelling. Not compact, not utility, not abstract right could for one minute convince people to obey political rules if that obedience were irrelevant to the survival of society and culture. It is the fact that the metaphor of social disintegration is not an extravagant act of imagination but a recognition of the clearly tenuous and conditional existence of civility and culture that makes the justification of political obligation significant.

Of course one may argue that the desirability of survival cannot be demonstrated with finality or validly inferred from its relationship to human existence. But this is surely a trivial point. Human life is in part defined by a network of needs, aspirations, and ideals whose very existence is dependent upon a social order and hence upon politics. Not merely culture, but moral life itself, the attainment and transmission of moral ideals – indeed the very understanding of ideals and the impetus and means to investigate them – are inseparable from the social order which makes culture possible and which in its turn is inseparable from politics. These considerations amply justify the phenomenon of political obligation. If it is possible to argue that the cost of dispensing with political obligation is the disintegration of culture and moral life, one has presented as compelling an argument for a moral position as it is possible to make – an argument which, if it stops short of analytical or objective truth, is nevertheless controvertible only at the cost of presuming the irrelevance to philosophy and morality of social existence. But the very possibilities of holding moral opinions, of contesting the justifiability of political obligation, of raising the problem of philosophical justification itself, are impossible without a social order and culture. In a very real sense, it is not the anarchist or nihilist, but the person with no moral opinions at all who may be said to be free of political obligation.

Politics thus goes to the heart of human existence and the demand for political obligation reflects the need to provide a mechanism for meeting threats to that existence. The most common form of encapsulating these threats involves the use of metaphors of communal destruction: the chaotic reduction of society to anarchy and man's entrance into a social wilderness, or the destruction of a particular order of society through conquest, enslavement, etc. But these metaphors need not be so apocalyptical. They may also be stated in terms of the desiccation of a culture and a common life which we may summarize by the phrase 'social disintegration'. Some of the most striking images of destruction are stated in this way. Consider the prophetic charge that God would forsake an apostate people, or the fears of Augustine and his contemporaries of the barbarism that would result from the fall of Rome. To these men, disintegration was not restricted to the casting of men into a permanent state of anarchic bestiality. It involved also, and perhaps more terrifyingly because more real, the replacement of a civil culture by barbarism.

This latter fear is notably present in the most famous literary example of social disintegration: the seventeenth century's state of nature. Of course we all know that the state of nature was never intended to serve as an historical account of the actual genesis of society. But neither was it, as many of us assume, merely an analytical postulate. The state of nature was also a prophecy of barbarism, a metaphor describing what human life might turn into if the conditions of civil association were seriously breached. For the social contract theorists, very much including Locke, the state of nature was primarily characterized by the psychological rather than political consequences of the absence of authority. Not mere unpredictability, nor even instability, but anxiety must be the chief result; and anxiety thus becomes the fundamental cause of civil association. But because the state of nature is not a picture of a primitive historic past, but an anxiety-breeding result of the failure of legitimacy and the degeneration of social order and culture, it remains a possibility for the future as well.

This possibility transcends the lapse of governmental authority and the relapse into anarchy. It is definable also in terms of the destruction of the capacity for specifically human life – in Locke, for instance, of the capacity for exercising God-given or natural rights. For the fact is that the relation between politics and culture is not one-way but reciprocal. If politics is necessary for the existence of culture and moral life, it is also based on culture and moral life. For politics to sustain a culture, it must be a politics based upon an appeal to something other than brute force. It must be based upon a notion of authority exercised according to certain standards – on an alternative to violence and barbarism, both of which defeat the very possibility of standards, culture, moral life, and even the stabilization of individual expectations and the protection of private life. The perversion of man's culture or moral life may plunge men into an anomic barbarism insufficiently distinguishable from anarchy – if distinguishable at all – in its results on the human psyche. Can we not understand the horrors of modern totalitarianism in this way? The conversion of a public or a people into an alienated, anomic, manipulable mass through the perversion of a culture and the substitution of controlled violence and terror for the order of society and legality produces precisely the opposite of what Locke understood by the phrase 'civil society' and stands as a genuine realization of common images of social disintegration. The twentieth century has taught us to take seriously both Locke's assumption that the destruction of civil order need not involve overt anarchy and chaos and Augustine's belief that the agonies and horrors of the last days may be played out against a background of apparently normal political authority. If barbarism is the negation of politics, the barbarization of a culture is as much an act of social disintegration as the destruction of its government.

It is not hard to see why this is so. It is encased in the very meaning of the concept 'politics' which has never, until quite recently, been interpreted as a neutral, value-free, wholly descriptive concept. This view is too well known to require extended discussion. It may best be stated by asking what the absence of politics seems to entail. The antithesis of politics is not individuality, or absence of authority and power, but anarchy, barbarism, violence, and arbitrary exercise of power. The point of political association is to make it possible to create a tradition in which the practices customarily associated with the concept of civility replace those associated with the arbitrary and barbarous condition of apolitical violence.

Civility means more than survival, stability, and the existence of culture: it is also and necessarily concerned with moral life, for the outlawing of barbarism and violence involves the understanding, attainment, and transmission of moral ideals; the justification of mutual restraint in interpersonal undertakings; and the consequent association of human action with moral decisionmaking and free moral judgment.

Thus, obligation derives from the imperative of survival which, as human life involves not merely physical existence but the presence of those specifically human capacities we summarize by phrases such as 'moral life', must be seen to include the survival of that level of human association which makes civility – political association, culture, and moral life – possible. Consequently, the justification of obligation entails an evaluation of the extent to which a particular set of political arrangements assures at least minimal attainment of these things. The most interesting and important questions regarding obligation concern the worth of the social order demanding obedience.

On a simpler level, it is possible to argue that the raw fact of obligation presents us with no choice at all. Political obligation is inseparable from at least current human experience. Men everywhere live in organized societies and the only question really relevant to the obligations imposed by these societies is not whether obligation is justified – we might as well ask whether it is right to breathe – but what that obligation may mean. This question may be approached by considering things like the worth of political authority, the proper limits of authority, the relation of authority to things like moral life.

The relation between politics and moral life takes place in the context of culture. There is an intimate and reciprocal relationship between politics and culture based on the fact that each influences the other and on the fact that both are modes of raising the level of human life above barbarism and violence, and thus contribute to the creation and sustenance of moral life. But, as I have suggested, politics may have this effect primarily as it creates the possibility of a culture of civility. I emphasize the word 'culture' because, in the absence of a sustained culture, civility is likely to remain a pious hope; for the traditions upon which social intercourse and civil behavior depend require more than authority to give them life. The problem of political obligation may be resolved only by asking what political arrangements meet the requirements of a culture of civility.

In one sense, the phrase 'culture of civility' seems redundant. For the very notion of culture is impregnated with civil implications. The word 'culture' necessarily stands for more than a description of the internal patterns of a community's social life: it stands for a notion of civility and conviviality as well.[1] For culture is nothing less than the attempt to create civilization – to develop traditions, ideals, standards, modes of transmitting knowledge and interpreting reality to meet common threats. It is a vehicle for the development of human aspirations, for the progressive satisfaction of needs. The very existence of a culture is a testimony to the notion of a common effort to outface barbarism, irrationality, brutishness, arbitrariness, violence. And one must underline the commonness of these threats and the dangers they create for whole communities. Whatever implications we may give to the notion of community, we must see it initially as inseparable from the notion of culture. Culture, civilization, is the attempt to create a life adequate to meet the threat of social disintegration. And this attempt can be made only in a context of conviviality – the cultivation of a common concern and association, the sense of the need to take account of others, to create a continual conversation among members of a community on the basis of trust and respect: in short, the capacity to create a common life.

We are entitled to ask how this may be done. As the process of identifying and evaluating human needs and aspirations goes on, how may a culture be adapted to deal with them? The answers may be many and complex but they must involve certain things without which the development of a culture of civility is impossible. They must involve the valuing of self-expression, self-restraint, reasonableness, openness, intellectual independence, diversity, free thought. The notion of a common life involves the creation of equal capacities to contribute to that life. A host of values is implicated in the notion of culture *because* we consider it not merely a description of the patterns of the internal life of a community, but as the opposite of barbarism and hence as something intimately related to the moral life of men. We are committed to optimizing the civil in culture by the need to outface barbarism – indeed, by the whole weight of reason. For civility is not only the very basis of reason, but the condition for its employment. And to the extent that reason is a condition of moral life – that is, of the making of moral decisions and the resolution of moral dilemmas – the values involved in a culture of civility are inseparable from that life.

The argument that political obligation is instrumental to culture and moral life and is limited in its scope by that relationship thus suggests some relatively clear boundaries. It suggests that the limits imposed by the concept of culture on political obligation can be understood in terms of the values just mentioned. Thus, if things like diversity, self-expression, free thought, equal capacities to contribute to a common life, and so forth, are inseparable from culture, they are necessary for the existence of a valid obligation. Neither consent, utility, religious tradition need be invoked to demonstrate this. It follows from the commitment to preserve society and culture from disintegration and barbarism – a commitment which I have suggested is, on rational grounds, unavoidable. I am never obligated to obey rules which restrict these values, except as it is necessary to restrict them to preserve the common life and to universalize them. Thus, self-expression may be restricted so that the self-expression of one is consistent with the self-expression of all others. I shall discuss my reasons for making such an argument shortly, although the argument is so obvious and common that extended analysis is really unnecessary. I shall also analyze these values and the way they function in a political order in a later chapter. My purpose at this point is not to present them systematically, but to show that the notion of culture need not be vague and conceptually useless.

The common life

I should now like to explore the notion of the common life. To say that political obligation is built upon a basis of common life may be to say too little or too much. It says too little if all that is meant is that politics requires association. It says too much if the phrase 'common life' is arbitrarily impregnated with egalitarian meanings.

Societies meet threats to survival and culture by acting on certain assumptions – the moral values of a society, like those of individuals, can be inferred from the maxims or assumptions upon which they act. But with the exception of a few well known, generally recognized, and apparently valid ideals – such as prohibitions against

murder – these assumptions are frequently subjects of great controversy. Under what conditions can they be imposed?

Consent is no answer, as I have tried to show. Moreover, like
absolute moral truths, consensually validated ideals do not apply
themselves and there is normally a good deal of dispute about when
and how they apply, what they imply in ambiguous circumstances,
how conflicts among them may be resolved, and, most important,
how to evaluate the circumstances to determine whether they are
relevant. Changing threats of social disintegration call for the
development of new and relevant values: to the extent that a social
order reflects moral visions, society must be seen as engaged in a
continuous and perpetual effort to create and justify new and relevant visions. Imposition of their moral visions by a wise and creative minority has always been an attractive answer – until it is
understood that wise men afflicted with self-interest do not normally make wise laws.

Moreover, two other things are obvious and true. First, people do
not engage in moral thinking automatically. They must learn what
can be evaluated and what moral thinking involves. Second, people
often receive moral enlightenment from others. From this, it seems
to me, we can draw four further conclusions. First, each person must
be willing to acknowledge his dependence on others for some or all
of his moral knowledge; second, each person must acknowledge
that, if he is concerned with moral evaluation, he is responsible for
transmitting this learning to others; third, each person must acknowledge that moral evaluation is impossible without exchanges
with others; fourth, each person must regard every other person as a
possible source for learning about moral values. The presupposition
of claiming moral values is thus a recognition that all other persons
can convey information about them. Since he can never know *a
priori* whether any particular person is a possible source of moral
knowledge, one concerned with moral evaluation must treat every
other person as possibly such a source. This knowledge may be
trivial – but it may be crucial. One cannot know in advance. Every
person concerned with moral evaluation must therefore treat every
other person as a potential source of crucial moral knowledge –
knowledge that may change his life. It is categorically wrong to
exclude anyone from the process of moral argument – wrong in
that it frustrates the enterprise of moral inquiry and moral life.

No person may be excluded from the process by which a society develops and articulates the ideals and values upon which its actions are based. If it is utopian to see this as requiring unanimous agreement, it is perfectly reasonable to see it as requiring that all people genuinely and freely have the opportunity to participate in the development and articulation of those ideals. Hence, valid political obligation requires the provision for all of equal possibilities to contribute to the common life.

To this point we have been dealing with politics only as it is instrumental to the development of a culture of civility. But politics may be more than instrumental: it may be valuable in itself. Politics may be a vehicle for the development of human personality and self-expression. Hence, as Mill believed, the justification for wide participation in politics is not that most people are wise or good, but that by participation they may be helped to become wiser or better. At any event, without identifying politics entirely with creativity, expression, development of personality, and so forth, it is right to say that politics may help to develop these things. Those who value them may then value a politics which helps to attain them.

I do not know of any argument which can justify the restriction of self-expression, creativity, development of personality, to less than all people. The types of expression may rightly be restricted, the direction of development influenced, creativity disciplined in appropriate and limited ways. But that some ought not to develop fully or be free to express themselves is an argument that cannot be sustained. Elitist arguments based on superior abilities, on nobility of mind or character, and so forth, are irrelevant. They merely state that not all people can develop or that social and political influence ought in some way to be governed by elite characteristics. They cannot show why these characteristics ought not to be possessed by all or why the attempt to develop them in all, or to create conditions in which they may be developed by all, is wrong.

If politics is a moral enterprise involving actions based on conceptions of value and persistent and continuing efforts to create and understand values, this very characteristic demands that all people be allowed to participate in the formulation, articulation, interpretation of those values. The common life is a common undertaking based on the presumption of equal liberty to contribute to that undertaking. What can such equality mean?

This question I will consider in some detail later. For the moment, I shall try to summarize, in admittedly sweeping terms, what I conceive to be its essence. My purpose now is not to present adequate arguments, but to summarize the basis of my approach.

No common life which demands that I surrender my right to judge its actions and demands retains its quality of commonality. It thus loses its principal justification for claiming my loyalty. A common life entails valuing the contributions to that life made by individual persons: it is a common life to the extent that its realization is a product of cooperative action in which individual moral visions and individual claims must be seriously considered and judged. It is possible only where every member is conceived to hold a morally significant place in the community and where he is as free as possible to contribute to it. Where these things are absent, no common life can exist and, hence, the thing which can rightly claim my loyalty evaporates.

Valuing the free expression of personality is a condition of the existence of a defensible common life, for free expression is the way men can contribute to it. But free expression is a mirage except under conditions of mutuality, where one test of the legitimacy of an expression of personality is whether it is consistent with the free expression of all other personalities. For a valid common life to exist, all claims must in principle be mutual and universal. The mechanism for recognizing claims which are mutual and universal is the translation of them into rights and the consequent translation of imposed responsibilities into mutual and universal obligations. Now from what I have been saying, it would indeed be inconsistent with any notion of a defensible common life to suppose that these rights and obligations can be restricted to particular persons, classes, or groups. For a common life to be the product of a cooperative effort, man must become known to society not as an identifiable individual, but as a representative of the general category 'man'. His status, rights, and obligations must attach to him as such an abstract representative. Insofar as he can be known to a regime, be the subject of rights and obligations, he can only be a juridical construct. Free man is juridical man.

We need do no more than recall the course of modern totalitarianism or reflect for an instant on the history of the American Negro to appreciate the immense significance of that concept. Its absence has been the constant which accompanies invidious legislation, deprivation of the rights of whole groups of people, repression. It is a long way from segregation to genocide, but both lie along the same road.

The concept of juridical man creates a definition of membership in a community based upon an equality of political significance. It strengthens the notion of the common life and encourages members of a society to define themselves in relation to their common life rather than in relation to other groups – race, class, sex, nationality, etc. The common life is subverted where the members of a community attribute their political significance to different sources, for sooner or later the social conflicts and group competitions endemic to social existence will begin to reflect those sources. This in turn will create a situation where the primary identification of individuals will be with groups other than the community; and it is only too likely that this system of identifications will result in attempts to identify the aims and aspirations of a particular group with those of the entire community and, hence, in legitimizing a particular version of social good to which others will have to conform. The replacement of juridical man by identified member – of race, class, sex, etc. – destroys, or at least subverts, the possibility of participation in a common life.

Let us pause for a moment to consider where we have come. I have argued that the justification of obligation is also a description of the limits of obligation: we are bound to do what is necessary to outface the threat of social disintegration and create the possibility of culture and civility. Such an objective can be attained only within the framework of a common life. A justifiable political order can only be one developed as a common undertaking where the articulation and administration of social values is a function of universal participation and equal liberty to contribute to them. I think that these conclusions, taken together with a recognition of the genuine and continuing controversy over values and the imprecision of our evaluations of circumstances allow us to draw a further inference: the widest possible diversity of social visions must be recognized not merely as tolerable but as legitimate. The boundaries of diversity are the threats of social disintegration.

The justifiable limits of obligation are given by the reasons why obligation is justifiable in the first place. The area of human activity outside of these limits corresponds to what we call basic human rights. To speak of these rights is thus to speak of activities which may not, except in the most limiting of circumstances, be restricted or invaded. Put another way, the articulation of basic rights is at the same time an articulation of the limits of political obligation.

The object of obligation

To whom or to what can we owe political obligation? For the most part, those who deal with the problem conceive that obligations are owed to states or regimes or to law itself. We discover arguments which hold that one has a *prima facie* obligation to obey the government or the law (more properly, law enforcement officials and judges) and so on. Such a view is deeply imbedded in our heritage, for most of the traditional discussions of obligation take place within the framework of obedience to the orders of formally designated officials. Divine right justifies obedience to the monarch, consent to those to whose authority one has assented. But such an answer cannot be given where political obligation is justified as a necessary mode of attaining certain ends or ideals.

What can it mean to say that the basis of our obligation is the common life? If it means anything at all, it must mean that our primary obligations are to a set of ideals and values, to a way of life we share with those with whom we are engaged in a common undertaking. For the common life is not merely a set of restrictions on a regime, but a way of life itself, a cooperative endeavor which defines our responsibilities and rights. To realize a common life we must understand that our primary obligation must be to those with whom we are engaged in a common undertaking. The government or the regime is an institution born of the necessity to administer and carry out the aims of the common life because these cannot be realized in its absence. The regime is thus an instrument of the common life, entitled to be obeyed when it carries out the aims and purposes of the common life, when it enhances the possibility of achieving the values that that life involves. We are obligated to obey the law to the extent that it is a formalization of the values of the common life. *But in no case can we say that our obligation to obey the regime or the law is primary, or that we have a* prima facie *obligation to obey them. We have a* prima facie *obligation to our fellows with whom we are engaged in a mutual enterprise.* We must take as our highest political responsibility the advancement of that mutual free expression, juridical status, and equality which are inescapably joined to justifiable obligation and which help to define a culture of civility. Our obligation to the regime – even to that savage and holistic abstraction known as the state – is at once secondary and prudential. It is secondary in that the test of our obligation to the regime is the regime's relation to the common life and its values. It is prudential in that the preservation of a culture of civility is largely a function of orderly and stable processes substituting formal methods of conflict-resolution for violence and self-assertion.

One further problem must be considered. Clearly, we may be said to owe moral obligations to those with whom we share nothing but ordinary humanity. But I have assumed that we owe different obligations to those with whom we share a common undertaking. Why does sharing a common undertaking make a difference in the obligations we owe?

Presumably, we cannot say that we owe different obligations to those with whom we share a common undertaking because we have joined with them, since that answer would seem to take us back to consent. It is not clear, however, that this is the case. Recall Ernest Barker's concept of the two social contracts. One contract creates a political association; a second determines political rights and the contours of political authority. But the justification of political obligation refers only to the second compact, for in contract theory our obligations arise not from the mere decision to associate, but from the content given to that association by further agreements. And it is by no means clear that the first contract entails a second. It is perfectly plausible to suggest that we can agree to form (or remain in) a political association whose rules governing rights and authority are necessarily determined by rational deduction from the concept of civility (or natural law, or whatever). I have suggested that this is in effect what Locke did. Thus, even if political association – the common undertaking – may be held to be a product of mutual agreement, the obligations it may rightly create need not – and, I believe, cannot – be. The question of the genesis of political association is different from the question of political right. An agreement to engage in a common undertaking still leaves open the question of what the goals and nature of that undertaking may be. And these need not be determined by agreement, but may – I would argue, must – be deduced from the requirements of civility.

But we need not resort to consent to understand the idea of a common undertaking or to account for the special obligations those who share such an undertaking owe to each other. We may also say that a common undertaking, creating special obligations, arises among those who are faced with common threats, whose actions habitually involve each other more than they involve others. Those affected by a common threat of violence and barbarism and whose attempt to create a culture of civility involves each other are united in a common undertaking, whether they agree or not.

In still another sense, the problem becomes a pseudo-problem. We are entitled to raise the question of obligation and the concept of the common life in the context of the types of states that exist in fact. If we are, in fact, divided into a world of nations, we are entitled to take this fact as basic to our inquiry and suggest that the common life is a mode of redefining the politics of the nation. If civility can be created only by creating a common life, and if the common life can be seen as largely a set of procedures and assumptions (as I shall argue in the last section of this chapter), then the existence of a common life becomes plausible for any type of political association. Although far from an ideal solution, it is not illogical or unreasonable to suggest that the concept of the common life can apply to any existing political association.

Individual and community

The concept of a common life implies the legitimacy of limitations on individual behavior. But what is the nature of the claims that the community may make on the individual? Perhaps we might consider, as a start, the approaches of Rousseau and Burke. Both Rousseau and Burke saw this problem as one abstractly posing the question of whether the community's demands in general are higher than those of the individual; and both agreed that the individual ought to find his freedom within the scope of those demands whose realization was necessary to preserve a certain type of community. For Burke, the concept 'type of community' referred to the institutions and practices which had grown up over a long period of time.

Here, the institutions and traditions of the community acquire prescriptive weight and gain a validity that is difficult to overcome. The community is given primacy over the individual and individual rights are deduced from the needs, demands, or traditions of the community. In such a situation, the conflict between individual and community demands is almost always settled in favor of the community and the notion that the individual has rights against the community is recognized only where these rights represent community norms or traditions.

One of the critical problems with the Burkean concept of tradition is that the traditions he spoke of were identified with the entire community despite the manifest fact that many groups and classes had systematically been excluded from the articulation of those traditions. Hence, the traditions that bound one to certain kinds of action, and whose prescriptive nature he identified with the very existence of the community, were not traditions of the *community* at all, but merely of a *segment* of the community. Whatever his intentions, Burke was not a defender of *tradition*, but of *authoritatively defined traditions* and of specific institutions which reflected the interests of a portion of the community. Hence, if the limits on political power are supposed to be deduced from tradition, then, in reality, the only limitations on power are the self-imposed limitations of those who, holding political authority, define the traditions under which the community is governed and their authority exercised. Burke thus limits the individual's obligations by nothing more tangible than the customs and good will of those who wield authority and impose obligations. The contest between individual and community is a contest between an authoritative elite which defines political right and a mass for whom political right is defined and whose rights are defined as obligations.

Rousseau deals with the individual–community problem in a different way from Burke, but agrees with him on one point: the values of the community – rights and obligations – are defined by the community and no limit is placed on this process save that the community as a whole must act and consult its corporate good. While Rousseau tries valiantly to preserve the freedom of the individual, such freedom is fundamentally inconsistent with the self-defining and self-validating character of community norms. Only let the norms be true community norms and there is no rightful disobedience to them. Consequently, the claims of the community over the individual are boundless. It is only by introducing the fiction of the general will, of the *true* will of the individual which is always consistent with the will of the community, that Rousseau manages to rescue, formally at least his commitment to freedom. Now the importance of the fiction of the general will is ordinarily thought to lie in the fact that it enables Rousseau to argue that the claims of the community are claims voluntarily imposed upon themselves by the members of the community and, therefore, that these claims are always consistent with freedom. That interpretation gives rise to criticisms of the general will (e.g., that it is psychologically arbitrary, that it presumes a false harmony between individual and group desires, that its coherence depends upon a falsely attributed organic unity to society, and so forth) and of Rousseau's theory of freedom with which we are all familiar. It may be that these criticisms are valid – I do not wish to pursue that argument now. But I do wish to pursue another intimation of the concept of the general will which, though apparently important to Rousseau, is often overlooked. I should like to suggest that Rousseau's theory imposes a limit on the claims of the community which, if inadequate by itself, is nonetheless of critical significance.

That limit derives from the convivial nature of the Rousseauean community. That is, whereas the norms (traditions) of the Burkean community are authoritative norms, laid down by an elite, the norms of the Rousseauean community are expressly the products of conviviality. A convivial society is one in which the creation of political procedures and the articulations of policies are based upon the recognition of the inter-relatedness of our lives and which, therefore, encourages the view that obligations are owed primarily to our fellows. Rousseau held – in one of his finest insights – that such a society demanded a continual conversation among its citizens, a political process built upon equality, participation, and persuasion. Such a community, he believed, would be one in which mutual accommodation and concern would be fostered. However much Rousseau might have overestimated the extent to which self-interest could be conquered, it is possible to accept that much of his theory which holds that a convivial society is one which is less likely than an authoritative one to impose grievous claims on individuals. We need accept this not as a necessary consequence entailed in the concept of conviviality, but as a general tendency of convivial and democratic societies, and supported not by logic, but by experience. That there are exceptions – even frequent ones – to this tendency only tells us that Rousseau was wrong in supposing that conviviality was the sole prerequisite for freedom. It does not negate the fact that convivial societies tend to impose the least burdensome claims upon individuals and that the other requisites for individual freedom are found most securely and persistently in those societies. Nor need we be much troubled by the threats to freedom that Rousseau raises, by his commitment to civic religion, or by his narrow view of civic education. In building on Rousseau's insights we are not bound to accept his excesses, nor are we bound by the contradictions and confusions – such as they are – of his general theory. Rousseau allows us a glimpse of the importance of conviviality – of a social relationship in which obligation is seen as owed to our fellows rather than to a state or regime, of the importance of seeing our fellows as equals, of the understanding that the basis of a common life is that each person shall be free to contribute to that life and judge its values. This, as I have said, may not be the whole of the case, but it is the necessary starting point upon which we may build.

The distinction between authoritative and convivial concepts of community is in part a distinction between traditions developed through a process of political socialization and traditions developed through a process of political education. Robert Pranger has pointed out the useful distinction between political education (meaning the education of free citizens in the practice of making independent political judgments) and political socialization (meaning the training of citizens to accept the civic responsibilities imposed upon them by social institutions and authorities).[2] The former takes place only within a context of citizen participation in 'the discovery of political values through common action by the entire membership rather than through the mediation of special authorities'.[3] Most of the conservative exponents of tradition see the process of political education quite differently: they, like Burke, support what Pranger would call political socialization. Michael Polanyi, for example, sees tradition – indeed the whole enterprise of conviviality – as referring to a consensus among elites accepted by society at large, which is 'responsive to the intellectual passions of this elite'.[4] An 'ideal free society' is one in which 'the shaping and dissemination of moral convictions should take place . . . under the guidance of intellectual leaders, spread out over thousands of special domains and competing at every point with their rivals for the assent of the public'.[5] He calls these leaders 'authoritative individuals' and that poses a problem.

How is the public to give its assent? Surely, the terms of public assent reflect the political education of the people, their responsiveness to authoritative leaders, the extent to which independent judgment is cultivated in them. But if the traditions which surely must guide a people's judgments are formed initially by authoritative leaders, will those traditions not encourage a pattern of acceptance of authoritative consensus? Political education (or socialization, as Pranger would call it) is largely controlled by political elites, and normally represents the institutionalization of conventional and regime-supporting values. Marcuse has pointed out – and he is certainly not the first to do so – that political socialization encourages a people to do no more than freely choose accepted ('establishment') values. In a similar vein, Shaw remarked that Englishmen would always be free to believe whatever the government and public opinion allowed them to; and Samuel Hobson sadly noted that the greatest triumph of capitalism was to make its victims proud of it. The justification of tradition as defined by an elite will always lead to the support of that elite. What is needed is a shift in our conception of what traditions are and whose understandings they are to reflect. A common life requires a political education which equips members of society with the ability to reject elite consensus, to participate in the formulation and articulation of social traditions. And this requires a concept of community built upon the evocation of liberty and equality and, perhaps more important for this point, upon a less passive concept of citizenship.

These things I shall explore in the next chapter. They are of interest at this time because they indicate that, while the claims of the common life naturally limit the assertion of one's personality and prevent one from being the sole judge of one's actions, those claims are closely bounded. The common life involves a relationship built upon explicit recognition of the extent to which rights like liberty and equality define its very nature. We can protect ourselves against social disintegration, barbarism, and violence only by creating a culture of civility; and we can create a culture of civility only where the demands of the community are consistent with the things that make a culture of civility possible. Put another way, the rightful claims the individual may make upon the community and the rightful claims the community may make upon the individual are limited to those things entailed by civility, conviviality, and a social life built upon the mutual and universal possession of rights. The claims of the community may override my individual claims – my freedom to act may be circumscribed – only where the community claims are rooted in the rights that compose the common life – where, that is, they serve to advance, or are consistent with, the causes of liberty, equality, citizenship, and accountability;[6] or where they are required to preserve the integrity or existence of the common life. Benefit or advantage to the community is not, by itself, a sufficient justification except in those instances where the rights of the common life are not involved.

The common life and the modern nation

One of the dangers of using a phrase like 'the common life' is, of course, that it recalls images of communal organization and tempts us to transpose our discussion of obligation into terms relevant to the polis or the intimate community. Clearly, the application of such images to the modern nation is absurd. The modern nation is not an intimate community and cannot be thought of in terms appropriate to the polis. Nor is it possible to think that the members of a modern mass society can create a common life based on their intimate experience of the needs and behaviors of others. Naturally, the idea of a common life may involve more than participation with equals in common political procedures. At its best, a common life is a way of living together, a translation of political obligations into assumptions about social and interpersonal behavior. Conviviality and a culture of civility grow as we value as equals those with whom we share a common life; as we replace intemperate self-interest with concern for our fellows and with traditions of restraint, forbearance, grace, tolerance, compassion. But I do not wish to confuse the search for the best or most preferable society with the search for the basis of obligation. What I write here is written only of the latter and this implicates us in a much less demanding notion of a common life. The values implied by the concept of a common life may similarly be reduced to mean that level of cooperative political behavior required to achieve a culture of civility.

There thus need be nothing romantic about our conception of the common life. We need not interpret it in terms of consent or see its realization as entailing an organically conceived community. By the phrase 'common life', we need refer only to that social order in which all are free to contribute to the development and articulation of basic values and in which conviviality is the condition of political life. These requirements may be met and a common life created in a complex mass society where three conditions are fulfilled: first, where there exists a set of procedures applicable to all, which insures that all persons may contribute to the development and articulation of society's basic values; second, where there is a general commitment to those procedures and to the values of liberty, equality, citizenship, and accountability; and, third, where the knowledge that there are such procedures and commitments and that there is such participation is in general widespread in society. Nor is such a notion of the common life overly formal or rationalistic, immune to the sense of conviviality. Conviviality need not depend upon the experience of intimate participation in a shared venture. It may result when the knowledge that there are procedures we participate in and commitments we share with others is combined with our participation and commitment in a context of equality. The knowledge I refer to may come in various ways. It may be direct knowledge or it may come through our consciousness of traditions which, because they *are* traditions, are surrogate evidence of shared purposes and common behavior. But the development and articulation of such traditions cannot be the preserve of a narrow and authoritative segment of society. If the purposes and behavior of which we are conscious are indeed shared and common, their development and articulation must be an open process involving all members of society.

One further word remains to be said. The structure of the common life is neither eternal nor unchanging. The things which underwrite civility and conviviality change and develop with the appearance of new needs and aspirations, perceptions and threats. The arguments of this and the next chapter reflect the developments of the present age and I do not conceive of them as timeless or conclusive.

4. *The conditions of obligation*

This chapter is a description of the rights intimated by the notions of the common life and culture of civility. In general, the rights described in this chapter constitute the conditions of obligation: that is, their fulfillment or promotion is a necessary condition to the regime's rightful claim to be obeyed. But I do not mean to contend that, unless these rights are realized, the regime is not worthy of obedience. As I shall argue in the next chapter, the question of the worth of the regime is a different question from the worth of a law. I do not argue, as some writers do, that one may only disobey the laws of an illegitimate regime. I argue that a law which invades rights may be disobeyed even if passed by an otherwise legitimate regime. The rights described in this chapter are descriptions of regime obligations, violation of which justifies disobedience.

Nor is this an outline of a utopia. I do not see any of these conditions as perfectionist demands. I do not argue that they must be wholly realized before a regime can demand to be obeyed. I submit, first, that laws which violate these conditions, which subvert them or erect barriers to their realization, cannot impose valid obligations; and, second, that the regime has, in general, an obligation to strive for their realization. But, as the contours and meanings of rights are never settled with finality; as we are constantly learning which conditions lead, in fact, to a fuller realization of the common life and which to its subversion; as human aspirations change; and as new threats to civility appear, we can only suppose that the regime is obligated to make a good-faith effort to do those things which appear to lead to fulfillment of these conditions. I hope that this will be made clear during the discussion.

First condition: citizenship

I have argued that the common life is that political order in which all members may freely judge and contribute to the development and articulation of the values of social life in a context of conviviality. In such a society, the member – or citizen – must be conceived

84

of in a very special way. What are the attributes of citizenship in a common life?

The citizen as a self-governing person. In general terms, we must see the citizen as a self-governing person. Self-government is an inference drawn from the concept of a common life. The procedures which underwrite the capacity of all to contribute and judge necessarily refer to something more than general traditions of social intercourse and behavior. They refer to the formal political processes of a society as well. We have learned through hard experience that the capacity of people to protect their rights, and especially their rights to contribute and judge, is inseparable from their capacity to participate in real ways in the political process. And only in this way is it possible for them to strive to realize their aspirations and protect their private order of expression, activities which, as I shall argue in the following section, are inseparable from freedom.

I am not interested in exploring the limits of self-government or in identifying some form of 'true' democracy with the common life. I am concerned with the justification of obligation and not with the articulation of a best possible political order. I take self-government to refer only to that level of participation necessary to guarantee one's capacity to contribute to the common life, to have a hand in the development and articulation of its basic values, to judge its actions, to protect one's rights, to sustain one's freedom. I take it as clear beyond cavil that if these things cannot be guaranteed by at least that level of participation and self-government characteristic of western democracy at its best, they are certain to be subverted in its absence.

It is also important that we not confuse self-government with consent. Consent is an attempt – albeit incoherent – to account for the legitimacy of a regime and justify obligation. Self-government is based on the assumption that a common life cannot exist if society cannot or will not enlist the participation of those who are affected by it. It is also the way the members of a society may, consistent with their participation in a common undertaking, delegate the direction of that undertaking. Self-government refers not to the means by which a regime is determined to be legitimate or to the way a justifiable political order may be defined, but to the nature of a regime's day-to-day process of policy articulation and decisionmaking. It speaks to the quality of the political life of the individual person, to the choices he may make, the things he may require of society and the things that may be required of him in the course of developing the actual texture of a common life. It is justified because it secures to each member his capacity to contribute to the common life and – although this is at the moment extrinsic to my concerns – because only the self-governing person possesses dignity and significance. It may also be an additional reason for obeying the laws of a regime: we may rightly be asked to obey even laws we oppose so long as we freely participate in the process by which all laws are made. But we may be asked to obey them *only where they are consistent with the conditions of obligation,* one of which – but only one – is self-government. If they are not so consistent, our participation in the making of them cannot make them obligatory or right. It may, as Neumann suggested, only make them a greater wrong.

One of the reasons why it is difficult to separate self-government and consent is that it is so often thought that voluntary participation in the political processes of a society is a form of tacit consent. It is not uncommon for people to believe that where I willingly vote or participate in some other way I tacitly accept the obligation to obey the laws which ensue. Such a theory is unjustifiable for two reasons: first, it places a cruel and arbitrary burden on the individual citizen. For it tells him that in the event of his profound dissent, he is required either to emigrate or to leave the protection of his rights to others. Second, it is illogical. It is surely possible for me to attempt to make the best of a bad situation by exploiting the opportunities offered to me without conferring on the society which offers them a legitimacy that may not be justified. Surely, exploiting these opportunities may be a sign of consent *only where I believe they are adequate,* in which case it is this belief which produces the consent. To reduce the matter to its baldest, would the attempt of Ivan Denisovich to make his imprisonment as tolerable as possible – even by cooperating with his captors – be taken as a sign of his consent to the concentration camp? Again, may I not participate in order to convert a presently unsatisfactory society into one which is at least justifiable? The belief that participation is a form of tacit consent, like the belief that one who accepts benefits owes obligation, is lawyers' conventionalism, the type of *quid pro quo* recommended by the desire to balance value by value. It is perhaps in place in a court of equity. But so long as obligation is translated into legitimacy and into the right to exercise authority, there must be a firmer basis for it than equitable compromise. Even if consent were coherent, consensual legitimacy could be inferred only where acts were done with the intent to consent. To infer legitimacy from the very human attempt to protect oneself, to assume that the drowning man who climbs aboard the pirate ship becomes a willing accomplice in crime, is to trivialize the notion of consent beyond credibility or to convert it into a means for enabling even the grossest tyrant to claim legitimacy.

The citizen as a public officer. The self-governing citizen is a public rather than private person, evoking the ancient truth that citizenship is a public office rather than a private status – that the function of citizenship is not merely to approve and obey, but to exploit the attributes of political authority available to it. The fundamental public function of the citizen is participation. The citizen aids in the making of political decisions and holds other office holders accountable for what they do.

That this is not now the case in the overwhelming number of political cultures is at least obvious. Whatever the official pieties, citizenship is now in fact a private status and we appear increasingly to take for granted the belief that the demand for real participation in the policy-making process is an intrusion upon the prerogatives of constituted authority. The relegation of citizenship to private status is supported, in effect, by a sizeable body of political scholarship. Some scholars suggest that widespread participation may threaten the stability of ostensibly democratic societies. One of the reasons offered to support this thesis is that a large percentage of non-elite citizens have little or no commitment to the values of civil liberty and democracy or to the rules of democratic politics.[1] It is, moreover, held to be unrealistic to expect widespread political participation, for man is 'by nature' politically apathetic: 'Homo civicus is not, by nature, a political animal.'[2] If these claims are justifiable, may it not be that the insistence on the public status of citizenship is self-defeating and that participation, far from sustaining a common life, will work to defeat those other things which make a common life valuable?

Yet these claims may not be justifiable. The evidence upon which they rely bears more than a single interpretation. Consider the American experience. As to commitment to undemocratic and illiberal values, it might be helpful to re-examine the beliefs of Americans at some future time when their leaders have not assiduously promoted acceptance of those values and equated criticism of the regime with subversion. If the rhetoric and action of leaders affects popular beliefs, may it not be right to attribute some of the popular suspicion of liberal values to their words and acts? Political power can be used in many ways. One might wish to speculate about the impact of the persistent use of power to manipulate public opinion to support vested interests. We should also want to know whether the elite's perception of social tensions and goals does not, in its essential conservatism, subvert its formal commitment to liberal and democratic values. Moreover, apart from their verbal testimony, the members of the American elite have shown something less than a passionate commitment to the legitimacy of dissent or the civil liberties of radicals: we are surely entitled to ask whether this behavior justifies faith in the genuineness of their libertarianism. It is true that many people do not want radicals to speak in their schools or blacks to move next door. But American political leaders meet radicals most frequently in court and the presence of blacks on corporate boards of directors is no more striking than in pleasant suburban neighborhoods. Those segments of the American elite which political scientists have found to be committed to liberal values do not seem to be as much committed in practice as in interview. Does this not permit us to ask whether their commitment to liberal values is hypocritical and perceived as such by the rest of the country?

The problem of apathy raises similar doubts. Apathy results when the poor and powerless see no stake for themselves in the system, where they see that, in every instance, they receive a disproportionately small share of the rewards that that system dispenses. Apathy also results from the perceived lack of encouragement to participate – when political leaders are presented, by themselves, their fellow leaders, and the media as constituting public authority while the citizen is consigned to a polite but insignificant role. (This lack of encouragement has not been accidental. One aim of political authority has been to construct barriers to accountability, to obstruct and render ambiguous the lines of responsibility between rulers and ruled.) And it is not only the underclasses which perceive politics in this way. The middle classes, having been promised the world, find their world to be one of crime, filth, and economic instability; and their interests, far from being paramount as their political representatives suggest, constitute the program of public authority only after the interests of elites are served. Social scientists have found widespread political cynicism to be nearly endemic in American life. May this not result from the individual's perception that his free and active public life is to a large extent controlled and manipulated by political elites and organizational cadres? Would this not impose real and practical limits on participation? May apathy not result from the individual's perception that his enfranchisement is often only a way to secure his tacit acceptance of policies he does not like?

If these things are so, apathy may be nothing more than a rational response to a social process in which participation is both discouraged and frustrating. Better turn one's attention to those aspects of life which may be productive, which may yield benefits and satisfactions and build up protection against the results of politics as practiced.[3]

Still another cause of apathy, which has recently received substantial attention, is the deadening work environment created by modern industrialism. The point was stated neatly by Lewis Lipsitz:

> Men in a work environment they cannot control may be to some unknown degree damaged in their sense of mastery and this damage may render them less capable of coping with and altering an environment they find unsatisfactory. To the extent that such damage occurs, men become victims rather than creators. To the extent that work life contributes to such incapacities, it needs improvement in modern societies. Industrial democracy may yet prove to be a prerequisite to political and social democracy.[4]

More recently, Carole Pateman has concluded that the individual's political attitudes 'depend to a large extent on the authority structure of his work environment . . . Specifically, the development of a sense of political efficacy does appear to depend on whether his work situation allows him any scope to participate in decision making.'⁵ Similar conclusions are documented by Almond and Verba.⁶

If these conclusions (and those of scholars holding similar beliefs) are correct, alteration of the work environment could spur increased participation. At the very least, it could result in a lessening of the anti-civil tendencies inherent in the modern work environment. Such alteration involves two things. First, the deadening work environment itself must be attacked and the assembly line varied so that workers assume responsibility for carrying out whole work processes rather than be limited to the repetitious performance of single functions. Second, and more important, the worker needs to be able to participate in decisions governing at least work processes and plant relationships. It is important to distinguish this form of participation from the greater involvement of trade unions in the governance of industry, which is what worker participation is sometimes taken to mean. Trade union involvement may at best forcefully articulate certain of the worker's interests as against management, but at the cost of creating a new level of authority over him. The need is to democratize an authority system, to make it accountable to those over whom power is exercised, to allow those greatly affected by decisions to have some part in the making of them, and, by giving the worker a degree of influence over this work environment, to develop his sense of political efficacy.

It is difficult to determine just how successful such participation may be, both in democratizing industry and in encouraging political participation. Empirical evidence is limited and the theoretical discussions not very informative. Certainly, the Yugoslavian experience indicates that there is not much ground for charges classically leveled against worker participation, such as that it would lead to inefficiency and industrial anarchy, or that it would develop into a form of syndicalism.⁷ Theoretical opposition may take other forms: it may be argued, for example, that worker participation invades the traditional right of owners to control their property or that it requires a decentralization of industry that would be wrong or self-defeating. Neither of these objections seems to me to be well taken. Even if we accept private ownership, the first objection is, in the light of the developments of the past half-century, nearly frivolous. Not only is industrial management no longer a prerogative of ownership, but owners of industry are often powerless to control the bureaucracies that largely run it. Again, modern industry is a system of power, seriously affecting the lives of those who work in it; and it is hardly consistent with the demonstrated need to control power to deny to those affected by power a voice in its exercise. Finally, as I assume that the modern corporation is in fact a segment of public authority – part of the government – the arguments based upon the rights of private ownership become irrelevant. As to the second objection, worker participation does not necessarily involve industrial decentralization;[8] but if it does, I believe such decentralization justifiable and will discuss it later in this chapter.

Other objections may undoubtedly be raised, but it seems premature to discuss them. They can be evaluated only in the light of more extensive empirical evidence than is now available. Examples of worker participation in American corporations are too isolated to provide reliable conclusions. Equally unreliable is the evidence concerning the performance of the guilds formed by British Guild Socialists after the first world war. For example, one of the best known of these guilds (the Manchester Building Guild Committee) failed after a period of genuine success. Part of the reason for its ultimate failure lay in the arbitrary restrictions placed upon it by the Ministry of Health – which, for instance, limited the number of building contracts between the Guild and local authorities to twenty – and part in the great upsurge in building which fairly ended the post-war housing shortage.[9] The relationship between guild organization and the outcome remains unclear.

Those who wish to assess the possibilities of worker participation in industrial decisionmaking frequently turn to Yugoslavia, where the principle has been carried out more fully than in any other nation. There, although the directors and technical experts of the economic units appear to have a disproportionate impact upon the decisions taken, workers do participate seriously in the decisionmaking process. Among the workers, however, participation varies: higher level and skilled workers exhibit high rates of participation, while semi- and unskilled workers exhibit low rates.[10] But the Yugoslavian experience may be only minimally helpful in gauging the possibilities of worker participation, especially in western societies. In the first place, the Yugoslavian system has been in operation for less than two decades. Second, the nature of Yugoslavian politics can certainly be taken to have created discouragements to participation in what are – despite ritualistic denials – state enterprises. Third, Yugoslavia's is an underdeveloped economy with great regional variations in economic status, political culture, and participatory traditions: contrast Slovenia with Macedonia. Fourth, it offers no guidance to the possibility of greater participation among workers in a more advanced economy which might strive to limit or eliminate the skilled–unskilled distinction by giving workers responsibility for a range of duties rather than create strict job classifications. And, clearly, the Yugoslavian governmental system gives us little opportunity to study the impact of worker participation upon participation in traditional political areas.

What can we conclude? We can conclude that there seems to be a genuine relationship between the conditions of the work environment and the motive to participate; and, from the Yugoslavian example, that worker participation in industrial decisionmaking is a real possibility, although perhaps overestimated by its advocates. Hence, by institutionalizing such participation and by altering the deadening conditions of modern work, we may encourage a real expansion of political participation. At the same time, we should seek to eliminate some of the discouragements to participation which I summarized earlier and thus embark on a policy designed to make citizenship a reality – or as much of a reality as it may become. At the very least, we are entitled to conclude that, *without the energetic pursuit of such a policy, we cannot assume that low rates of participation are natural or inevitable and that the idea of an active citizenry is vain.* While the assumption of apathy may, in the end, prove true, the evidence needed to support it is by no means conclusive. Before we decide that self-government cannot be advanced, or is a utopian condition of political obligation, we should have to know more about the reasons why it is thought to have failed.

This brings me to my final point. Political scientists spend too much time discussing the possibility of widespread participation and too little discussing the regime's responsibility to encourage it. But this seems to me to be the real point in issue. In the context of democratic theory (which is where the question of participation is usually raised) it is surely insufficient to show that people tend to be apathetic, or to assume that the postulate of apathy precludes further inquiry and raises no question about regime obligations. In the context of my discussion of civility, a similar point may be made: the issue of apathy is irrelevant to the consideration of regime obligation. If we are to justify the secondary obligation owed to the regime, we can do so only to the extent that the regime's laws advance the common life and make a culture of civility possible. *The performance that is in question here is the performance of the regime, not of the citizen.* Now if citizenship is a cardinal element of the common life, and if what is involved is the validity of the obligations owed to the regime, the question is not whether citizen participation is natural or unnatural, but *whether the regime passes laws and acts in ways that encourage or tend to increase participation.* The question is the good-faith effort of the regime to correct known impediments. If this is seen to entail, e.g., democratization of the work environment, then the promotion of a democratization sufficient to encourage widespread participation becomes a regime obligation. If such democratization proves a chimera, or if a genuine effort fails to encourage participation, the regime has at least done what it is obligated to do.

Participation in decisions affecting his life is one mark of a free man. Equally important, it may be an activity inescapably tied to the *development* of freedom and civility. We have known since Mill that participation is valuable not because people *are* free and civilized, but because through participation they may *become* freer and more civilized than they actually are. Perhaps Mill was wrong. But the evidence is not in and we may comfort ourselves with the thought that each advance in participation was met with prophecies of immediate political disaster. Like Froissart's knights, who saw in the elimination of their right to rob and pill the end of the good life, those who now participate may view the entrance of new multitudes into the political process as a social catastrophe. History, perhaps, suggests otherwise. Participation is no panacea and is sometimes truly dangerous. But its plausible role in the development of free and civilized people suggests that the attempt to encourage it is a risk worth taking.

The citizen as a juridical person. From the very beginning, we have understood that self-government is radically inconsistent with legal privilege. That understanding is not merely a conventional assumption accepted because of its antiquity. It rests on firm evidence as well as on the commonsense realization that legal privilege formally reduces or obliterates the governing powers of the non-privileged. I do not believe that it is necessary any longer to demonstrate that membership in a self-governing political community must mean the same thing for all and that laws cannot create favored classes or groups with greater formal control over the governing process than others. A self-governing person is one who is addressed by the law in the same way as all others.

It is equally the case that, as self-government can only be coherent where the effect of laws upon individual persons is the same, so that the powers that some exercise are not mere fictions, the rights and obligations of all persons in a self-governing community must be mutual and universal. The condition for claiming a right, and therefore being able to compel people to do something, must be the supposition that that demand can be made by all and that the obligations imposed are imposed universally. Thus, rights and obligations must be framed in general terms, must be equally applicable to all, and must be allocated on the supposition that a right exercised by one may be exercised by all and must not deprive others of their rights. The absence of universality and mutuality either robs those deprived of their ability to contribute to the common life or places such roadblocks in their way as to make their contributions largely fictitious.

The absence of legal privilege and the universality and mutuality of rights and obligations necessarily means that all persons claim rights and owe obligations not merely as persons, but as abstract representatives of the general category 'person'. That is to say they are, for these purposes, abstract legal constructs, deprived of specific personalities and knowable to the regime and capable of being addressed only as legal constructs. They are juridical persons – purely creations of law. This abstraction from reality makes legal equality possible and provides the only possible formal basis for self-government. It insures against the assignment of rights and obligations on the basis of class, race, sex, group membership, and so forth. One does not have to probe far beneath the surface to understand the extent to which such operative classifications destroy the reality of self-government. Privileged and non-privileged classes cannot be members of a common political order nor have the opportunity to contribute equally to its life and values.

The common life is an undertaking of juridical persons. It is important to remember that the concept of the juridical person is a formal notion, concerned with the equal assignment of rights and obligations. It is an attempt to equalize the status of people subject to the law. However crucial this objective is, it is at the same time a limited one. Since it is obvious that social and economic conditions greatly affect the individual person's capacity to exercise his rights and to take advantage in fact of the opportunities he is offered in law, the realization of formal equality cannot be presumed to conclude the problem of equal rights. If equality of rights is thought to be a necessary ground of the common life, we must turn our attention to other and substantive questions. We must ask which conditions of social life need to be equalized and what degree of equality needs to be promoted in order to create a society of juridical persons. Indeed, I shall shortly argue that equalization of certain of the conditions of social life is a necessary prerequisite to the creation of a society of juridical persons. This argument is a variant of the old but valid claim that freedom cannot be realized unless social and economic conditions are such that formal equality enforces a fairness and rightness built into the laws that are equally enforced. Blake rightly understood that one law for the lion and ox is oppression. It is only where conditions are such that lions and oxen are equally able to take advantage of the law and to vindicate their (equal) rights that one law can be liberating.

The citizen as a rational person. Self-government requires a presumption of the rationality of each citizen. This presumption is the commonest element in the liberal theory of man and it is one element that is surely justifiable.

In the eighteenth and nineteenth centuries, liberals thought that human freedom and self-government required formalizing man's relations to the state – making those relations matters of law. The presumption of rationality was, of course, necessary to such a theory, based as it was on the calculable consequences of laws and behavior. But this theory seems hopelessly utopian today and a better justification for the preservation of rationality must be given. This justification may be found in the notion of authority. Presumed rationality is a prerequisite to holding a member responsible for apprehending authoritative communications. For authority, whatever else it may be, is possible only where the persons to whom a communication is addressed conclude that obedience to that communication is right and are moved to obey it by something other than their desire to avoid unpleasant consequences. They must believe, for one reason or other, that they *ought* to obey it. Such an 'ought' means that justification of an authoritative communication must – at least potentially – be capable of being reduced to reasons. Compliance with authority requires that the persons to whom communications are addressed be capable of giving reasons for their obedience, of justifying it in terms of choices made within a moral framework. Authority can be exercised only over rational persons.

One crux of self-government is the individual's responsiveness to authority rather than to power. Self-government is not the same as anarchy. It may be consistent with obedience to laws made by a government rather than given by individuals to themselves, but only where the laws which demand obedience are in some way authorized, are consistent with the society's understanding of or intention regarding the substantive and formal limits of policy-making. Self-government is the prerogative of rational people.

The presumption of rationality is, of course, a juridical presumption and says nothing about the psychological realities of human behavior. It is demanded by the need to convert the exercise of mere power into authority. Yet, clearly, the fact that people may in fact be less than rational or moved by irrational motives or appetites cannot be overlooked. One no longer needs to be told that self-government, like the whole enterprise of political freedom, is a gamble and that what we call human nature works both for it and against it. But if freedom and self-government are gambles worth taking – if, that is, the human political enterprise possesses a degree of moral validity when it satisfies, even to some extent, this passionate aspiration of people to share in the determination of their destinies, the presumption of rationality becomes a moral imperative. However limited the actual scope of human rationality may be, it is impossible to believe that the eradication of self-government and the presumption of rationality it entails will strengthen or enlarge it. Self-government is our political tool to build actual human rationality.

The juridical presumption of rationality, being an inference from self-government, is non-rebuttable. It cannot be altered by law since the notion of the juridical person requires that each person be known to the law as an abstract construct. Hence, the presumption applies universally.

The presumption of rationality makes the imposition of an obligation an invitation to explore its implications. The traditional and formal ascription to law of *prima facie* justifiability must become suspect, and political conventionalism – the disposition to agree to the terms of new laws – must be seen for what it is: a moral disease of the body politic. The presumption that people are rational commits us to value only that type of social undertaking where challenges to a regime are accepted as performances of a citizen duty and where resort to political vilification, manipulation of vague fears, and the like, come to be seen for what they are: attempts to by-pass the duty to reason and therefore crimes against the common life.

Second condition: freedom

Freedom is inseparable from civility and hence from the justification of obligation. In one sense, of course, the very conception of political obligation as problematical – as subject to dispute and refutation and as requiring justification – itself demands a notion of freedom; for the problem could not exist if it were not for the belief that the limitation of a person's freedom of action requires justification. The assumption behind this belief is that in the absence of justification, no limitation of freedom is defensible.

Now it is true that such a presumption proves nothing about freedom, but merely indicates that a certain type of inquiry cannot be carried on without it. Yet this presumption is not merely gratuitous for behind it is an indication of what we should have to surrender if we did not view freedom as a profoundly important ideal. We should have to abandon, for instance, our attempts to discover if and how social life can be made to be consistent with human aspirations and basic needs; perhaps even the attempt to decide which needs are entitled to fulfillment and which not. We should have to ignore the political significance of man's efforts to transcend the limits of the human condition, to create, think, energize his social world. We should have to give up altogether the concep-

tion of moral life – at least as it applies to politics – on the ground
that men may not choose and be responsible for their choices. And
we should have to surrender the notion of human rights.

This last point is worth considering for a moment. H. L. A. Hart
has argued persuasively that 'if there are any moral rights at all, it
follows that there is at least one natural right, the equal right of all
men to be free'. By this, Hart means that 'in the absence of certain
special conditions which are consistent with the right being an
equal right, any adult human being capable of choice (1) has the
right to forbearance on the part of all others from the use of coercion or restraint against him save to hinder coercion or restraint
and (2) is at liberty to do . . . any action which is not one coercing
or restraining or designed to injure other persons.'[11] In order for
us to be able to speak about rights in the first place, it must be supposed that any person has a right to require any other person to
forbear from interfering with his freedom, with the choices he may
make, unless the person interfering can produce overriding moral
reasons for doing so, reasons based 'on such grounds as we give
when we claim a moral right . . . '.[12] If Hart is right, then the
absence of a right to be free is tantamount to a destruction of the
entire conception of general rights and also deprives us of any
way, short of divine or oracular revelation, to specify grounds on
which forbearance to interfere can be based. But it is impossible to
see how even a minimally satisfactory social life could exist in the
absence of a network of forbearances. In an age which cannot
return to the inspiration of Plato or Augustine, the concept of
freedom alone gives the justification of such forbearances its
coherence.

Freedom is demanded by the notion of a common life, for only
where men are free can social life be common. A common life
cannot exist in the absence of a universal freedom to contribute to
that life, to judge and criticize its values, to inform others about
moral goals. The very texture of moral life is also altered where
freedom is subverted, for the communication of moral ideals and
the making of moral decisions would be stunted if not destroyed.

In understanding the relation of freedom to the common life, we
must be clear about what it is that is common. People share some
aspirations and commitments but not all, and there is a good deal of
dispute concerning others. Valuing freedom means valuing these

differences as well as similarities and protecting the right to hold
different aspirations and commitments so long as they are consistent
with the freedom of others. It is inconsistent with this vision to hold
a free society to be one devoted to a harmonious realization of a
stated ideal (no matter how worthy) or to interpret freedom as
action in accordance with the ideal or with a defined concept of
rationality. While there are some commitments we can be said to
share politically, these commitments can only be the rights necessary
to the creation of a common life and the realization of freedom.
Otherwise, what we share is participation in the procedure by which
we safeguard rights and commitments.

One who participates in a common life is a private as well as a
public person: elements of his existence are intimate, outside the
gaze and interest of a society as a whole, largely unregulated but
informally governed by personal agreements, customs, and accom-
modations. This private sphere is especially significant because it is
the sphere of intimate commitments and aspirations developed out
of the individual's own needs, desires, and interests. It is the sphere
where one may be alone with oneself and hence think – do that
which allows one to participate most fully in the affairs of the
world.

In a very real, as well as literal sense, freedom is the protection
of a private order of expression. By this I do not mean that the
bounds of freedom are our private interests or needs. I mean that
those aspects of freedom which are thought of as public owe their
significance to the function they play in protecting our ultimately
private selves. (I need hardly add that the freedom to be alone with
oneself and to develop commitments and aspirations is not synonymous with an absolute right to be let alone. The idea of a common
life implies restrictions on my being let alone as I shall suggest in
this and the following section.)

Human aspiration, commitment, and thought – the type of thing
I mean by 'private order of expression' – become public not merely
when they are advanced in public, but when they become subjects
for public consideration. My thoughts are in the public realm when,
so to speak, they are taken out of my hands and become common
property. The public realm develops through the development of
the private realm, through the making public of what was private.
A common life is a life in which individual aspirations, commit-

ments, and thoughts may become subjects for public considera-tion. Since a common life must guarantee to each of its members the possibility and opportunity to contribute to the common life, it must undertake to protect the integrity of the private. But protecting the integrity of the private involves more than passively guaranteeing the private against undue public interference: it in-volves encouraging and nourishing private expression. This is perhaps the single most neglected notion in traditional theories of freedom.

Consider what protecting the private order of expression is nor-mally taken to mean. On the one hand, it is sometimes taken to mean valuing individual choice and hence valuing a plurality of aspirations and commitments and protecting disharmonious visions. On the other hand, it is sometimes taken to mean valuing the pri-vate self, the individual's self-determining capacity. Although there are obvious relationships between these views, philosophers who stress one or the other frequently conclude different things. Stressing the former seems to put the emphasis on the kinds of acts men may do and encourages us to see freedom as the absence of restraint on action and on the expression of aspirations and com-mitments. Stressing the latter seems to put the emphasis on the autonomous or self-directive nature of action and encourages us to see freedom as self-governance, as being subject to no will but our own.

Robert Paul Wolff is only the latest philosopher who has sug-gested that freedom can be interpreted only in terms of autonomy.[13] Wolff maintains that the whole enterprise of morality is impossible unless we are willing to take responsibility for our moral decisions, to determine ourselves what we ought to do. This obligation does not free us from taking into account the thoughts and demands of others, nor does it insulate us from moral criticism or argument. It merely requires that we ourselves be the final judge of the validity of those ideas, that we act on premises we recognize as valid rather than on premises whose validity we accept because of the prestige or power of their source. As we must express these moral decisions to ourselves in the form of laws or imperatives, Wolff argues, we must be *autonomous* – that is, we must submit only to laws we have made for ourselves. We may obey the laws of a regime not because we are told to do so or because the regime itself somehow deserves obedience, but because its demands (or laws) appear to us to be right.

To this argument we may raise several objections. It is certainly possible that the preservation of justice, order, and civility demand that our fundamental political judgments concern not individual laws or choices, but general matters or procedures. But either form of judgment is consistent with the concept of autonomy. That is, Wolff gives us no principle to determine what is the character of the rules which must be given to oneself. May they be rules which define procedures and general goals or must they be rules regarding every act that can be done? Is it wrong to say that the belief that the former type of rule is preferable is inconsistent with the demand for autonomy? Do I relinquish my moral responsibility if, upon reflection, I make such a decision? The notion of autonomy runs aground on the same rocks of ambiguity as utilitarianism: neither contains a principle which allows us to decide non-arbitrarily whether we must be concerned with individual or general rules. Yet the consequences of deciding that autonomy is consistent with decisions regarding general rules of social procedure rather than decisions regarding each individual law are certainly momentous. For the former allows us to conclude that we are bound by laws we think wrong so long as they have been enacted according to proper procedures, while the latter forces us to conclude that we are bound only by laws we hold right.

Second, the resort to autonomy may allow us adequately to define freedom from the point of view of the individual. But we are entitled to ask when a *society* may be said to be free, or how freedom may be universalized. Clearly, a free society or the universalization of freedom cannot result from a universalization of autonomy unless we presume the universal acceptance of fundamental values and the possibility of an underlying social harmony. Neither of these assumptions is exactly plausible. Many of the claims men make are distinguished not by the justice they entail, but by the narrow self-interests they serve. Hence, my exercise of autonomy may deprive others of the opportunity to pursue their own freedom. Acting consistently on self-interested premises, I may autonomously refuse to accept as valid obligations which restrict my freedom to choose for the sake of providing greater freedom of choice to others. The universalization of freedom is possible only where people are sufficiently equal that some cannot use superior power over others without restraint. Now, as equality in complex societies can only be a product of deliberate social policy, the universalization of freedom requires that limits be put on autonomous action. But if a free society is one committed to preserving autonomy, how, without contradiction, may it restrict autonomous action? And if it cannot, from what may the restrictions on autonomy needed to universalize freedom derive?

Having begun on a Kantian note, Wolff might want to continue by arguing that I cannot give a law to myself unless I would grant all other men the right to give it to themselves. Hence, autonomy may be restricted where I have no right to give a law to myself. Kant suggests this when he argues that freedom, defined in terms of being independent of the will of another, is a right only insofar 'as it can coexist with the freedom of all according to a universal law . . .'[14] But who is to say whether it can coexist with the freedom of all? Whoever can make that determination is clearly capable of laying down the basic rules for a society. Hence, we are forced to conclude, as Kant was, that the decision whether co-existence is possible is a decision which can be made only by public authority.[15] This imposes a rather extraordinary limit on autonomy, giving public authority, in effect, a veto over individual behavior.

To speak of autonomy under such circumstances strikes me as dishonest. If I limit autonomous decisions to decisions which are consistent with a moral rule (whatever it may be), I am saying that men ought not to be autonomous. To hold that they may be autonomous under such circumstances is to hold that restrictions on freedom are not restrictions on freedom but the realization of freedom itself. This type of argument is not exactly unknown in political philosophy, but its frequency does not make it more respectable. It is one thing to say that people should be free. It is quite another to say that there are justifiable reasons for limiting freedom. But the reasons advanced to limit freedom should be stated honestly and directly as reasons to limit freedom, not passed off as elements of freedom or as irrelevant to the question.

In 'Two Concepts of Liberty,' Isaiah Berlin suggests that such circumlocution is practically demanded by the theory of positive freedom – that is, freedom as self-direction or self-governance – of which autonomy is one version. Self-governance may mean freely doing anything I wish. If it does, then freedom is indistinguishable from arbitrariness and anarchy and the free man may be a slave to his lowest impulses. Typically, however, advocates of positive freedom have held that self-governance requires self-mastery, the control of one's lowest impulses. To be free is to act according to reason. We are thus required to make the distinction – classically associated with positive freedom – between the 'real' or autonomous self and the empirical or 'heteronomous' self and to identify freedom with self-governance by our real self. Normally, this distinction is pictured as a conflict between a self which represents rationality and purpose and a self which represents irrational impulses and passions, demands for immediate gratification, and the like. 'True' freedom is the triumph of the real over the heteronomous self. Hence, restrictions on the heteronomous self, however hateful and repressive they may seem and however they may contradict actual desires, are not restrictions on freedom but are the very realization of freedom. And this conclusion holds whether these restrictions are self-imposed or state-imposed.

Once I take this view, I am in a position to ignore the actual wishes of men or societies, to bully, oppress, torture them in the name, and on behalf, of their 'real' selves, in the secure knowledge that whatever is the true goal of man (happiness, performance of duty, wisdom, a just society, self-fulfillment) must be identical with his freedom – the free choice of his 'true', albeit often submerged and inarticulate, self.[16]

Of course, what is 'real' is difficult to specify, even for advocates of positive freedom who differ sharply among themselves as to what it is that is the 'real' self. And the very notion that there is a conflict between, say, the rational and irrational in man argues the arbitrariness of the notion of the real self since it is impossible to say that any part of us is more real than any other part. The distinction between real and heteronomous selves can only be coherent – not to mention consistent with basic theories of psychology – where the 'real' means the 'morally good'. Whatever the philosophical pretenses, that is in fact the way this distinction is persistently drawn: it is at least a remarkable coincidence that every philosopher's conception of man's 'real' self is always consistent with his conception of the highest moral ideal. But that is clearly an arbitrary use of the concept of the real and an arbitrary approach to freedom. Do we not gain a more honest and profound insight into moral dilemmas by frankly acknowledging that the obligations imposed by our ideals in fact often run counter to our actual desires? Can we ignore the extent to which the preservation of certain ideals requires restricting human behavior? Is anything gained by defining freedom in such a way that evidence of actual human desires is irrelevant? Have we not learned that where men may be forced to be free they are likely to encounter rather more force than freedom? It is true that men may occasionally be made happier and ultimately even freer by being compelled to act against their wills in a particular case. But that does not make the compulsion freedom nor does it force us to identify the initial compulsion with the ultimate result. And certainly it is false that these consequences always or usually occur.

The danger of positive freedom (a danger realized in the conclusions of many of its advocates) is that freedom may paradoxically be reduced to obligation – to bringing one's will into line with someone else's moral ideal. The difficulty with autonomy is that it is not possible coherently to universalize it. To escape these objections, we may turn to a different approach to freedom. We may think of freedom as an outcome of actual desires: I am free when I am able to act as I wish, to make the choices I wish. A free society is one in which this capacity to act and choose is universalized. Obviously, since complete free choice and action is impossible, limits may be set on freedom. These limits, or restraints, need to be justified and these justifications must be significant enough to override the importance we attach to free activity.

This notion of freedom has been called 'negative freedom' and is associated with much of liberal theory. Freedom in this interpretation means nothing but the absence of restraints: I am free insofar as my acts and choices are not restrained by the intervention of other men. I am free when I am able to act and choose. Now, as the only relevant restraints on my action are those imposed by other men and not by nature or fate or God, it should follow that I am free to act when others refrain from preventing me from acting and, therefore, that defining freedom as the capacity to act and choose and defining it as the absence of restraint are, to all intents and purposes, the same thing. But they are not. There has always been something incomplete and unsatisfying about the concept of negative freedom, although this incompleteness is not necessarily logical. It is merely that we are not encouraged to follow the concept of freedom as far as it may carry us.

Liberty is an act of defiance in the name of rights, human independence, and the integrity of the private self. Freedom, Dostoevsky has said, is the right to say No. This can hardly be passed off as excessive or literary. What can be more basic, more essential to human freedom than the capacity of individual persons to assert their commitments; what more vital than that people be able to express themselves publicly? Yet this capacity can be reduced or destroyed in various ways unrelated to overt restraint. There was a time, not too long ago, when advocates of liberty had to argue that the reduction of economic privilege and the equilization of economic power were at least as relevant to the increase and universalization of liberty as the containment of the arbitrary power of the government and that the man who was prevented from choosing and acting as fully as he might because of his poverty was no less restrained than the man who was forbidden by law to vote or speak. Mill was not being extravagant when he noted, over a century ago, that the life of the average workingman was in many respects no freer than that of the slave. The relevance of economic restraints to liberty has now become widely accepted: poverty, disinheritance created by the deliberate policies of men – whatever their motives – is a limit placed on human activity and as such is a restriction on freedom.

But the twentieth century has discovered other restrictions on human activity and choice more subtle and harder to deal with than those against which Mill, Hobhouse, and Tawney inveighed. We have discovered that social conditions may create a sub-culture whose members are disabled from asserting their rights because those conditions engender fear, apathy, alienation, or distrust of the legal system. We have discovered that radical insecurity and anxiety inhibit the expression of desires and needs. We have discovered that the deadening work environment so characteristic of contemporary industrial technology, by nurturing the recognition of the inability to influence satisfactorily an important segment of one's immediate social environment, leads to passivity and alienation and hence to a failure to assert one's desires or will. We ought not to blind ourselves to the obvious fact that self-assertion or self-expression is not the automatic product of legally-guaranteed rights, but is the result of a complex and subtle social process which works to encourage the public expression of commitments and needs.

The conditions which encourage self-expression and which enable men to make demands or assert commitments are as much a part of human freedom as the legal and political guarantees which protect those demands or commitments once they are made. If freedom means the capacity to act and choose, then the existence of social conditions and consequent psychological attitudes which subvert or inhibit the expression of acts and choices are as clearly limitations on freedom as imposed restraints. They have precisely the same effect: they prevent people from acting and choosing. The fact that they operate not as overt restraints, but as subversions of the conditions precedent to self-expression is at least irrelevant and at most dangerous for being so insidious. For inhibiting conditions subvert free expression before the question of restraint normally arises and so frequently prevent us from detecting the actual limits on freedom. If freedom means the ability to act and choose, it means striving for the attainment of those conditions which make it possible for people to act and choose. Among these conditions is certainly the limitation of restraints on human action. But it is impossible to conclude that this is the only condition. We must be equally conscious of the need to create those social supports upon whose realization the expression of needs and commitments waits.

It is of course possible to speak of these social conditions as restraints and hence to rescue the theory of negative freedom. I do not see the purpose in that, however. Clearly, the problem with negative freedom is not its logic, but the way it narrows our vision of human social life. 'Restraints' normally means 'overt restraints' and to insist upon defining freedom as an absence of restraint turns our attention toward the legal, political, and economic activities which openly restrict human behavior – that is, toward the overt exercise of power. Indeed, the entire question of human freedom is most often discussed in terms of our ability to control power. That is certainly how the great battles against illiberal government and dominating economic enterprise were fought. Most often, freedom meant a diminution in the power of the government or the corporation and it was the evidence of that power that supplied the great incentive to redefine liberty.

But freedom may be limited by widespread patterns of social behavior, by commonly-held beliefs, by social traditions, by the consequences of a particular structure of social organization. While these are all products of power, however indirectly, they are normally not perceived as such by society in general. Commonly, when social movements to limit power arise, they have as their objects important and visible individuals or institutions: it is a sad fact, but a fact nonetheless, that movements to limit power are frequently little more than searches for culprits. Widespread traditions, which are not looked upon as exercises of power, are also not looked upon as wrongful limitations of freedom. That is, their reform is rarely placed on the political agenda. To create a concept of freedom which depends upon the limitation of power may thus blind societies to the lack of freedom perpetuated by their most fundamental activities.

The typical interpretation of negative freedom also glosses over other aspects of the problem. Let us briefly consider some of these. We should all agree that, other things being equal, the rich man is freer than the poor, the wise man than the fool, the strong man than the weak, the educated man than the ignorant. Clearly, one reason for this is that the rich, wise, etc., are better able to assert themselves and combat attempted restraints. But there is another reason. To be wealthier or more capable than one's fellows is to possess the ability to create new choices and to perceive more fully the range of choices available. It is to enlarge one's perceptions of the social world, to reveal opportunities frequently hidden to others, to possess a greater sense of personal efficacy and therefore to be motivated to engage in a greater and more fruitful variety of activities. Even in the presence of identical restraints, the rich and capable are freer than their fellows.

May this freedom – created not so much by the greater ability to outface restraints as by the greater ability to perceive existing courses of action, to create new ones, and thus to enlarge the range of choices open to one – be attributed to the absence of restraints? In one sense it may be. But I fail to see why it would be advantageous to twist language to do it. It is less the absence of restraints than the presence of abilities that is at stake. And while some of these abilities often reflect the unequal gifts of nature, they more often reflect nothing more than the unequal distribution of social resources or the attitudes built into the cultures of different social classes. What is required to correct this and to universalize freedom, so far as these are possible, is not so much a reduction in restraints as positive and creative steps to correct the conditions – many of them unconsciously produced or unintended – which in fact lessen freedom: that is, to move in the direction of equality.

Let us consider another problem. It is not enough to say that I may choose between competing alternatives. These alternatives must also be important because if they are not I should be controlled in the important aspects of my life. But who decides if they are important? Who assesses the significance of the alternatives offered to me? If that assessment is made by a public or oracular authority, that authority would have the power to control my life in the name of freedom. My freedom is a mirage unless I am able to invest the options open to me with significance and to influence the nature of the options open. Obviously, I may do this only where there is a significant limitation of the restraints put upon me by public authority. But I must also be able to act and think. I must perceive myself as able to affect at least my immediate social world. I must be psychologically capable of asserting my needs and demands. How can this be except in a society which encourages the development of my private self, which strives to protect and nurture my capacity to express my commitments and aspirations? Before we speak about human choice-making we must ask, what must be nurtured in man in order to make that choice-making significant to him?

Political concepts, said Tawney, are for use, not display. Freedom becomes significant where we understand the importance of human activity and where we see the employment of creative energies as valuable. If the attempt to create a common life and a culture of civility entails valuing the contributions of diverse human beings, if the outfacing of barbarism and violence requires continuing creative effort, the necessity of a commitment to freedom becomes obvious. But such a commitment can only be understood in terms of the kinds of human activities which may be done, in terms of the choices individual persons may make. Freedom is increased where the variety of choices and activities open to men is increased. If it were true that the variety of choices and activities open to men were a constant, expanded or contracted solely in proportion to the restraints placed on men, then the definition of freedom as absence of restraint would make sense. But the variety of choices and actions is not a constant. It is expanded not merely when men are not prevented from acting, but when their minds and psyches are nurtured, when they are provided with the conditions which allow them to expand and develop, to employ their imaginations, to discover new choices and actions relevant to the situations in which they find themselves, to develop new and hitherto unheard-of aspirations. Freedom is a process by which men create their own social worlds.

It is hardly a coincidence that the profound concern with freedom which characterizes modern political philosophy arose at the time of the Renaissance. For the Renaissance was concerned, over and above all things, with the importance of human activity. The artists and philosophers of the Renaissance celebrated the dignity, indeed divinity, of human creativity. It was activity, the release of intellectual and creative energies, pointing toward the progressive development of man's capacity for heroic action – *virtu,* virtuosity, Machiavelli called it – that was at the root of Pico's notion of human dignity, Rabelais' social law ('Do as you will'), and Machiavelli's passion for politics. Human action and creativity, stunted by the restrictive and narrow culture of medieval Europe, were now to be revalued and placed at the center of morality and politics. But we must understand the significance of Machiavelli's insistence that such a morality could arise only where society and the state gave it positive encouragement. It was not enough to cut away the repressive restrictions of medieval life. These restrictions and the culture they created corrupted a people – made them weak, passionless, manipulable; caused them voluntarily to put aside noble and exciting aspirations and embrace limitation, disunity, passivity as a way of life. To bring a people out of corruption, to make them capable of heroic action, required the creation of encouragements to action.

We need not accept Machiavelli's solution, which involved state-worship, or his interpretation of *virtu,* which involved, among other things, conquest and the passion for power. But we cannot pass over his insight into human activity. The growth of human activity, the enlargement of the choices men may make and the actions they may do are products of the increasing opportunities for action created by a social order. To free people, in the sense of removing restraints on their action, does not necessarily enlarge the scope of choices and actions available to them. They must be prepared, intellectually and psychologically, to develop new choices, create new courses of action.

Isaiah Berlin, in offering support for the concept of negative freedom, mis-states the problem in a typical and therefore instructive way:

> It is true that to offer political rights, or safeguards against intervention by the state, to men who are half-naked, illiterate, underfed, and diseased is to mock their condition; they need medical help or education before they can understand, or make use of, an increase in their freedom. What is freedom to those who cannot make use of it? Without adequate conditions for the use of freedom, what is the value of freedom?[17]

What is misleading about this statement is the artificial line drawn between freedom and the conditions for freedom. If certain conditions are necessary for freedom to exist, if other conditions enlarge the choices we may make, are these conditions not entailed in the notion of freedom itself? Must freedom necessarily be a simple concept, easily definable, or may it be at least as complex in definition as it is in life? To say that I am free in proportion to the choices I may make is to say that those conditions which make it possible for me to choose are as much a part of the concept of freedom as the absence of restraint. A society which, by universal assent, valued ignorance would certainly be one of limited freedom even if its only law was, Do as you will. No one need quarrel over the question whether freedom may be defined solely in terms of choice. But we are interested in understanding a concept, not in defining a word. Freedom, like many political activities, takes place in the practical world – it is a practical activity. To understand it, we must see it in the practical contexts of that world.

Freedom is self-motivated activity. To act in this way we require the absence of restraints. But we also require a satisfactory capacity to act. It is this insight which, I believe, created the impetus to go beyond the absence of restraint and to define freedom as self-governance. That approach is, in its fullness, unsatisfactory and yields dangerous and arbitrary results. But the inspiration behind it is sound. Freedom must mean more than the mere absence of restraint. It depends for its significance on the existence of an active assertive populace. It exists only to the extent that our private selves are developed, to the extent that our capacity to have and assert commitments and aspirations helps us to create a satisfactory range of choices and courses of action. These choices, I have insisted, are not created merely by cutting back on restraints, but by creating conditions which make their discovery, development, and assertion possible. The social and psychological conditions which make possible the robust and determined assertion of one's self are part of the meaning of freedom. The absence of restraints is, among other things, a way of protecting and guaranteeing the integrity of the private self.

Freedom and privacy are thus intertwined and inseparable. For not only is freedom largely the protection of a private order of expression, but the development and nurturing of the private self makes it possible for people to develop for themselves, to discover and enlarge, the choices which reflect their needs, commitments, and aspirations.

Third condition: equality

I do not propose to engage in a thoroughgoing analysis of equality, tempting as that is. While I believe that equality is a noble and eminently justifiable social goal and that a good deal more equality than is currently accepted would be desirable, my purpose is only to deal with equality as it bears upon the notion of obligation. Such an inquiry deals with what is minimally satisfactory, what is acceptable, rather than what is ideal. If the account of equality which emerges here is unsatisfactory to egalitarians, I ask them to remember the restricted question I am dealing with.

Neither do I propose to devote energy to rebutting the argument – now rather embarrassingly old-fashioned – that equality is inconsistent with liberty. That argument is true, of course, if equality is taken to mean an imposed levelling of everyone or if it implies the illegitimacy of the freedom to deviate from social norms. But partisans of equality who also care about liberty have never suggested that equality means imposing a robot-like sameness upon all members of society. Their concern is not to treat all men the same, but to correct those social and economic conditions which keep some in bondage to privilege and prevent others from developing into fully human beings. These ancient objections seem, therefore, somewhat irrelevant. Their purpose is to transport the discussion of equality into that territory where fancy and hyperbole can do the work of reason.

Opponents of equality are correct when they argue that the promotion of equality must mean a reduction in liberty for the privileged. But extensions of liberty as well as equality often involve such reductions. Freedom for the wolf is death for the lamb. If we are to protect the lamb, the wolf must be restrained. The freeing of slaves was a reduction in the liberty of slaveholders. The protection of workingmen against starvation wages or barbaric working conditions was a reduction in the liberty of employers. The question in cases like these is not whether the liberty of some has been reduced. It is whether there is a net gain in liberty, whether the liberty represented by this gain is justifiable, whether it is worth the constraints put upon those who lose liberty. Liberty is always based upon constraint: the constraint of the powerful, the wealthy, the unscrupulous, the savage is the condition of the liberty of the weak, the poor, the honest, the civil. If liberty is as good a thing as libertarians believe, it ought to be universalized where possible; and where equality may work to increase liberty by creating conditions which make it possible for people to develop and express commitments and aspirations, the results may justify the constraints needed to produce it.

Equality is a precondition to the exercise by the poor or disinherited of liberties thought to be essential. Poverty, ignorance, powerlessness may not extinguish liberty in a society, but they prevent those afflicted with them from exercising rights and claiming liberties. Libertarians are right in insisting that adequate incomes and decent housing are not the same things as liberty and in warning us that an increase in the former does not automatically lead to an increase in the latter. But they are wrong if they believe that the attainment of the former is a goal to which advocates of liberty need not aspire. It is hypocritical to say that people have a right to fair legal treatment provided they can afford to pay a lawyer or that they have a right to an education if education if possible only where certain economic and social disabilities, which we do little to correct, are removed. It is less than significant to identify liberty with things like free expression of ideas or political participation where conditions exist which discourage a substantial portion of the population from developing the capacity or will to do these things. Unless liberty is to be reduced to privilege, equality must be seen as an aid rather than a danger to it.

Equality is a condition of a common life because it is a prerequisite to the integration of the poor, deprived, powerless into the common life. Economic and social deprivations make such integration impossible, create crippling psychological disabilities which discourage it, or create roadblocks to self-expression so powerful that they may be overcome only by the most heroic efforts. Membership in a common life can coexist with differences in social and economic conditions. But where those differences are radical, where a portion of the population lives in misery and filth, dies younger, works less, suffers crime more, is more often cheated of its rights, is provided with inadequate schools and hospitals, pays more for poorer quality food, purchases goods whose sale is governed by the rules of piracy, lives in homes fit only for the rats who overrun them, and is daily faced with degrading reminders of its own inadequacy and uselessness which prevents it from developing that sense of self-esteem and dignity prerequisite to active and civil participation in social life, it is only the most childishly literal mind, the mind closed to the realities we daily experience, that can treat this membership as substantively real.

But we must be careful not to equate equality merely with the relief of the lowest strata of society. The demand for equality is not satisfied by creating an economic floor below which people do not fall. The lack of equality damages those with adequate incomes also. Let us consider, for a moment, what should be painfully obvious to everyone. Adequate incomes are no protection – as the American middle class has discovered – against unfair taxation or arbitrary corporate power. When school budgets are cut, rich children are not packed into classrooms or deprived of new programs. Service in the combat branches of the army is not exactly a prerogative of the wealthy and public construction is not known to displace them from their homes. The sacrifices demanded by new social objectives – from racial desegregation to reduction of defense budgets to economic austerity – are rarely borne equally. Most important, the unequal distribution of political resources leads to gross differentials in the ability of different classes to manipulate the instruments of power to realize their aspirations or interests.

It is true, of course, that the complaints of the middle classes are –

whatever their own interpretation – less urgent than those of the poor. It is also true that egalitarians are right in stressing the condition of the poor and largely ignoring that of the middle classes. First things come first: the prevention of starvation is more important than the equalization of political power; too many rats is worse than too many taxes; the universal possession of bread takes precedence over the universal possession of caviar. But in an abundant society, people are entitled to demand amenities as well as necessaries; and they are entitled to demand that the sacrifices required by society be borne in some rough proportion to the benefits derived from it.

This last point requires some elaboration. Equality refers not merely to a way of distributing the goods and resources of society, but to a way of distributing its burdens and sacrifices as well. Where people share a common life, they may be asked to share equally its obligations. This seems to be entailed in the very conception of a common life. Political theorists tend to ignore this aspect of equality, perhaps because it is less dramatic than the problem of glaring economic inequality which works such hardship upon lower classes and racial minorities. Perhaps, too, inequality of obligation is thought to be a reflection of the unequal distribution of political resources, correctible only as political resources are redistributed upon a basis of equality. But the fact that inequality of obligation can be corrected by the equalization of political resources does not argue that obligations cannot be made more equal without it. Equality is not a seamless web, to be attained once for all in full. Equality is composed of equalities. It is a condition made up of many types of equality – a condition to be achieved by progressively correcting different types of inequality. One does not 'equalize political resources' except in argument. In the practical world, the equalization of political resources can only be the result of a series of developments in which various differentials are corrected. The existence of a radical inequality of obligation works against this correction, preventing the equalization of other resources. Hence, egalitarians ignore it at their peril.

Those who are concerned only with the relief of the lower strata sometimes fail to see how the absence of equality of obligation prevents them from attaining their goal. For the truth of the matter is that, in an inegalitarian society, the burden of relieving the lower strata falls heavily on the lower-middle and middle-middle classes. Such an unequal distribution of sacrifice breeds resentment of the lower classes by the middle, causes them to seek political leaders willing to neglect – however benignly – the relief of the lower strata, and contributes to the latter's continued dispossession. Equality of obligation comes to be less and less important as greater equality of condition is attained. But in an inegalitarian society, or in a society that comforts itself by pursuing only equality of opportunity, equality of obligation – the equal sharing of burdens and sacrifices – comes to be a goal of great urgency, making it possible for the middle classes to accept egalitarian policies by relieving them of the principal burdens and risks entailed by them.

What is the relation of equality to the common life and a culture of civility? In the first place, equality is a precondition of the attainment of a civil culture. By this I do not mean to deny that great advances in civilization are often produced by outstanding individuals or creative minorities or that responses to grave social threats require a degree of diversity and social differentiation which a literal leveling would destroy. I mean only that the infusing of civility in a culture or society requires a development of the sense of community and of shared concerns and commitments which equality promotes. 'The relation of superior to inferior', Shaw noted, 'excludes good manners.' A civilized society is one in which, among other things, people are civil to each other and accept the need for restraint and forbearance in their dealings with one another. Rules prescribing restraint and forbearance are effective among legal equals. The habits of restraint and forbearance depend upon our capacity to treat with each other on relatively equal terms, to recognize that, as far as that portion of our life which requires restraint and forbearance is concerned, the senses in which men are alike are more important than the senses in which they differ. Equality is a sign of mutually recognized dignity, of that value put on the phenomenon of humanness which, whatever logic holds, seems in fact to be at the root of our capacity to share values, to value common enterprises, to engage in cooperative undertakings. Men do not share their prized values with inferiors, nor seek to engage in common enterprises with those with whom they have no qualities in common. Mutual regard, esteem of others, acceptance of diverse contributions to and opinions of a common culture are not exactly exotic components of a common life and a mutual civility. But these are not possible in the absence of that move toward equalizing those things upon which the expression of personality, the capacity to act, the assertion of rights and liberties, the real participation in self-government depend. A common life and a culture of civility are possible only among those who have attained that degree of equality that allows them to be considered members of a common enterprise. Besides being instrumental in guaranteeing the individual a significant place in the community and helping to make possible the exercise of rights, such equality helps to make self-governance a reality and to create the conditions in which members of the community can contribute to it and judge its actions. Equality is both an inference from and a condition of free membership in a political community.

Equality does not mean (except, perhaps, to anti-egalitarians) that all persons shall be treated alike in all cases – that, as Benn and Peters put it, 'rheumatic patients [are] to be treated like diabetics'. Although proponents of equality frequently suggest that the ways in which men are alike are more important than the ways in which they differ, they also recognize that people are not equal by nature; that some possess intellectual, artistic, physical attributes which others lack; that people have different needs; that some may be said to deserve different rewards or treatment; and that, as people differ in their conceptions of the goods of life, treating all alike may mean imposing upon them an overriding and alien conception of good, submerging those goods which cannot be thought of as common, discouraging diversity. What is important is not that all men be treated alike but that they be equally able to assert their rights, exercise a satisfactory control over their lives, realize their legitimate aspirations.

Equality is the belief that existing differentials in the distribution of resources or values or in treatment are inconsistent with an overriding moral ideal and should therefore be eliminated. The scope of egalitarian commitments is as wide as the justifiable ideals they are based on. As we do not suppose that there exist moral ideals which mandate always treating everyone alike, we may assume that equality is a demand relevant to less than all aspects of social life. The beginning of wisdom, then, is to see the word 'equality' as standing not for an overall state of social organization or distribution, but for an equalization of resources in designated and particular areas of social life. That is what I meant when I said that equality is composed of equalities and that the attainment of equality is a process of progressively equalizing the things that the common life and culture of civility require be equalized.

The question I propose is, What does equality mean in the context of political obligation? In what ways must those who share a common life be equal? They must, first, be equal in the sense that the obligations imposed upon them are equal – that is, proportionate both to the benefits they draw from society and their capacity to meet burdens. I have already indicated my belief in the importance of this form of equality and in its strategic role in equalizing other aspects of social life. While a detailed discussion of the equality of burdens is outside the scope of this book, it might be helpful to have some examples of it. The most obvious example is the progressive income tax. Another is the bearing by society in general of the burdens created by major policy changes: for instance, rather than allowing those put out of work by a reduction in Federal defense contracts to bear the major burden of this policy shift, a defined program can be worked out to retrain and reemploy them. A third, and extremely critical example, would be the correction of the current practice of allowing the poor, the marginal worker, the aged, and the unemployable to bear the heaviest burdens imposed by the need to reduce the rate of inflation.

Second, those who share a common life must be equal in the sense that the distribution of resources relevant to participation in the common life must guarantee to all the capacity to participate in that life on equal terms. Whatever differential in resources may be justifiable, it should never be great enough to give to some persons or classes a disproportionate share of political power. Such an eventuality defeats the very notion of participation in a common life by reducing the participation of some to the formal opportunity to speak and be disregarded. Put another way, social conditions which reduce classes of people to powerlessness, or to relative powerlessness, or which give some groups – defined by wealth and social position – a disproportionate share of political power, are inconsistent with a common life.

If the disproportionate power of wealth is the commonest example of the political results of inequality, it is hardly the only one. Where inequalities are most harshly felt – that is, among the poorest segments of society – we discover another roadblock to effective participation: the continuing subversion of some members' juridical personalities. I suggested earlier that those who participate in the common life must be regarded as juridical persons and I stressed the importance of conceiving of rights and obligations as being addressed to abstract legal constructs. We must now reflect on the obvious question whether or not the destruction of juridical personality is a matter solely of formal rules of law or whether it is a function of something else. To suggest an answer to this question, it might be helpful to think of the rights possessed by juridical persons as being of several kinds. There are, first, those rights classically associated with the liberal aspirations of the Enlightenment. The purpose of these rights is to protect the citizen against the government and they are commonly stated in terms of prohibitions against specified types of state action or guarantees of specific rights against invasion. The writ of *habeas corpus*, the rights enumerated in the first eight amendments to the American constitution, the prohibition of bills of attainder or *ex post facto* laws are common examples of this most famous conception of rights.

The second variety of rights developed out of our experience with the vast social changes wrought by industrialization. These rights are not merely limits on state action, but are claims for performance by regimes – for things like the provision of education and housing, the guarantee of economic security, adequate living standards, the right to a livelihood. Whatever was thought to be true in the past, we now know that if ignorance, disease, squalid housing, poverty, economic dependence create an environment which prevents millions from taking advantage of their rights and subjects them to a different and subtler form of control, the promotion of freedom requires that these obstacles be overcome. To be a right-holding creature means to have roots in a social environment which makes the claiming of rights feasible. The articulation of this theory promoted extensive changes in our thinking about rights. Nevertheless, what these changes have for the most part accomplished has been to add to the conception of rights those things necessary to make the basic eighteenth-century rights functional. For most liberal nineteenth- and twentieth-century writers and statesmen regarded rights to economic security, education, and the like as justifiable not so much for their own sakes as for the sake of that classical liberty which was impossible without them. This second variety of rights I would call – not without trepidation – *functional rights*.

Yet functional rights perform one other service, whose implications we are only just beginning to understand. Things like economic security and education are important because in their absence the deprived person *has no opportunity to become integrated into the community of right-holders*. Private behavior and social conditions may operate not merely to deprive people of their capacity to exercise specific rights, but to deprive them of the ability to claim rights in general. Social and economic deprivations create classes of people ignorant of their rights or afraid to exercise them. Frequently, regimes tacitly support – through inadvertence or the determination not to interfere – private or social sanctions which follow attempts to exercise rights. These result in the wholesale disenfranchisement of groups of nominal citizens, in their abstraction from the normal processes of law and politics, and in the creation of an essentially lawless relation between them and the regime. Social, economic, and cultural deprivations thus amount to something quite remarkable: the near-equivalent of statelessness. It takes no special insight to perceive that the relations between black and white in the American south were extra-legal or that law was only slightly less suspended in the north. For all of the provisions of the American constitution, for all of the equalizing talk of presidents, the conclusion is unavoidable that the Negro possessed no real legal status in America and that his present occupation of such status is tenuous. The practical unavailability of legal redress converts classes and groups into people with special – and hardly enviable – legal relations to the regime.

The notion of juridical man founders on the rocks of social behavior, not constitutional theory. For if a person is disinherited, we find his special disability to be not that he is known to the law as a second-class citizen or inferior class member, but that he is simply *unknown to law* and has no rights.

Typically, the twentieth century has found new images to picture its lower classes: we call them disinherited, submerged, invisible. For these people, a status of formal legal equality is subverted by submergence. They are victims not merely of oppression, but also of lawlessness. Against them claims may be asserted which amount to grants of privilege for the asserters. Housing laws, ostensibly written to protect them, go unenforced. The police act toward them as a primitive army of occupation might act toward a captive people. The laws regulating daily economic transactions are built upon their disadvantages, frequently being little more than formal and complex sanctions for robbery or fraud. Their political participation – which they anyway perceive as pointless – is actively or subtly discouraged. Their ignorance, fear, expectations of unfair treatment are the cornerstones of their relations with the rest of society. Their disabilities are not corrected by law so much as taken advantage of by it. This has lately been reinforced by their state of powerlessness in a pluralist political system whose policies are so much a function of the power that conflicting parties bring to the bargaining table. Their participation in the making of law is not sought and is often discouraged or refused. Their interests are unprotected and their rights unlitigated. Administrative or legislative correction of lawlessness directed against them is, in general, rare and haphazard.

What this amounts to is, as I have said, something analagous to statelessness. It is true that the disabilities of people denied juridical status by the impact of social and economic deprivations are not as total as those of stateless persons. The latter are denied the rights to act and have opinions.[18] The former may not be wholly deprived of these rights, but they find them enforced selectively and arbitrarily. The disabilities of stateless persons are the result of their belonging to no political community. The disabilities of the disinherited are the result of lawlessness on the part of the political community to which they ostensibly belong, of the arbitrary and haphazard legal identities which they are given. They lack, to adapt another of Arendt's concepts, a constant space of legal appearance.[19]

This lack is definitive. The space of appearance, as Arendt understands it, encompasses the conceptual space where one appears to others and others to him. It is the thing that makes men significant, not in any special moral sense, but in the sense that other men may take account of them and they of others. To be deprived of a space of appearance is, then, 'to be deprived of reality, which, humanly and politically speaking is the same thing as appearance. To men the reality of the world is guaranteed by the presence of others, by its appearing to all . . . and whatever lacks this appearance comes and passes away like a dream, intimately and exclusively our own but without reality.'[20] To lack a space of legal appearance is to lack that quality of reality which makes legal protection possible, as slaves have always discovered. It is to be ruled by lawlessness.

This lack need not be total. The members of a disinherited class may not be wholly deprived of a space of legal appearance. But their juridical recognition may be haphazard and arbitrary: they may occupy a space of legal appearance – be treated as juridical persons – only on unpredictable occasions. But the possession of an ambiguous legal reality, the transient occupation of the space of legal appearance on unpredictable occasions destroys one's capacity to claim rights because it limits arbitrarily one's capacity to call upon others or the regime to vindicate rightful claims. Such a status creates an unbearable tension and an anxiety not unlike that attributed by seventeenth-century theorists to inhabitants of a state of nature. For the fact is that the anxiety which they saw attending life in such a state derived not merely from the wholesale subjection of one's personality and aspirations to the arbitrary whims of a despot, but to one's ambiguous status in a social order in which rights were indifferently and uncertainly secured. The evil of tyranny lay in the fact that the members of such a state lived in perpetual tension, never sure of how, or whether, the sanctions of law would apply or the guarantees of rights would be honored.

It thus becomes necessary to speak of a right to have rights, a right encompassing more than Arendt's right to belong to an organized community.[21] For we must face the curious and terrible fact that *members of an organized community can be deprived of their rights simply because they are not integrated into the community of juridical persons.* Such deprivation need not be a matter of law, as with slavery. It can be the result of the absence of law; that is, of the failure of the regime to correct social and economic – in a word, 'private' – deprivations which operate to deprive certain groups of their legal reality. If citizenship is a condition of obligation, then the obligation on the part of the regime to guarantee juridical personality to each person, to vindicate his right to have rights, is inescapable. Laws which directly or indirectly perpetuate conditions which lead to the destruction or suspension of juridical personality cannot be binding and the systematic deprivation of juridical personality to a defined group – provided this is not justified in the most precise possible way by the clear necessity of temporary paternalism – is a fundamental component of the judgment of illegitimacy. A regime which either directly supports the subversion of juridical personality *or which fails to take steps to correct such subversion as is made known to it,* violates its obligations and retards rather than advances the realization of the ideals of the common life. At this point, the whole apparatus of disobedience and resistance becomes relevant and the question becomes one of deciding which form of disobedience may be employed.[22]

What I suggest, then, is that we conceive of a third variety of rights: *integrative rights.* Possession of these rights is prerequisite to one's becoming a real member of a political community, to his occupying a space of legal appearance and thereby being known to the regime as a juridical person, to his contributing – on an equal footing with his fellows – to the common life. To the extent that such integration is subverted by social and economic conditions or by the results of social and economic conditions, it is incumbent on the regime to recognize the correction of those conditions as a *rightful obligation* upon itself and not as a dictate of equity or paternalism. *The members of a political community have a right to those economic and social things which, like adequate living standards, education, elimination of invidious social discriminations, are the social and non-legal bases of their juridical personalities.* And I cannot insist too firmly that the whole of our recent experience indicates that these rights are no less significant or more difficult to conceptualize or apply than the traditional rights to formal legal equality. The right to be equal before the law entails the right to be known to the law equally with all others. The obligation to secure that right cannot be avoided on the grounds that it imposes new or unconventional duties upon the regime or that it requires substantial revisions in the duties regimes are accustomed to undertake. And as it can hardly be suggested – in the face of decades of social inquiry and official policy commitments – that these rights are indeed newly discovered, this obligation comes down to a demand that regimes do what for a long time they have in fact paid lip-service to.

Obviously, it is not possible to deduce the things which affect the right to have rights from some *a priori* standard or from the consideration of the meaning of legal ideals. Where the elementary requirements of formal equality have been met, knowledge of the subversion of the right to have rights comes from the evaluation of emerging empirical evidence relating to the effect of behavior and conditions upon the integrity of the juridical personality. The very fact that we have only in the past generation been able to appreciate the impact of statelessness or to realize that, in a liberal democracy, social and economic factors can not merely hinder the exercise of rights, but subvert juridical personality itself indicates that it would be absurd to hold a regime responsible to anticipate the variety of things which may affect the right to have rights. What we may hold a regime to is the obligation consistently to seek for evidence, or weigh evidence presented to it, which suggests ways in which juridical personality is subverted. The obligation of the regime is thus fourfold. It must constantly be aware of the signal importance of guaranteeing and fostering the right to have rights. It must be aware that that right may be subverted by means other than formal deprivations of juridical status. It must accept as one of its prime responsibilities the obligation constantly to assess the extent to which this right is actually being realized and to evaluate such evidence as is turned up to indicate whether and how it is being subverted. It is responsible, where such evidence is discovered, to redress the wrong: it must act affirmatively to correct the conditions which perpetuate disinheritance as it once acted to remove formal and legal constraints on the exercise of rights.

The third egalitarian requirement of the common life is that the distribution of resources must be such as to make equal freedom a reality. I have already pointed out that freedom can be reduced by social and economic conditions which inhibit the active and robust expression of commitments and aspirations and which promote apathy, alienation, fear, and the like; which restrict one's perception of the social world; which crimp one's ability to understand and create choices, to assess their significance, to influence the nature of the options open to one. The concept of a common life demands the elimination of such conditions, for their presence prevents the realization of equal freedom and often trivializes such rights as are available.

This is a conclusion which it is impossible to avoid. But we have tried to avoid it. We persist in attacking the problems caused by inequality by creating legal rights which are supposed to correct its results and which are frustrated by the same forces which frustrate the realization of other rights. Where freedom depends upon equalized economic and social conditions, it cannot be realized by failing to equalize those conditions and attempting to compensate for the disabilities they cause. Such a procedure merely creates new artificial rights. Participation by the poor in welfare programs is less than revolutionary where the programs in whose administration they participate are pitifully inadequate. The easing of academic standards by universities reaches only a small percentage of those who might, if the conditions of their lives were different, be eligible for admission to college on equal terms with their classmates. A generation of fair housing laws has not prevented slums from degenerating into ghettoes nor opened the suburbs to the poor. Fair employment laws do not guarantee employment, especially at adequate wages. If economic security, the right to a livelihood, non-discriminatory housing, education are considered essential to freedom, it is clear that only a substantial improvement in the conditions of life of the poor can make freedom a reality for them. The substitution of legal devices gains us nothing.

The requirement of equal freedom once again makes it clear that the demand for equality cannot merely be a demand to raise the living standards of the lowest portion of society. The point is that it is not enough to insure that some people do not suffer from great disadvantages, but to make certain that none have great advantages which allow them to assert their interests to the prejudice of others. For equal freedom means more than the equal possession of rights: it also means the equal ability to realize interests and aspirations. It is true that things like protection from arbitrary imprisonment or punishment for speech are important. But a conception of freedom which ends there and omits the realization of legitimate interests and aspirations is simply inadequate for it omits the things which make free speech and the like so valuable: the ability of men to define their own lives, to reach for their own private goods. If freedom means guaranteeing the private order of expression it must be seen to involve the capacity to realize private goods, to assert interests in those cases where interests may rightly be asserted. But inequality of condition leads to an inequality of the capacity to assert interests and aspirations and gives to some a greater opportunity to realize their private goods than to others.

The protection of freedom also means that people must have some capacity to influence those factors which involve their intimate relations with others and which can be identified with their commitments and aspirations. They must be capable of resisting manipulation of their private lives. They must be given the social, economic, and psychological wherewithal to protect their private lives by themselves.

There is a social environment of privacy, an environment in which man's most intimate activities are located. We may think of this environment in terms of conceptual space – the space in which, while we may appear to others, we appear fundamentally as private persons. This conceptual space can be translated into institutional terms: we may think of this environment as an immediate or proximal environment, comprising one's household, work, property, neighborhood, and other elementary social relations. Freedom means the capacity to assert one's aspirations and commitments in this environment quite directly, to be able to resist the manipulation of that environment which is, after all, the one in which one's most passionate and personal life is lived. It is not unusual, although it is illogical, for people to consider themselves free where they may move freely and satisfactorily within this environment, even if they lack the full apparatus of political and legal rights. The extent to which this proximal environment nourishes aspirations and commitments; defines, especially in our earliest years, the texture of our ability to live in the world; creates the possibility of satisfying our physical or affective needs, can hardly be exaggerated. The ability to influence our proximal environments is something profoundly and rightly cherished by men.

It is also, as we have been given to understand, important to the assertion of rights and aspirations. We have good reason to believe that men faced with deadening work environments 'become passive and alienated, feel unable to control their fates and [lose] sight of the significant issues of political life'.[23] Passivity and resignation are evident in Lane's studies of lower middle- and working-class life. Ghetto residents and the rural poor – two groups who have nearly no control over their proximal environments – are less likely to vote, to call upon lawyers to help them vindicate their rights, to organize to defend their interests than their more fortunate fellows. And they are, as I have argued, less likely to occupy a space of legal appearance. In short, their world is one in which their rights are expendable and unsafe, their freedom illusory, and their ability to claim rights and freedoms undermined by the attitudes their environment nourishes.

The capacity to influence one's proximal environment is, on both of the above counts, inseparable from the condition of freedom. But the universalization and reality of that capacity waits upon the equalization of conditions of social life. Such equality need not be thought of as literal identity, but as an approximate equality of social environments and a distribution of resources sufficient to assure that some groups or individuals will not possess, by mere control of economic resources, disproportionate power or ability to control the lives of their fellows. A common life demands that

> while the occupations and incomes of individuals varied, they would live, nevertheless, in much the same environment, would enjoy similar standards of health and education, would find different positions, according to their varying abilities, equally accessible to them, would intermarry freely with each other, would be equally immune from the more degrading forms of poverty, and equally secure against economic oppression.[24]

Nothing less could satisfy the requirements of the opportunity to participate equally in the articulation of social values and to be equally free, capable of influencing one's proximal environment and developing one's private self. If it is utopian, its utopian quality is a measure not of its fanciful nature, but of our hypocritical abjuration of the values we supposedly profess. Not democracy, not freedom, not even legal equality is possible on other terms.

Such equality is subject, of course, to the limitations imposed by nature. Under perfectly equal conditions, some men will prosper more than others, realize aspirations more, and so forth. I do not suggest that we alter this. But we must be careful not to use nature as an excuse for inaction or moral blindness. If a genuinely egalitarian society is, given the nature of man, impossible, it is nevertheless possible to avow a loyalty to the ideal of equality and strive to realize as much of it as possible. On the other hand, we must never forget that there was a time when learned men solemnly declared the impossibility of popular government, or believed that people would turn to savagery if Christian churches lost their power to control morals, or feared that the destruction of aristocratic legitimacy would irrevocably lead to barbarism. Advocates of equality do not have to place their trust in a benign, optimistic picture of human nature. Equality cannot be produced by the force of moral argument any more than Christianity. And it may be that, as with Christianity, we shall have to settle for a very poor and very pallid substitute. Equality will be produced – if at all – by the articulated demands and political power of billions of unequals whose claims can be satisfied only by equalizing the distribution of available resources. This, as Schumpeter brilliantly described it, reverses the Marxist causal theory: an egalitarian society will be the product of political democracy, shallow and incomplete as it may be. That is a very good reason for valuing democracy – even bourgeois democracy – and for taking care not to destroy it. Democracy provides the means by which men may create a genuinely common life. I do not by any means wish to imply that this creation is inevitable. Like non-doctrinaire Marxists, I believe in the need to give history a little push in the right direction.

Fourth condition: accountability

The senses of accountability. The fulfillment of the conditions of obligation requires that the regime be accountable. It takes little imagination to see that things like freedom and participation are nothing but polite fictions where the regime is under no compulsion to account for its actions to its citizenry. Indeed, one of the central insights of liberal constitutionalism is that irresponsibility of public authority inevitably leads to the repression of rights. The benevolent despot always turns, on examination, to be more despotic than benevolent. To possess rights means to be able to compel the regime to act in certain ways. To be self-governing means to be able to influence the direction of policy. The capacity of members to develop, articulate, and judge the values of the common life and the actions taken under them is pointless where the regime cannot be held responsible, where the member becomes a judge without power and a delineator of abstract ideals.

A regime is accountable where the members of a society can

compel it to observe the conditions of the common life, where there exist real mechanisms to enable members to vindicate their rights. In those areas of political behavior where rights are not involved and where wants may legitimately govern policy, the members ought to be consulted about what they want and have at their disposal the means of enforcing their conception of wants under the regime. In practice, the mechanism for doing the latter can be provided by the institutions of democracy; for where wants and interests conflict and rights are not involved, the fair and practicable way of resolving those conflicts is to make the ultimate decision a matter of majority will.

There are two senses in which a regime may be said to be accountable. It may be accountable in the sense that decision-makers are in fact answerable to those they represent for their decisions and actions. It may be accountable in the sense that there is a legal model of accountability to which the regime adheres. This second type of accountability is a formal type and we have come to regard such formalism with suspicion: the real question, we are often told, is not whether decisionmakers are responsible in law, but in fact – whether, that is, they can be made to live up to what the law demands.

There is certainly no reason to minimize this objection. But at the same time, we surely must realize that any time a regime is said to be accountable, there must be legal or formal reasons for holding it so. If a government is responsible through elections, then the relations between the government, electorate, parties, and so forth, must be specified in law. Accountability divorced from law is mere moralizing or else it is something to be invoked only where strong interests demand it. But to say that a regime is only morally accountable is to say that it is not accountable at all, as medieval political theorists who argued that the prince could be bound only by the 'directive [i.e., moral] power' of law and not by its 'coercive power' sadly discovered. And to make accountability a function of political power is to render it arbitrary, haphazard, and unprincipled – subject only to the movements of the dominant interests in a society. Accountability divorced from law also deprives us of the advantages of using law against an unwilling regime, or to exploit existing tensions within the regime, or to invoke the sometimes critical aid of courts. If a regime is to be accountable in fact, law is indispensible: it alone can provide a coherent theoretical framework for imposing accountability and make available the tools such imposition requires.

The difficulty with many discussions of accountability is that they are not general enough: they are too frequently concerned with justifying or analyzing a particular mode of imposing accountability. We have been told, e.g., that accountability is a function of citizen participation, or of decentralization, or of particular constitutional or legal reforms. The problem is not that any of these contentions is wrong, but that they are all likely to be correct, although limited in applicability. We cannot pose the question by asking how we can make 'social institutions' accountable: different institutions can be made accountable in different ways. What is needed is an understanding of the different ways accountability can be attained.

That vast and complex problem is beyond the scope of this book. To examine accountability in detail, evaluate the dense and often contradictory evidence, and propose a supposedly definitive set of recommendations would require prolonged study as well as something approaching analytical genius. But the point of this section is not to set out a definitive program. It is to show that a common life cannot exist unless the political institutions of the regime are accountable. That point is made once we recognize that it is impossible to guarantee that the members of a society will be able to contribute to the common life if the institutions within which that contribution is formalized may go their own way. To justify this requirement, it is necessary merely to show that accountability is not vain, that it is, in principle, possible. Hence, I propose to do no more than suggest that there exist ways, whose possibility is supported by empirical evidence and reasonable argument, to impose accountability upon the great political institutions of modern industrial society.

Accountability in mass society. Democratic politics has, I believe, shown that accountability is in principle possible: political participation, in a context of rivalry and competition between opposing forces, has succeeded in imposing at least a degree of accountability upon elected officials. Such accountability undoubtedly varies and flags from time to time and place to place; and it may be that it is, on the whole, less than satisfactory. But enough evidence exists to support the proposition that the development and extension of equal citizenship will serve to strengthen it.

We have also seen that a legal system that offers adequate opportunities for recourse to the courts may be used by citizens to impose another kind of accountability upon public institutions and officials: it may hold them to the performance of their duties as specified in law.

Another mode of imposing accountability is disobedience. In some instances, acts of disobedience have focused public attention upon particular injustices or invasions of rights and have impelled sometimes recalcitrant public officials to move toward correcting them. In other cases, acts of disobedience have made it possible to litigate serious questions which, for various and often petty reasons, could not be brought to the attention of courts in more traditional ways. The extent to which disobedience may help to impose accountability is surely a fascinating, if generally overlooked, phenomenon. Unfortunately, I cannot discuss it in advance of the argument developed in the next four chapters. There I maintain, among other things, that disobedience is sometimes a right and that a more permissive attitude toward disobedience is justified, if not demanded, by the idea of the common life as well as by democratic theory. If these arguments are valid, a more permissive attitude toward disobedience may increase the number of occasions where a breaking of the law leads to greater accountability. But these ideas cannot be presented in advance of the discussion ahead. I can merely ask the reader to reflect, at the end of the book, upon the relevance of the arguments in Part Two to the question of accountability.

The modes of imposing accountability just mentioned – however much they may show that accountability is in principle possible – have a major drawback. They do not seem particularly effective against the two major public institutions of mass society: the corporation and the bureaucracy. Indeed these institutions seem beyond effective control – so much so that there are probably many who would be satisfied to know that the degree of accountability imposed upon elected officials, haphazard and inadequate as it may sometimes be, attached to them as well.

Consider the corporation. The enormous and varied powers of corporations to regulate, to make decisions regarding relocation, investment, development, price, which affect millions are public powers for which they are not systematically accountable. Of course, they are accountable in certain limited ways. In American law, they may be required to observe the restraints imposed by the constitution upon government where they can be shown to be agents of a government or to be acting in sufficiently close involvement with a government. On occasion, legislatures impose specific duties upon them which are, in theory at least, enforceable in court. There is an ongoing attempt to make them responsible to the public through regulation by independent commissions; but we have discovered that the regulatory agencies have largely become advocates for the industries they regulate and the responsibility they impose is minimal.

What steps might be taken to correct this? A generation or two ago, the answer to that question seemed obvious: the corporation must be formally made a public body. There seemed several ways to do this. The most drastic, of course, was nationalization. The least drastic was regulation, combined with the legal imposition of duties toward the public. Between these extremes were various possibilities. Some of the suggestions of R. H. Tawney, though more cogent than most, were typical. The question, he noted, was not who owns a corporation or even who manages it, but whether owners and managers compose a 'body representing the nation'. In addition to outright nationalization of critical major industries, Tawney suggested

> the extension of public utility companies working under statutory constitutions, the acquisition by public authorities of a controlling interest in private undertakings and the appointment of directors, the assistance with capital and credit of approved concerns which comply with conditions as to operation prescribed by the State, the control of raw materials and primary products by import boards, and the introduction of the public costing system.[25]

He had earlier argued that, under properly organized conditions – that is, where ownership of capital in an industry is unified and where the industry could assume collective responsibility for all competently managed firms – the basic function of the shareholder could be reduced to the provision of capital when investment money was needed. Such a proprietary interest would not entitle the shareholder to exercise control over the operations of the company in which he has invested or, because unified ownership largely obviates risk, to demand profit as his reward. He would be entitled to demand only interest.

Capital is an instrument the function of which is to assist the labour of human beings, as a man uses a bicycle to enable him to get more quickly to his work. A price must be paid for it, which is interest, because it cannot be got without it. But when the owner is paid its price, he has been paid his due, and any surplus which he receives is waste.[26]

Whatever the merits of these proposals, whatever the strength or elegance of the arguments which originally supported them, they sound badly on contemporary ears. Why is that so? Partly, I think, because we have found that the transfer of corporate power to public ownership or the creation of governmental supervisory boards has not increased the accountability of those industries and has created a new class of administrators and bureaucrats with a new set of institutional devices to mask responsibility. But there is another reason. Proposals such as Tawney's seem written for the inhabitants of another world, a world of different realities and expectations. The very postulates which those who sought to restrict the power and activities of the corporation regarded as necessary and natural seem eccentric today.

For the corporate mystique has changed. We really seem to be convinced that there is no alternative to the corporation, that protest against it is as foolish as Canute's commanding the waves to stop. In fact, few of us any longer conceive of the corporation as something to be replaced or superseded. This at least passive acceptance of the corporation as the permanent economic institution of modern society has enabled it to develop a new popular image. It is coming to be seen not as a symbol of exploitation or of fantastic economic development, but as a rational mechanism providing the most efficient means of ordering the economy of technological society. Corporate leaders are largely seen as capable professional managers employing rational techniques of production, deliberating like statesmen over the role and responsibilities of corporate power, striving to find a proper balance between private initiative and government regulation.[27] Where the corporation is perceived as a danger, the realistic appraisal that it is useless to protest against it or to try to alter the corporate economy forces programs like Tawney's into an historical limbo out of which they seem unlikely to emerge.

The acceptance of such a belief discourages the proposal of all but legal and constitutional palliatives which, while sound in themselves, are dramatically inadequate. Consider the suggestion (advanced by Berle among others) that, in the United States, the constitution be extended to cover corporations as well as formal governments – that constitutional restraints on government be held applicable to the corporation and trade union.[28] The groundwork for such an extension was laid a generation ago when we began to realize that 'the modern state has set up and come to rely on, the corporate system to carry out functions for which in modern life by community demand the government is held ultimately responsible'.[29] This approach is beset by various difficulties. First, its development has not surprisingly been slow and uneven: constitutional and political traditions are not lightly upset nor powerful interests easily subjected to new legal restraints. Such accountability as has been imposed upon corporations has been accomplished only under the fiction that some sort of government involvement took place or that the corporation was, for the purpose involved, essentially an agent of the government.[30] Second, our commitment to the existing system of corporate ownership and management cannot be altered merely by constitutional interpretation. At the most, the constitutionalization of the corporation in present circumstances can only mean the imposition of limitations upon things like racial discrimination, or increased protection of free speech and assembly, and so forth.[31] In other words, the constitutionalization of the corporation in present circumstances can involve little more than the application to it of certain segments of the Bill of Rights. If it were taken seriously, and seriously applied, that would undoubtedly be progress of sorts. It would mean that General Motors could not arbitrarily forbid a shareholder from speaking at one of its annual charades; that United States Steel could not (as it did) sidestep its responsibility to promote racial equality in Birmingham; that trade unions could not close their ranks to blacks. But if the application of constitutional limitations is to result in genuine accountability, it must extend beyond the Bill of Rights and cover as well those activities – such as price setting, capital investment, or plant relocation – which constitute the rule-making powers of the corporation. Such an extension of constitutional limitations would involve an enormous reshaping of our social processes. It would require the transfer of some corporate rule-making powers to the formal government. Further, the rule-making powers of a constitutionalized corporation would have to be thought of as legislation or administrative regulation and hence necessarily subject to constitutional rules of delegation and to other restrictions contained in or intimated by the constitution. A corporation so restructured could not continue to be controlled merely by private shareholders or represent only their interests in collective bargaining and agency contracts. Thus, it is not clear that the total constitutionalization of the corporation is consistent with the maintenance of private ownership of capital; and it is certainly inconsistent with private management of capital. Hence, the constitutionalizing of the corporation must either involve some form of nationalization or else must, in stopping short of nationalization, be a limited and not very effective remedy. If the corporation were constitutionalized only in the sense that it became subject to certain Bill of Rights provisions, the question of the enormous power it wields would not be resolved. The corporate bureaucracy could remain unaccountable and its rule-making powers – its power to direct much of our social life – would not necessarily be touched.

On the other hand, nationalization of the corporation would not, by itself, be sufficient. The behavior of nationalized industries and great bureaucracies gives us little reason to assume that responsibility to the public would follow from the fact of nominal ownership by the public and actual control by a new managerial elite.

The size of the corporation – private or nationalized – may defeat any attempts to impose accountability. Sufficient evidence exists that the giant conglomerates and the supercorporations cannot effectively be controlled, that they wield greater power than it is wise to entrust to men and that their acts are frequently inconsistent with the maintenance of freedom. This is an old perception, but the experience of the past generation adds new power to it. It is perhaps time to reconsider (though possibly with some alteration of the dollar figure given) this suggestion of Henry Simons:

> There is simply no excuse, except with a narrow and specialized class of enterprise, for allowing corporations to hold stock in

other corporations – and no reasonable excuse (the utilities apart) for hundred-million-dollar corporations, no matter what form their property might take. Even if the much advertised economies of gigantic financial combinations were real, sound policy would wisely sacrifice these economies to preservation of more economic freedom and equality.[32]

It is at least worth considering whether corporate accountability is possible in the absence of a radical restriction on the size of the corporation and a consequent break-up of existing giant corporations into many successors. The decentralization of the industrial system may be the only remaining way of imposing, or beginning the process of imposing, accountability.

One of the ways the decentralization of industry might help to impose accountability is by reintroducing the conditions and controls of the economic market. Such reintroduction might eliminate the authoritative and rule-making powers of the corporation while making it less able to resist the demands of the public or its representatives. Moreover, what better mechanism than the market exists to determine a people's material needs and wants, to coordinate economic activity without resort to authoritarianism and undue coercion, to channel investment in such a way that mistakes can be revealed?[33] But it is questionable whether the developments of contemporary technology – especially in the areas of coordination of information and administration – would make a return to a classical (i.e., capitalist) market possible: as Robert Paul Wolff has pointed out, 'reliance on the market is fundamentally irrational once men know how to control it in order to avoid its undesired consequences'.[34] This point is especially significant in the context of decentralization, where an extremely sophisticated technology would be required to maintain an acceptable level of production. Hence, controls must be placed on the manipulation of the market and on the tendency of private economic actors to replace the market with less unpredictable forms of organization.

The classical market encourages – if experience is any guide – a corruption of the economy where the production of goods is subrogated to the pursuit of wealth. It supports acquisitiveness, exploitation, and a destruction of the sense of community in economic affairs. Hence, while the market mechanism can be employed, in appropriate circumstances, to impose accountability upon and limit the rule-making powers of corporations, a too-great reliance on the market as the basic element of an economic system can lead to the subversion of the very idea of a common life – indeed, even to the subversion of the things the market was originally expected to realize. In the context of a common life, the market must be reduced to its proper role as a mechanism of economic coordination, a tool of society rather than its master. This argues a need for planning, for a degree of regulation not possible (again on empirical grounds) within the confines of a classical market, and for limits placed upon the market in the name of the values of the common life.

A possible mode of doing this (although it is by no means an ideal solution) is to federalize the economy. Within a constitutionally determined set of values and clear, though broad, planning boundaries, production and exchange could be carried on by a congeries of independent, competing, public corporations. These bodies can be bound by clear legal guidelines, be required to report in accordance with a single agreed-upon accounting system, and be subject to the usual constitutional restraints placed upon public bodies. With the direction of the decentralized corporations placed in the hands of workers and representatives of the public as well as professional managers – perhaps a senior civil service — and with appropriate restrictions on overlapping directorates and terms of office, such a system could substantially limit corporate rule-making, impose a degree of accountability upon economic bodies, and avoid the legendary disadvantages and dangers of bureaucratic socialism and centralized planning.

The coherence of such an economic system is undoubtedly problematical and its justification would require much more analysis than I am prepared to give it here. As I have said, my purpose is not to propose a definitive program, but to indicate the direction of the reforms necessary to impose accountability. I do not assume that serious problems of accountability would not exist under the system I suggest. I merely assume that such a system is possible and that it would impose a greater degree of accountability than presently exists. Nor do I assume that it is possible in the circumstances of the western industrialized world to attain it. It may be that the accumulation of corporate power is already so great that no attempt seriously to restrict or tame it can succeed; or that we are on the threshold of a process whereby the economic institutions of the present are irreversibly developing into the political institutions of the future, much as the *latifundia* of Rome developed into the fiefs of feudal Europe. I do not address myself to these problems. I only state that if a common life is to be attained, corporations must become accountable; and if they are to be accountable, some such dramatic change as I have proposed is necessary. If this cannot be done, we must face the fact that we cannot establish a common life or realize civility. In that case, the whole problem of politics takes on a new and more terrifying dimension.

The establishment of control over the bureaucracy is a somewhat less intractable problem, although by no means simple. In his recent critique of 'interest group liberalism', Theodore Lowi offers some interesting suggestions.[35] Lowi argues that much of the abuse found within the administrative process is the result of broad and ill-defined delegations of power to the bureaucracy.[36] Administrative agencies, in other words, are frequently forced to operate without adequate legal guidelines and this forces them to rely on bargaining as a standard mode of procedure. Now bargaining is frequently necessary and proper in the administrative decisionmaking process. But the absence of clear and precise delegations of authority forces agencies to bargain not merely over the decisions they make, but over the rules which are to govern the making of those decisions. Reliable standards disappear, arbitrary and apparently contradictory decisions occur, proceedings are extended, costs rise. Much of the bureaucracy operates, in this view, in a legal vacuum, without benefit of clear standards to guide its behavior. What is needed is the restoration of a strict law of delegation: a constitutional requirement that legislatures not delegate legislative authority to the bureaucracy and that all permissible delegations of power be 'accompanied by clear standards of implementation'.[37] This would, among other benefits, making the bureaucracy more amenable to judicial or legislative check and would place the job of creating fundamental standards for decisionmaking where it belongs – with the elected representatives of the public.

Lowi also argues, following Kenneth Culp Davis, for 'early and frequent administrative rule-making' – that is, for greater formality in the administrative process.[38] Within its proper scope of delegated authority, the administrative agency ought to be responsible for formulating, in clear and formal terms, the rules upon which decisions are to be based. In addition to making the administrative process more efficient, such formalism would increase the possibilities of appeal to the legislature or the courts. Further, Lowi proposes that a statutory tenure of from five to ten years be placed on the life of every administrative agency. This would insure substantive review of the agency's activities as its tenure draws to a close and its continuing existence comes to be considered.

We may ask whether suggestions such as these go far enough. There are many types of bureaucratic organizations whose purposes are to administer programs rather than regulate industries. These organizations – which range from school systems and urban service agencies to the great Federal departments – have, largely because of their strategic political positions, become extremely powerful and it is unlikely that Lowi's reforms would be sufficient to impose adequate accountability upon them. In the case of these agencies, we must institutionalize accountability procedures within the agencies themselves and open the administrative policymaking process to the public.

Twenty years ago, Norton Long suggested that we structure into the bureaucratic agencies a 'loyal opposition' to present policy alternatives to agency heads.[39] Such institutionalization would be especially valuable in regulatory agencies which are frequently charged with favoring the industry, or part of it, that they are supposed to regulate. In addition, the commissioners of these agencies are frequently not professional civil servants whose career is within administration, but employees or executives of the industry regulated who regard government service as a temporary hiatus in their private careers. It might be wise to institutionalize departments within each agency, staffed by senior civil servants, and specifically charged with representing public interests or interests opposed to the industry regulated. In agencies whose job is the administration of programs, these departments might function as controllers, but with policy as well as fiscal responsibilities, or as intra-agency ombudsmen.

More important, there is a demonstrated need for public participation in the process of administrative policymaking. We have labored too long under the myth that administration is solely a matter of professional expertise to be controlled by professionals and experts. But many of the decisions made by bureaucrats are not properly related to expertise at all: they are value choices. The best administrative structure for a school system, whether a piece of public land should be park or wilderness, which of several competing groups should be granted a broadcaster's license are questions involving values and preferences as well as technical matters. Where policies are matters of value or preference, of choices which, whatever their rationales, affect the public in serious ways, no claims of expertise and efficiency can justify excluding the public from participating in the making of those policies. The truism that policies cannot be administered by the public is irrelevant. It does not mean that the contours of administrative policy should be made without consulting the public. Administration is government and public involvement in the making of important governmental policy is demanded by the notions both of the common life and democracy. From these demands, the bureaucracy is not exempt.

Nor does it help to argue that public participation would hinder wise and effective administration because the public is often shortsighted or because particular groups tend to place their interests above those of the community or identify them with those of the community. It is also true that administrators frequently hold views that reflect their own often narrow experiences, develop self-serving values, and view criticism defensively as at best a product of ignorance or bias. Confrontation with the public, the need to answer public criticism, can sometimes correct these shortcomings. Besides, on most major issues, the public – or that part of it interested in the issue – is rarely blind: there are experts and professionals outside of the bureaucracy and the interests supporting a particular administrative policy.

How can the public be brought into the administrative process? The answer, in most cases, is only indirectly. But indirect participation may be enough to establish a satisfactory degree of accountability. It may also enhance the possibility of early and effective rule-making. Let us consider both of these benefits in the context of an institutionalized loyal opposition or, as I shall call such bodies, administrative policy controllers. An important corollary to the controller recommendation would be a formal requirement that policy decisions meet the arguments and objections that the administrative policy controllers might make. This would require that policymakers' decisions be formally made and supported by reasoned argument. Suppose now that we go a step further and require that such decisions be submitted enough in advance of their application to allow public opposition formally to demand to be heard. A formal appeal could be made to the agency head – or, in lesser cases, to a designated representative – who would then have to render a decision affirming, rejecting or modifying the one under attack. In appropriate cases, the administrative policy controller might be given the power to require the decision be made by the legislature.

Such a procedure would have several advantages. It would, first, allow the public to be heard. Second, it would ventilate the issue, bring it into public view, reduce the deplorable tendency to make what are in effect secret decisions. Third, it would make possible a formal statement of policy which, in the context of an adequate law of delegation, might be appealable to the courts. Fourth, in issues which created substantial controversy, it would encourage the legislature or executive to involve itself publicly rather than privately in the outcome.

Nor would such a procedure unduly delay the administration of programs. The specter of constant appeals to agency heads is not a convincing one. Experience with agencies which provide for appeals and which operate under fairly precise delegations (such as the NLRB) suggests that neither the public nor interested groups care to get involved in costly dilatory proceedings. Indeed, an agency which establishes a reputation for fairness and which issues clear rules is likely to be challenged less frequently than otherwise. Public involvement might encourage such practices and hence increase efficiency.

A second type of public involvement might be somewhat more immediate. In especially important cases, where policy governing the basic activity of an entire agency is at stake, we might consider creating public commissions to investigate policy alternatives. Where serious conflicts between commission recommendations and agency desires emerge, law might dictate that the decision be made by the legislature.

It is also possible that, for major agencies, basic policymaking be done in consultation with legislative committees, adequately staffed. The legislature should have the power to hold open hearings on particular issues, especially where the public seeks to be heard.

The most direct form of public involvement would take place where a bureaucratic agency is decentralized and a measure of community control introduced. It is probable, though not certain, that this form of organization is apt only for certain kinds of agencies (such as school systems and urban service agencies concerned with things like health, sanitation, legal representation). Here, participation may take the form of having communities elect local boards to oversee the administration of the service; or it may take the form of creating community governments to oversee a number of services. Recommendations in this area must be tentative because of the lack of evidence: only hesitant steps in this direction have been taken and those quite recently. However, a respectable and growing body of literature on decentralization exists[40] and points to the feasibility of such programs where seriously undertaken.

Concluding remarks

As I stated at the outset of this chapter, none of the four conditions of obligation is a perfectionist demand. They are less goals to be attained than ideals to be striven for. They are conditions of a common life in the sense that a common life can develop and a culture of civility be more nearly realized as they are fulfilled. But in the absence of general agreement on these conditions – on their meanings, implications, and worth – in the absence of generally agreed-upon evaluations of regime performance, and in the absence of comprehensive knowledge of the social conditions which lead to their realization, it would be absurd to make their full attainment a prerequisite for obligation. Furthermore, we must make allowances for developing and changing conceptions of rights and for the introduction of new aspirations. And we must respect the ancient truism which states that the attainment of social goods is a continuous process of adjustment and development.

But if these reservations make it unreasonable to demand that the conditions of obligation be wholly fulfilled, they do not make it unreasonable to demand that the regime make a good-faith effort to realize as much of the conditions as possible. The fact that the conditions of obligation are not perfectionist demands modifies not regime obligations, but the strictness of our evaluations of regime performance. The legitimacy of the regime still depends upon its fulfillment of its obligation to help to create a common life. The legitimacy of the laws made by the regime still depends upon their being consistent with the conditions of obligation, reasonably interpreted. Hence, a law or action which frustrates or subverts or unreasonably postpones the attainment of any or all of these conditions can impose no obligation. But so long as a law represents a good-faith effort to realize these conditions, so long as the regime cannot reasonably be required to go further, obligation can be justified.

This is not an attempt to draw the teeth of the theory. The burden of showing that a law represents a sufficient step toward the realization of these rights logically rests with the regime, which imposes duties upon us and to which we owe only a secondary obligation. In my view, this burden cannot be entirely carried by any existing regime, as I believe the rest of my argument will make clear. But as it is not my intention to evaluate the actual performance of any existing regime, but merely to set out the standards we should refer to in the course of making our evaluations, I shall not pursue this question any further.

Part Two

DISOBEDIENCE

5. *The right to disobey*

Beyond protest

Most discussions of disobedience concern what has come to be
known as 'civil disobedience'. I confess I do not know what that term
means except as it may refer to disobedience of law within conventional boundaries of civil behavior – that is, behavior which is conscientiously motivated, public, non-violent, etc. There have been
numerous attempts to define it more precisely but it is fair to say
that no definition has been widely accepted or possesses that degree
of precision and clarity which would entitle it to be widely
accepted.[1] In addition, most notions of civil disobedience involve
disobedience of rules or laws made by governments, which might
be taken to mean that the obligation which disobedience negates is
one owed to governments. I, on the other hand, conceive obligation as something owed to a community of juridical men in the
name of a common life to which the government is little more than
a formal party. And the recognition that nominally private institutions are actually public complicates the notion of obligation
beyond ordinary measure. Finally, most notions of civil disobedience tend to be descriptions of *how* one may confront public
authority, whereas I believe the critical problem to be one of speci-
fying the reasons *why* one may do so and the conditions under
which one is not *bound* to obey. In considering this question it is
not enough to say we may disobey evil laws, for it is by no means
obvious or self-evident that the goodness of a law by itself determines our obligation to obey it. A law passed *ultra vires* imposes
no obligation, whatever its worth.

Insofar as it can be summarized, the most prevalent approach to
disobedience sees it as a form of conscientious, public, and non-
violent protest against a law or act which one considers unjust.
Now conscience is, of course, a rather subjective thing. Furthermore, in an otherwise legitimate society, conscientious protest is
thought to be directed against evil laws and not against the law
itself. Hence, to recognize the limits of conscience and the sanctity
of law, the disobedient is usually asked to justify his act by will-

ingly submitting to punishment should his disobedience be judged wrongful. The subjectivity of conscience and the consequences which might attend every man's acting solely upon it have further convinced some writers that one ought to disobey only where the wrong is clear and palpable and capable of being judged so by applying common moral standards rather than esoteric or private ones.

On balance, I find this view to be pitifully inadequate. In the first place, it turns disobedience into a form of dramatic communication which may then not be justified where reasonable and lawful channels exist to publicize dissenting viewpoints. Second, it limits disobedience to a surprisingly narrow class of cases. Third, it involves a questionable kind of justification. Disobeying the law is always a serious act and one not to be undertaken in the absence of reasonable justification. But conscience is an imperfect arbiter of right, different men's consciences differ, and, of course, the king has a conscience as well as the subject. It is not at all clear that conscience is a sufficient justification for disobeying laws which most people hold valid.

These objections to the conventional view, though serious, are not in themselves fatal. What is fatal is the objection that the conventional view forces us to overlook one of the most obvious and critical facts of disobedience. Let me explain.

The conventional view is in fact based upon the remarkable hypothesis that all acts of disobedience are grounded in the same type of claim: that they are expressions of protest directed against immoral laws. But if there is anything obvious about disobedience, it is that that hypothesis is insupportable. Many acts of disobedience are justified by the contention that the law in question is not merely immoral, but that it violates rights. Now, in the political realm, the distinction between *having a right* and *being right,* however elementary, is enormous. Having a right invokes consideration of the obligations which the law may rightly impose. If I have a right, I have a justifiable claim to limit another's freedom of action: I may justly compel another to act or refrain from acting in a particular way. Being right implies that the other person ought to regard his conduct or assertion as wrong; and that, if he may be said to have any obligation to do what is right, that obligation is a moral one rather than a legal one. In some cases having a right and being right are conjoined, while in many others they are not. I may, for example, have a right to make certain promises to a friend which I do not intend to keep, although I may not be right in doing so. Being right does not necessarily (although it may) entail any consequences with respect to legal obligations. Thus, to claim I have a right may involve a wholly different conception of obligation and wholly different consequences. Obedience to law is justified where some obligation to obey that law can be shown. When I say that I have a right to do *a,* I am addressing myself to the limits of my legal obligations with respect to *a:* the word 'right' stands for conduct or choices, the restriction of which I am never obligated to accede to.

Now it is sometimes true that the assertion of a right involves the disobedience of a law which infringes upon that right. Suppose I am arrested for refusing to sit in that section of a courtroom marked off for blacks even though I am black; or for calling the President a war criminal in deliberate contravention of a law forbidding such criticism of him. Such acts of disobedience are at the same time assertions of rights: the right to be treated equally in certain ways and the right to speak freely. They arise in circumstances which make it necessary to disobey laws in order to assert rights. But this disobedience, because it cannot be separated from the act of asserting a right, is a right in itself. It is a denial of the legitimacy of the duty imposed upon me. My disobedience consists merely in doing something I have a right to do.

A right to disobey is asserted not in title of itself – except for certain types of claims of illegitimacy – but in title of a right which has been violated: the right to disobey law *L* means, in effect, nothing more than the right to do not-*L*. Now a law which is merely wicked does not necessarily lose its power to bind me to obey it. But a law which contravenes rights does. It imposes upon me a duty which may not rightfully be imposed: it is a law whose passage is outside of the authority of the regime and which I am no more obligated to obey than a policy declaration by my greengrocer or a tax levy of Queen Zenobia. Of course, some invasions of rights are trivial and disobedience in such a case may be a greater trouble than it is worth. But no society predicated on the assumption of the importance of the common life – no society which may initially be the object of obligation – may require that the invasion of serious rights, however formally legal, be accepted as binding and authoritative. I may disobey this kind of law precisely because I have no duty to obey it in the first place. If I have no duty to obey it, I have a *right* to disobey it in the absence of compelling factors which might counsel forbearance. If I have a right to disobey, I have no duty to submit to punishment for the exercise of that right.

A right to disobey exists because the protection of certain rights is the condition of the authority of the regime and the legitimacy of the common life it represents. I can never be asked to surrender, or acquiesce in another's surrender of, the right to judge the quality of and contribute to the common life. I can never be asked to accept a morally insignificant place in the community, or forgo my juridical status, to surrender my freedom.[2] For the need to realize these things is what creates obligation in the first place: they define the contours of the common life. The recognition and protection of rights converts the mere power of a regime into authority, which is the only thing I may be obligated to obey. The destruction of rights largely destroys my capacity to be morally responsible – that is, to exercise moral judgment on matters relating to the common life and to many parts of my private life as well. But if I cannot exercise such moral judgment, I cannot be obligated, for obligation, if it means anything at all, must be a product of moral argument which eventuates in judgment.

An argument that is frequently made and which, if correct, would seem to invalidate the idea of a right to disobey is that while one has a right to revolt against an evil state, one has no right to disobey the laws of a just or legitimate one. Where disobedience takes place in a basically just society, it violates a justifiable obligation we owe to that society and to the principle of lawfulness. To hold otherwise would not only undercut legality; it would allow each citizen the right to pick and choose which laws he will obey and thus invite anarchy or chaos.

I believe that this argument is wrong because it reverses the principle that obligation is owed directly to one's fellows and only incidentally to the state. But even if that principle should be thought invalid, this argument is little more than a red herring. Adherence to a standard of lawfulness is not undercut by disobedience provided only that that disobedience is principled. Lawfulness, after all, refers to something besides a stable and consistent pattern of authoritative decisionmaking. It also implies that those decisions are not arbitrary, that the standards of decisionmaking are principled. For however purged of natural law and moral inflections the concept of law may be, it clearly possesses one requisite other than being authoritative: law is not arbitrary. A law is, at its positivistic minimum, a rule informed by standards and it is only by seeing it as such that we may distinguish it from other types of political communications. It is not merely the logic of law, but the whole tradition of legal theory, the appeal of law, the supposition that legality is a desirable quality that impels that conclusion. If this is so, principled disobedience is no enemy to law. It is behavior based upon the claim that, in this case, the standards which define lawfulness are absent. The purpose of such disobedience is to introduce or reintroduce them and thus to strengthen rather than weaken lawfulness.

This relationship between lawfulness and principled standards may of course be denied, but not by those who would appeal to lawfulness in order to condemn disobedience. The virtue of lawfulness for them cannot be merely the stabilizing of authoritative rules – at least not if the appeal to law is more than rhetorical. For they would then be appealing to no more than stability in general and seeing law as nothing more than an element of stability. If it can be shown that stability is not much threatened by disobedience – a showing I shall attempt to make in chapter 7 – their objection is answered. Further appeal to law is, on their own terms, redundant because the only condition law is held to relate to has been satisfied.

This element of the argument against disobeying the laws of a just state, then, turns on the unspoken assumption that picking and choosing which laws to obey is an arbitrary process, subject to no manageable controls or standards and consequently unprincipled. Of course people can (and do) arbitrarily disobey laws. But so long as we are not helpless in dealing with that, so long as we can define – in a rough but serviceable way – the principled standards that ought to guide our assumption of obligation, the charge that disobedience must involve lawlessness may be dismissed as rhetoric. Indeed, on the question of picking and choosing, I would go further and suggest that, with appropriate standards, a citizen cannot avoid picking and choosing which laws to obey without abrogating his claim to being a morally responsible person and thus depriving even his obedience of moral or civic significance. Obedience is not docility. It is always easier to maintain stability and protect legality by universalizing obedience. But it is not easy to protect freedom that way or to raise legality above the level of certainty. Picking and choosing among laws is precisely what a free and responsible man does. The only question is, How may that picking and choosing be rationally and morally defined and limited? For if the free citizen is an agent of lawfulness – as he surely must be – then principled picking and choosing is his contribution to the definition of legality.

A second difficulty with the argument that it is never right to disobey the laws of a legitimate state can be explored if we start with a limiting example. Suppose a law required everyone to sacrifice his firstborn. We may expect – indeed hope – that those who raised the cry of picking and choosing would choose to disobey that law. On what basis could they do so, consistent with their earlier principles? We might expect them to argue that such a law would render the state illegitimate and thus deserving of no obedience. But this only shows how worthless the standard of legitimacy is in this context. Can a single bad law – even a law as bad as this – render a state illegitimate? If it can, what becomes of the rationale of stability and the fear of anarchy? For it is clear that, in most societies, there are many laws which are destructive of human liberty and dignity or wasteful of human life. If they are less diabolical than the example I have given, they are no less unjust. How does my example differ – on the question of legitimacy – from a law which supports racial subjection with all of its attendant horrors; from one which supports the continued imposition of indefensible hardships upon the poor; from one which mobilizes military force to destroy a foreign nation? Are we to assume that each of these laws, if shown to be actually in existence, would lead to a judgment of illegitimacy? If so, what becomes of the fear of chaos and anarchy in the face of many claims that they do render a society illegitimate? And how would one show that any of these laws would not render a society illegitimate? Is it self-evident, or obvious? Clearly not. Well, then, one must engage in argument. But how is argument on this point clearer than argument on disobedience? Or, put another way, does the contention that these laws render a society illegitimate (or do not) invite clearer standards of judgment than the argument that they ought to be disobeyed (or not)? In the absence of a belief that disobedience is never right, there is no way to avoid the difficulty of choosing which laws to obey and which to disobey. It is no answer to say that one may disobey only those laws which render a society illegitimate, for we are then left to decide what it is that renders a society illegitimate. This argument settles no difficulties; it merely transfers them into another context.

This last objection applies to any argument which ties disobedience to illegitimacy, even if the question of whether a single law can result in illegitimacy is passed over. Except in the most limiting of cases (such as Nazi Germany or Stalinist Russia), the legitimacy of a state is no easier to determine than the wrongness of a law. Proponents of the theory that one may disobey only the laws of illegitimate states have an obligation to show why that distinction is easier to draw than the one between binding and non-binding laws. Moreover, upon what ground is it wrong to pick and choose among laws but right to pick and choose among legitimizing principles? If we universalize each type of behavior, the latter is surely more dangerous and anarchic. If we are concerned with legality, we cannot be certain that the reasons given to undercut legality will be clearer or more manageable in the latter case and the consequences for legality are certainly much greater.

Governments act through laws, not through basic legitimizing principles. When we say that a government is illegitimate or that a state is illegitimate (and if we put aside as irrelevant illegitimacy caused by usurpation, etc.), we mean that the rules it lays down and the things it does are in some way or other so unjust that they vitiate the state's authority. The lack of obligation to obey a state is thus a function of its passing non-obligatory laws. Consequently, the decision that a state is illegitimate can never precede the question of the obligatoriness of its laws, but is always an inference from it. Law and legitimacy cannot be separated. It is senseless to say that we may rebel against a state because it has passed laws we are obligated to obey. It is precisely because its laws do not obligate us that we can raise the legitimacy question in the first place. The justification of disobedience is a function of the obligation imposed by the law being disobeyed. The fact that it is right to rebel when unjust laws accumulate does not mean that it is wrong to disobey when they come individually. Indeed, the judgment that it is right to rebel makes sense only where the non-obligatoriness of the laws is taken into account.

Finally, I should like to point out that the legitimacy argument may be self-defeating. I have tried to show that the judgment of illegitimacy is not easier to make than the judgment of non-obligatoriness of a law. I should now like to argue that it is no more stabilizing. If people are offered a choice between compliance and revolution, it is not likely that those staggering under what they consider to be unjustifiable oppression will choose compliance. They are more likely to take facts which could be viewed as reasons for disobedience to be reasons for rebellion, to strike the balance in favor of illegitimacy earlier than necessary and thus to threaten greater chaos. The prohibition of disobedience encourages more direct and violent forms of resistance. Even the most cynical conservative must appreciate the function of disobedience as a mode of releasing pent-up social tensions. To deprive a society of this mode of release is not to contain social tension, but to encourage it to turn to something which is, from the conservative's point of view, worse.

We are left, then, with the conclusion that, on principled and prudential grounds, a right to disobey must be recognized in every case where the law in question is held non-obligatory. I shall consider later the restrictions on this right, the occasions when forbearance may be right or wise, and similar questions. At this point, I merely reaffirm my point that a right to disobey, as distinct from protest against immoral or unwise action, is a coherent and justifiable concept.

But the right to disobey has limits; not every instance of disobedience may be rightful. Consider, for instance, a case in which I am arrested for trespassing, with others, on public property and claim in my defense that the restrictions on the use of that property are unreasonable. Such a defense may mean nothing more than that the government's policy is wrong or unwise. In that event, I have produced no reason to justify my claim that I am not bound to obey it. For it does not necessarily follow that I need not obey a law merely because it is unreasonable or even immoral: a bad law may still impose an obligation.

Certain kinds of behavior may exist in a sphere where the relevant moral norms are matters of preferences rather than right, or interest rather than principle. On issues of this sort opinion may rationally differ and society may have a perfect right to decide which opinion shall represent its formal judgment. The salient fact here is that, while I may have a right to have my preference consulted, I have no right to have it followed. My preference that a vacant parcel of land be turned into a children's playground rather than a tennis court, my belief that the continuation of an aggressive war is a moral horror, my demand that public monies be spent on public transportation rather than superhighways are examples of beliefs not commonly considered rights. They are examples of a broad category we may call, for want of a better term, policy choices. When we say that something is a matter of policy, we mean that it exists within a sphere of discretion where it is permissible for the government to choose among competing alternatives. In such a situation, no matter how unwise or wicked a choice may be, no matter how profound and basic my opposition to it is, I can have no *right* to disobey a law embodying that choice. Of course, nothing precludes me from showing that what is thought to be a policy choice actually involves rights. So, for example, I might undertake to show that the London Agreement, upon which the Nuremberg trials were based, or the concept of civility itself, gave to American citizens a right to resist the prosecution of an aggressive war, or perhaps imposed a duty upon them to do so. But unless it does involve a right, no act can be the subject of a right to disobey.

To sum up: a right to disobey a law exists where that law is not binding upon us, where no adequate reason can be given to justify our obligation to obey it. If it is possible to say that certain laws bind us while others do not, it is possible to create a broad distinction between acts of disobedience based on that claim and acts of disobedience based only on conscience. It is possible, then, to argue that no good purpose – whether moral or logical – is served by conceiving of all disobedience as conscientious protest. For my assertion of a right can never be merely a protest against a wrong. My assertion of a right is an assertion of the limits of public authority and personal obligation. That an assertion of a right may also be an act of conscience is surely irrelevant. It is not my conscience which ratifies its validity, but its relation to the values of the common life, to the realization of liberty, to the perpetuation of juridical man. No principle short of sheer authoritarianism justifies obedience to laws which override these things. To deny that disobedience may at times be a right is to assert that all laws are morally binding. To argue that voluntary submission to punishment legitimizes disobedience is to make martyrdom a condition of the assertion of rights. And because rights are frequently developed from startling and unorthodox assertions, to demand that disobedience be justified by appeal to commonly accepted standards of right is to subvert the historical role of disobedience in the development and articulation of new and valuable rights.

Who may disobey?

Is disobedience the prerogative of the victims of repression? Some writers would have it so, while others seem merely to *assume* that it is the behavior of the victim that is in question. At any rate, much of the discussion appears to center about formulations such as this one by Lewis Feuer: 'Civil disobedience is justified when an oppressed group finds itself deprived of lawful channels for remedying its condition because of an arbitrary obstruction in the democratic workings.'[3] The question of democracy apart, such an approach has a profound effect on subsequent discussion. The whole problem is colored by the assumption that it is the victim's conduct that is in question – the more colored because the almost subliminal and unanalyzed nature of the assumption means that few people ask the searching questions about it they might ask if it were presented as a matter of principle.

On occasion, an argument on principle is presented which would tend to limit justifiable disobedience to the victim. But these arguments can be sustained only on the ground of the preservation of order or the restriction of disobedience to its minimum. Such an argument, however, only tells us that, in many cases, the course of wisdom is to resort to disobedience only as a last resort and that the surest sense of the existence of the last resort is held by the victim.[4]

In part, the reflexive treatment of disobedience as an act of the victim reflects the overwhelming concern of the modern western world with social contentment. Traditional consent theory – which is popularly considered to be the basis of political obligation – has been converted in the popular imagination into a private agreement between individual persons and their government. Consequently, it is frequently thought to be a sufficient answer to a protester to remind him that he personally is 'doing well', that he has been dealt with fairly. In the mist-ridden past, primitive romantics might have believed that so long as some men were enchained none of us was free. But such naive ideas were swallowed up in the economic and technological triumphs of the modern West and swept aside even among the thoughtful by the hard-headed, skeptical liberalism of post-war social science. What this taught us was that the pursuit of one's interests within certain formal restrictions was what democracy and freedom meant; that the absence of external moral standards to guide conduct was actually the highest of standards; that interest group liberalism was the truest foundation of freedom; that western constitutional democracy provided the surest possibilities for equalizing opportunity – and what else could anyone realistically want?

Putting aside the question of whether liberal social science needed only a modernized invisible hand to make it complete – a suggestion few social scientists would be comfortable with – we can see where such a theory has led. True, the confident conclusions of polyarchists were somewhat embarrassingly upset by rioting blacks who seem not to have read their books. True, some thinkers argued stubbornly that the apparatus of scholarship had been devoted less to critical analysis of a social system than to a vapid mobilization of support for existing institutions and values. Nevertheless, the result generally has been to reeducate a whole generation in the science of self-interest or, to be somewhat fairer, to add the weight of scientific social inquiry to the forces already legitimizing self-interest.

This legitimizing of self-interest makes the restriction of disobedience to victims of repression popularly credible and contributes to its acceptability. But it does not contribute to its rationality. What reasons can be advanced to justify limiting disobedience to the victim? I can conceive some trivial reworking of consent theory which might hold that if I am bound to consent to a society whose protection and benefits I accept, I may not withdraw my consent on the ground that similar protection is not accorded to others unless I have reasonable grounds for expecting that such repression will shortly touch me or unless I am willing to renounce society's protection. Assuming that consent theory can rightly be stated in this way – an assumption I believe to be quite indefensible – it follows that I may withdraw my consent only when I become a victim or when I voluntarily join the ranks of the victims. However, if consent theory is read in tandem with natural law, or if it is conceived to reflect the hypothetical agreements rational men might make, such a construction would be inadmissible.

It is equally true that the restriction of disobedience to victims cannot reflect any invalidity on the part of a law or illegitimacy on the part of society. A law cannot be invalid nor a government illegitimate as to one part of a population and not another. If victims of repression may justifiably disobey, they may do so only because the repressive law itself is invalid and therefore non-binding. But a law which is not binding is not binding on anyone. The reasons it does not bind reflect a defect in the law, not in the persons to whom it is addressed. Any other construction would violate the principles of mutuality and juridical status.

But the reasons for rejecting this restriction of disobedience are more immediate than these. Surely, after Nuremberg, we cannot seriously argue that a non-victim is obligated to obey a repressive law or that his disobedience of it is wrong. Surely we cannot seriously wish to restrict disobedience to those who are least able to sustain their case, least able to persuade the rest of society of their plight, least able to attain justice. By what stretch of the imagination can we deduce that a society which has dealt badly with them when they were obedient will deal justly with them when they break its laws? In the modern West, the chief victims of repression are poor, ignorant, insecure. Is it right to demand that they resist repression alone? Is it right to suggest that those who are aware of their repression may not join with them in fighting it? Are we really to suppose that a legal system which penalizes me for being my brother's keeper when all else has failed is worth obeying or defending?

Against this, there is only the demand to keep disobedience as limited as possible, to make recourse to law the rule. These are very laudable purposes. But they can mean only that disobedience ought not to be undertaken frivolously or that certain prerequisites ought to be met before one engages in it. They cannot mean that, in proper circumstances, I must obey a wrongful law because it does not bear upon me.

No one need be told that a political opinion may encourage views which are not entailed by it and which may even be inconsistent with it. The importance of an idea, as frequently as not, lies not in the deductions it entails, but in the way it encourages us to see the world. The belief that only victims of repression may disobey repressive laws encourages the view that those who have been favored by society have an obligation not to resist by disobedience injustice done to others, but to support at least passively the authority in whose name such injustices have been committed. I should have thought that any political philosophy with a title to decency and honor would suppose the reverse: that disobedience by those who have everything to gain and nothing to lose by obedience is a sign of that healthy altruism and concern for one's fellow men which is the ostensible hallmark of free and good men. But, sadly, that is not the case. The middle-class origin of many contemporary disobedients is taken as a sign not of healthy conscience but of spoiled petulance; or as a sign of ingratitude for what society has done for them. The young man who refused a draft deferment and burned his draft card was whisked off to prison while statesmen and judges clucked over his inability to appreciate the hard-won benefits he enjoyed. In a world in which the overwhelming number of people live miserably stunted lives, in which a sizeable number in even advanced societies are poor, frustrated, and unfree, those who are free and capable, who claim the greatest share of the benefits offered by social life, are applauded only when their sense of shame is not too great to inconvenience their peers while those who understand the enormity of our offense against humanity are dismissed as malcontents, ingrates, and criminals.

None of this might matter very much if it were true that the laws we generally observe cast their benefits equally. But no one in the twentieth century need be reminded that they do not. The overwhelming advantages which the law gives to the capable minority must be obvious even to a demented inchworm. So too is the relative freedom with which public authority and pillars of society may disregard and disobey laws. The capacity of the powerful to define legality so that it serves their interests was a cliche in St Paul's day.

Given this, what justice is there in insisting that only those who are too weak and powerless to manipulate the law in their interests, who are least favored by law, may act against its worst excesses, leaving the capable, powerful, healthy members of society free to observe their struggle?

More than this may be said, however. I think that, from what I have already said, the non-victim has more than a right to disobey repressive laws: in appropriate circumstances, he may have an obligation to do so. How is this obligation derived?

Michael Walzer has tried to show that an obligation to disobey may arise from the '*prima facie* obligation [men have] to honor the engagements they have explicitly made, to defend the groups and uphold the ideals to which they have committed themselves . . .'.[5] Such a view is open to serious criticisms. Does it mean that we have no duty to disobey in the name of groups or persons to whom we have made no explicit commitments? If one's commitments are always *prima facie* the ground of one's primary obligations, does the social tie not depend, in the end, upon the fortuitous concurrence of egoistic interests? Must the explicit engagements one has made be defensible as a matter of moral principle? If these engagements conflict with the duty of obedience to law, upon what principle is the disobedient to rely in weighing one duty against another? Is loyalty to one's comrades always to be put ahead of loyalty to the community?

Yet somehow it is hard to deny that Walzer is more right than wrong, that he is on to something of great importance, that the implied egoism which is the basis of obligation in his formulation ought really not to be there. For the duty of the non-victim to disobey need not arise from explicit commitments any more than the obligation to obey need arise from explicit consent. Let us recall the conclusion of chapter 3. Political obligation is based upon the need to attain a culture of civility and, hence, a common life. The notion of a common life means that our primary obligation is to our fellows with whom we share a common life and with whom we are engaged in a common undertaking. But obedience to or toleration of repressive laws is not a way of realizing a common life, but of destroying it. It is acquiescence in the deprivation of our fellows' rights, in the destruction of their juridical status. It is the participation – albeit tacit – in the destruction of the mutuality and equality which is the heart of the common life.

We have known for a very long time that moral responsibility attaches not merely to active acts of evil, but to passive acquiescence in it as well. I am responsible for what I do, but also for what I tolerate with equanimity, what I acquiesce in, what I support by inaction. Suppose I see a man about to throw a child into a pond. Suppose also that if I intervene I can save the child from drowning. If I refuse to intervene, am I not in some way responsible for the child's death? Does it matter that I am not the active agent of its death, that I am not primarily or legally responsible for it? To the extent that my intervention might have saved the child, does my refusal to act not implicate me in the responsibility for its death?

What inversion of ordinary humanity is implied in such passivity! What sense of isolation from ordinary human relationship does it mark! And are we to assume that a common life can exist in the presence of such isolation, in the absence of an acceptance of the moral responsibility which a demonstrable obligation to our fellows involves? Are we wrong in assuming that the quality of American life was profoundly affected by the passive toleration by kindly whites of racial discrimination and repression? Or that a community cannot approach a culture of civility while one part of it limits its response to the dispossession of the other to voicing its disapprobation and continuing business as usual? The notion of a common life is inseparable from the assumption of responsibility for our fellows; and the conception of obligation as being primarily owed to them includes the frank acceptance of a responsibility to act to relieve their repression. In the absence of this, the common life becomes a euphemism for mutual disregard and political obligation is rendered meaningless.

Nor does it help to speak about a *prima facie* obligation to obey law because laws are the formalizations of the rules of a common life. The obligation to obey the law cannot be justified for its own sake but for the sake of those things which make obedience to law compelling. If we are obligated to obey laws, it is because we are obligated to realize those things, however they are conceived. A *prima facie* obligation is an obligation that is not absolute but rebuttable – a belief that laws are entitled to respect and obedience where they do not conflict with the obligations which give them life. If laws ought to be obeyed, then the reasons why they should be obeyed are equally reasons why certain laws should be disobeyed.

It is wrong to give the notion of a *prima facie* obligation to obey the law a greater force than this. It can be said that the obligation to obey the law is so important and compelling that it can be reversed only in those rare circumstances where the repression of rights is unambiguous and severe; and the notion of severity can be so formulated as to make *prima facie* duties over into relatively strict and irreversible ones. Such a theory, which is mostly asserted for rhetorical purposes, is, I think, fundamentally inconsistent with a political philosophy built upon a foundation of an ultimate respect for human rights. For the assertion that any important right has intentionally been invaded immediately calls the duty of obedience into question. It may be that a strict duty to obey arises out of the theory that obligation is something owed primarily to the state. But we have seen that such a theory is incoherent: our primary obligation is to our fellows. Our obligation to the state is prudential.

I do not mean to dismiss that obligation by my use of the word 'prudential'. If it is true that prudence is not the highest of political virtues, neither is it the least and only a fool fails to understand its importance in political affairs. To say that a certain duty is prudential is not to deny that the quality of social life may depend upon a proper exercise of prudence or that the exercise of prudence is itself a principle of great importance. To draw a distinction between prudent behavior and principled behavior – as is sometimes done – is to miss the point that the thread of social existence often hangs upon what Hart has called forbearances, upon the willingness to employ sensible restraint in the pursuit of principles which may divide societies or cause unnecessary friction. Prudence is the reasonable man's weapon against the passions of fanatical idealism, against the over-zealous or premature introduction of measures which, however compelling they may seem to their adherents, would serve to inhibit rather than realize the values which underlie them. The burden of part of this book – like the burden of many discussions of disobedience – will be to show that the decision to disobey often depends upon a sane weighing of the factors other than human rights that bear upon its justifiability. It is prudence which allows us to see when disobedience of a repressive law is not the best way to vindicate the rights repressed. In such a case, the refusal to disobey may not be merely a tactic: it may be the highest duty we owe to those repressed if it allows us to relieve that repression through other means.

Prudence might seem to warn us that, where a regime reasonably tends toward the realization of a common life, where rights are reasonably protected, where means other than disobedience – even if less efficacious – exist to right wrongs, then disobedience which threatens to destabilize that society or to stiffen a significant portion of the population's abhorrence of the wronged is itself wrong. But here is where it becomes important to distinguish between prudential and rightful obligations. It is too easy to use these prudential objections loosely and thus to deny rights for very bad reasons. The threat of instability is almost always exaggerated: the experience of human society is that men tend toward obedience rather than disobedience. Men tend to overestimate the usefulness of alternative means to vindicate rights or to forget that the formal existence of an alternative is a very different thing from its practical usefulness. Rigorous attention to the fundamental obligations of men is thus a corrective to the temptations of prudence. To understand that we owe final obligations to our fellows; that we can never, as Thoreau put it, be the agents of injustice to others; that the protection of human rights and juridical status and equal liberty is fundamental, allows us to place prudential weighing of the results of disobedience into a fitter perspective. It matters a great deal whether we say that our obligation to our fellows is primary, to be limited by our prudential obligation to the law; or that our obligation to the law is primary, to be limited by our obligation to our fellows. For upon this choice rests our decision as to which initiative is right, which position comes into court armed with the critical advantage of *prima facie* justifiability, which position is to be regarded as secondary or as a brake upon our initial commitment.

We have a right to disobey laws when that disobedience is at the same time an assertion of a right. But the very rationale of this right creates at the same time an obligation in appropriate circumstances to disobey laws which subvert the common life or which frustrate or foreclose the attainment of a culture of civility. Moreover, in appropriate circumstances, we have an inescapable obligation to help vindicate the rights of our fellows by disobedience or, if that is impossible or impractical, by support of their disobedience if that is the only way our obligation to them can be carried out. We are entitled to accept as reasonable the contention that, as our primary goal is the vindication of rights or the realization of the common life, we ought to disobey only where disobedience is the best way to attain that goal. We are also entitled, as I shall try to show in chapter 6, to accept certain conditions as prerequisite to the exercise of disobedience. But saving these, the notion of a justifiable obligation is inseparable from both a right to disobey and an obligation to do so.

As I have discussed them here, a right to disobey refers to the claim asserted by the disobedient against the regime, while an obligation to disobey refers to the moral commitments which motivate that disobedience. We can be said to have an obligation to disobey when the reasons for disobedience are so compelling that, if we take political obligation seriously, we cannot avoid disobeying. I realize that this is a very inexact, not to say inefficient, method of dealing with the obligation to disobey, but I do not see what could be gained by making it more precise. Clearly, we cannot be said to have a duty to disobey, in the sense of having a formal obligation to do so, for the creation of such a formal obligation would be meaningless. At the same time we can recognize the difference between the conclusion that we ought to disobey and the conclusion that that ought is simply not subject to rational question or challenge.

Democracy and disobedience

Is disobedience justifiable in a democracy? And if so, when and under what conditions? The question is by no means as simple as it is occasionally made to sound by those who assume that the existence of channels for the righting of wrongs, the freer communication with authority, and the participation by the community in making the laws renders disobedience superfluous or ultimately harmful. One difficulty of discussing the relationship of democracy to disobedience results from the difficulty of evaluating the complex empirical research relating to the democratic process. Unfortunately, such an examination is outside the scope of this book. It is possible, however, to consider whether, in principle, there is any relationship between democracy and disobedience.

It is by no means obvious that democracy – as it is commonly understood – is even relevant to the issue of disobedience. While it is true that obedience is very much a function of the worth of a social order, it does not necessarily follow that it is a function of the worth of any particular form of social order. The worth of a social order is determined by consulting the quality of its common life. If democracy is relevant to this issue, it is because democracy is the form of government which in fact most furthers the attainment of a decent common life and of a culture of civility. To the extent that this is so, the forebearance we ought to exercise when contemplating disobedience of a democracy's laws is a function not of the intrinsic worth of democracy, but of the relation of democracy to a good common life. It is arbitrary to conclude that disobedience is less justifiable in a democracy than in a non-democracy without showing, first, that democracy is in theory closely related to the attainment of a good common life and, second, that the actual democracy whose laws are in question operates this way. Thus, to be relevant to the question of disobedience, democracy must be seen as more than an arrangement for a specific type of political participation: it must be shown to be related to the values of the common life as well – either as a moral vision implying them or as a system of politics which best realizes them.

One of the things which complicates the discussion of democracy and disobedience is the fact that democracy is not often defined as a set of moral values related to common life. Rather, it is seen as a set of procedures and protocols regulating the conduct of public business. In other words, democracy – as it is commonly understood – defines only the manner in which social ends are to be achieved and not the ends themselves. Nevertheless, these procedures certainly include moral ideals necessary to the functioning of democratic government such as equal liberty, equality of opportunity, and so forth. But, of necessity, they cannot specify the whole content of justice and right, or reflect the opinions concerning these of all members of society. What they must include is an agreement to respect differences of opinion concerning justice and right. Now if we agree that such a system is the best practicable one, it is reasonable to expect that we should be bound to obey laws made under it and consistent with the principles that define it. Even if a law violates our sense of justice, we should obey it provided it is consistent with those principles.

Broadly, this is a reasonable argument and it has been defended quite ably, in a slightly different and consensual formulation, by John Rawls.[6] There is no inconsistency, Rawls believes, between a right to disobey and democracy so conceived, where the right in question is a formalization of one of the agreements defining democracy. Passing over the consent issue, we may so far agree. But a problem arises where the right in question is something else. Suppose injustice is done to people outside of the context of these agreements, such as colonials: does such legislation justify disobedience of right? The agreements we are dealing with do not necessarily – though they may – include ends valuable in themselves but in no way instrumental to the proper functioning of democracy. The right of a black to marry a white may be an example of one of the most valuable of all human rights, but it is no way relevant to a democratic political process. Unless we are to define democracy in such a way that it necessarily encompasses all valuable human rights – a better definition, I believe, than the procedural one but not the one we began with – a right to disobey laws which violate democratic principles is narrower than the right I have proposed.

Is this narrowing of the right to disobey justified? I think not. It is arbitrary to conclude that the procedures of democratic government necessarily provide an adequate basis for obligation. Political obligation can be accounted for only if there are elements of a common life which make a culture of civility possible. Obligation is justified precisely because a common life is a prerequisite to such a culture. But the preservation and promotion of such a culture requires the protection of many rights concerning the judgment and expression of private goods which are not necessarily entailed by democratic procedures. Thus, democratic procedures can never describe the boundaries of one's right to disobey laws which invade these rights.

It is certainly possible to define democracy so that it is coterminous with the values of the common life. It is possible to argue that the attainment of mutually compatible private goods is entailed by democracy; or that democratic participation may require things like free expression, equal opportunities to contribute to the common life, juridical status, a universal presumption of individual significance, and so forth. But while defining democracy in this way may be legitimate, it deprives democracy of any special significance in the attempt to account for obligation; for to say 'democracy' would be to say 'common life' and 'culture of civility'. In that case, the invocation of democracy adds nothing to the argument.

It may be supposed that framing obligation in terms of *consent* to democratic procedures might justify narrowing the right to disobey to the rights entailed by those procedures. But even if we believe consent capable of providing an adequate account of obligation – even if the objections raised in chapter 2 can be answered – there is no reason to assume that consent will entail democratic procedures. The fiction of consent is quite arbitrary when it is used to justify specified political arrangements rather than to account, in a general way, for the legitimacy of creating public institutions and obligations. While consent may limit the range of legitimate political arrangements (for example, by excluding those which deny future members the right to consent), it is by no means true that it entails very many specific political procedures or human rights. The entailments of consent are functions of the imagination and cleverness of the philosophers who write about it and few advocates of consent have managed to agree on just what it is that men consent to. That is actually not unreasonable since it is obvious that the arrangements men would consent to would probably constitute a bewildering and inconsistent variety of processes and institutions. The only way to show that a set of democratic procedures and specific rights would be consented to is first to decide what it is that men *ought* to consent to and then to presume that, in fact, they have done so. That seems to be the typical pattern of consent theories: no consent theorist to my knowledge has decided that men would consent to something which he thought especially wicked. It may be thought that specifically democratic agreements might emerge if consent is imagined to take place among equally free and rational men ignorant of their position and status in society. But I do not understand how this assumption is of much help to us. There is no compelling reason to suppose that such men would opt for democratic procedures or that an especially clever man would necessarily agree to abide by the future decisions of his less favored fellows. It is just as likely that such a situation would preclude coming to an agreement altogether, unless we assume that by the terms of the discussion the parties are bound to. (But if the consenters are to be considered equally rational, clever, altruistic, and so forth, and their consent presumed, it seems to me that the democratic agreements produced by consent would be outcomes of the terms of the discussion and the justification for using those terms the real justification for associating democratic procedures with obligation.) Even if they are bound to come to an agreement, it is arbitrary to assume that that agreement will be limited to the acceptance of democratic procedures. The only guide to the agreements produced by hypothetical consent is, I repeat, the imagination of consent theorists. Any set of agreements so derived is open to the charge of arbitrariness. Hence, we must rely on reasoned argument rather than inspired intuition to produce the conditions of justifiable obligation; and I have argued that such reasoned argument cannot yield a justification for restricting obligation to the observance of democratic procedures.

There is reason to believe that, in a general sort of way, democratic societies are more likely than others to protect basic rights. This may mean that we have a prudential obligation to refrain from precipitate actions which might endanger democracy and to balance carefully the danger of our disobedience to democracy against the wrong we seek to overcome. But such an obligation is limited and it can never mean that the mere existence of a democratic government limits our right to disobey in principle. Further, the fact that, in a democracy, people normally have greater access to policy-makers and a larger number of channels of appeal than in other governments, means that there are more legal routes to redress of grievances which ought to be exhausted prior to engaging in disobedience. But these things are all that an appeal to democracy can mean. It cannot mean that disobedience is never right or that a democracy's laws have a greater moral validity than a non-democracy's. The fact that a law is the product of a democratic process does not affect its obligatoriness. A law which deprives people of their rights or juridical status, or which is based on the existence of such deprivation, imposes no obligation whether it is passed democratically or not. The voice of the people is not necessarily the voice of right. As Franz Neumann put it, 'A wrong cannot possibly become right because a majority wills it so. Perhaps it, thereby, becomes a greater wrong.'[7]

The existence of repression may be a sign that the democratic process is breaking down, particularly if we associate certain rights with democratic government. A democracy is not a democracy because its constitution says so, but because its actions make it so. The existence of repression or the invasion of rights is at least a sign of democratic failure. In that case, the course of wisdom is not to demand unquestioned loyalty to a faltering process; it is to see how the failure may be redressed. And recent experience with the democratic process has shown us that disobedience is sometimes an excellent way to do that. At any rate, it would be foolish to argue that, in principle, disobedience is wrong at this point, for that would mean that we have no recourse but to trust that the process which has worked to deny a right may be counted upon to retrieve it. Sometimes, of course, it can. But frequently it cannot and that circumstance cautions us to reconsider the justifiability of disobedience in a democracy.

The fact that democracy provides people with more legal routes to redress of wrongs than other forms of government is also irrelevant in certain cases. It applies, of course, to many wrongs whose present and immediate vindication is not especially critical. If I am denied the right to vote, it may be that I can vindicate that right through lawful channels and the fact that I cannot vindicate it in time to vote in the present election may not be especially significant. But if my child is denied a reasonable education, or a decent diet, the use of time-consuming legal channels may lead to the vindication of a right at a time when it is no longer valuable and when serious damage has been done. There are times when we cannot take the long view, when the invocation of legal processes means the consignment of another generation of human beings to a life of waste and futility. It is not certain that their disobedience – or ours— will rescue them. What is certain is that a society which is prepared to exact such a price to perpetuate its traditional processes is not one which may easily declare disobedience illegitimate, even if those processes satisfy a voting majority.

As a practical matter, it is simply false that all critical rights are satisfactorily protected in a democracy: one need only mention the American Negro. In addition, whatever the mythology fed to helpless schoolchildren and patriotic adults, opportunities for serious dissent *are* limited, the perversion of justice for political purposes *is* employed, public opinion *is* molded and mobilized to support the regime. These practices are not calculated to open and make accessible avenues for expression of dissent. It is childish to assume that the mere existence of democratic procedures prevents those procedures from being perverted into means of repression.

To demand that channels for reform other than disobedience be used requires these channels to be open in fact rather than fancy and requires that they be capable of providing the relief which justice demands. Where this is not the case – where the conventional channels provided to powerless minorities are inadequate – it is hypocritical to demand that conventional channels be used and that disobedience be resorted to only to protest against unpleasant policies. Where in practice no way exists for me to do the things I am supposedly entitled to do, the requirement that I accept that practice as defining the boundaries of my justifiable political behavior is a requirement that I assent to my repression and a demand consistent not with democracy but with its opposite.

Disobedience need not only apologize to democracy. There are times when it is not merely consistent with democracy but the very condition of its growth and development. Where traditional political channels are closed or unfairly limited, or are incapable of fulfilling legitimate demands, disobedience becomes a strategy for the attainment of goals and rights. The function of disobedience in that case is to accomplish what voting, coalition-formation, bargaining, and observation of the rules of the game could not. Its goals are positive rather than negative; it seeks to create rather than resist; it is programmatic rather than moralistic. It is utilized because the disobedients believe that their only alternative is submission or that the political opportunities open to them in law are either inadequate or closed in practice. Such behavior is justified by the very absence of those opportunities whose existence is the condition for its condemnation. But if it succeeds, it may create wider opportunities and extend the availability of rights. Equally important, it may result in the inclusion of a hitherto alienated group of people into the workings of the community. The examples commonly cited to show this are too well known to require analysis: the plotting of the American revolutionists, the Underground railway, the agitation of the Puritans against Charles, are a few of them. They support rather vividly the conclusion that, where democratic procedures fail or are non-existent, disobedience may be a mechanism for restoring or creating them.

6. *The varieties of disobedience*

Typology of disobedience of right

It is unfortunate that the word 'disobedience' is used indiscriminately to refer to many types of behavior. This carelessness blurs the serious distinctions between the different types of disobedience and confuses the responsibilities, sanctions, actions, and justifications appropriate to each. To understand disobedience, we must see it not as a generic activity, but as a number of related activities which often differ in many respects however much they all involve a refusal to obey a law or rule. Just as we cannot lay down rules for education without considering the differences between the kindergarten and the university, we cannot talk about disobedience without considering the differences between asserting rights and encouraging revolution.

My purpose in this section is to discuss the various forms of disobedience of right. What unifies these forms is that they all may be justified by claims of right, by the argument that I have no justifiable obligation to do what the law commands. But here the necessary similarity ends.

Disobedience as the direct assertion of a right. There are two varieties of this type of disobedience. The first and most obvious type is the assertion against a law or rule of an existing positive right. Here, the arguments asserted in chapter 5 are most clearly relevant. In the American system, this type of disobedience frequently occurs when someone disobeys a law on the grounds that it is unconstitutional. A black man refuses to sit in a section of a courtroom marked 'colored' in face of a judge's order that he do so; a physician prescribes a birth control device in violation of a state law prohibiting it; a student wears a black armband as a political symbol despite a school ban on doing so. In each case the disobedient seeks to justify his claim by arguing that the law or rule violates a right granted by the constitution.

There are some who do not regard this type of behavior as dis-

169

obedience. If I violate a law in order to raise the question of its constitutionality, am I disobeying or merely resorting to a traditional method of bringing the issue before a court? If I disobey an order of a police chief on the authority of the Supreme Court am I truly disobeying? Or is the chief? Is this not actually obedience to a higher authority? If I am fairly confident of being vindicated, can my disobedience be considered disobedience?

On the whole, I think that it can. When we consider how few cases are appealed to courts or to higher authorities, how rarely the question of violated rights is litigated, how often the even glaringly invalid rule is obeyed and if disobeyed punished, this objection loses its force. In the real world of politics, where people are often unsure of their rights, unable to afford to litigate them, pressed by extra-legal means (such as loss of job or community harrassment) to accept sanctions for actions which, in the world of logic and hornbook, are wholly insupportable, an act of disobedience must be defined by the simplest common denominator known.

An act of disobedience takes place where a rule which is valid in form, or is asserted by a power-holding public authority to be valid, is intentionally disobeyed; or where a public authority, acting within its scope of authority, or what it asserts to be its scope of authority, is intentionally disobeyed. It does not matter, for the purpose of calling it a disobedient act, that the rule is likely to be overturned by a higher authority or that it is probable that the authority demanding obedience will be held to have acted outside of its scope of authority. So long as a formally valid rule or formally recognized public authority is disobeyed by someone within its ostensible or apparent jurisdiction, the act is disobedient. The *present* rule or order is the one against which an act of disobedience is to be judged to be such. A reversal or invalidation of that rule in the future does not change the act into something else. However solid, however predictably valid the disobedient's legal case is likely to be, his refusal to obey even a *prima facie* invalid rule or order is still disobedience. It is solely when he challenges a law only for the purpose of raising the legal question in a court, while tacitly agreeing to abide by the court's decision, that we may question whether he has committed disobedience. The ground for this question is that his apparent disobedience is in reality an attempt to challenge the rule by employing a traditional legal means to do it and his challenge is at the same time an avowal of ultimate obedience to the system. Yet even here one would be entitled to insist that the act be called disobedience, although much of the challenge to authority is diluted and some of the uncertainty (e.g., regarding punishment) is mooted. For if the case is lost, it is probable that sanctions will be applied. Of course this means that discussions of disobedience can become trivial: if the outcome is reasonably certain it is foolish to speak about it as if it were a heroic defiance of the civic gods. Yet this merely tells us that such cases are not interesting and that no fruitful discussion of disobedience can take place if we focus solely upon them. The point is, however, that such cases are the exception rather than the rule because only rarely is it even probable that the results of disobedience can be foreknown with reasonable certainty. Even more rarely is it the case that serious acts of disobedience are vindicated by higher authority.

Disobedience of a law on the ground that it violates an existing positive right is, however insignificant it may appear, a serious and complex matter. In the first place, it is not always clear that the public authority being disobeyed is in theory answerable to a higher or different authority. Authority is an ambiguous concept and the scope of one's authority is equally ambiguous. The legitimation of an authoritative act sometimes depends upon the judgment of whether the actor was acting reasonably: it is often impossible for a reviewing authority to decide he was not. In American jurisprudence, the authority of a peace officer to act to preserve public order, or the authority of a state to regulate intrastate economic activity are frequently beyond control by 'higher' authority. The claim that a certain speech will lead to riot requires the exercise of judgment and discretion which reviewing authorities cannot easily challenge. A state legislature's opinion of what constitutes public welfare is, if neither arbitrary nor unreasonable, binding in normal circumstances upon the Supreme Court.

Second, a disobedient cannot always know whether his disobedience will be vindicated by higher authority. His decision to disobey must normally be predicated on the assumption that it is at least as likely that he will be punished as not. To argue that an act of disobedience which is subsequently validated is not really an act of disobedience is to confuse the future resolution of an act with the act itself, to classify the act according to an outcome which was unpredictable when it was done.

Third, it is only too clear that the meaning and contours of positive rights are often contestable and difficult to state with confidence. That is partly because the language of law is no more precise than the language of philosophy, partly because social experience or necessity may force us to interpret legal language now liberally now restrictively, and partly because the facts of each case provide ample ground for arguing whether or not an asserted positive right is relevant to it.

Finally, while the validation of an act of disobedience may resolve the threat of legal punishment, it does not guarantee the disobedient protection against the varieties of social and informal reprisal which often result from his action. How can we disregard the possibility that he may lose his job, be ostracized, be the target of community venom or even violence, that his children may suffer, his home be vandalized? He may be deprived of normal police protection, harassed, or framed by the authorities. These sanctions, sometimes done with the overt or tacit indulgence of the authorities, make many acts of disobedience costly, even where they are legally vindicated.

Thus, this simplest form of disobedience of right is not as simple as it may appear. Since the assertion of a positive right does not preclude its arbitrary denial, or the limiting of its application, or its restrictive interpretation, it imports only a small degree of certainty into the dispute. Hence, it is legitimate to regard this form of disobedience as disobedience, admitting at the same time its limited utility in helping us to explore the general problem.

Where an act of disobedience is itself the assertion of a right, the right in question need not be a positive right. Perhaps the most classical expression of disobedience occurs where the right being asserted by the disobedient is unrecognized in law. Here, the disobedient seeks to enlarge the dimensions of legal rights by attempting to show that an act not now recognized as a right ought to be, or that existing legal language is not interpreted to apply to this act, but ought to be. Whereas the assertion of a positive right is justified by legal argument, this variety of disobedience can be justified only by moral argument whose purpose is to redefine the law. This is where the most fundamental conflicts over the right to disobey arise.

I have argued that human rights are formalizations of the values of the common life and civility and, as such, describe the limits of justifiable obligation. Consequently, one is never bound to obey a law which violates rights, since such laws cannot impose justifiable obligations. Now any rationale of rights short of one which claims absolute and infallible validity necessarily admits the possibility of developing new rights. To deny that we may develop new rights is to assume that by 'rights' we refer to a static and known body of final truths, to deny the relevance of human experience to the definition and articulation of rights – in short, to condemn the free body politic to death by dogmatic strangulation.

If we suggest that a disobedient may justify his act by relying only on positive rights, we must affirm that rights are not merely final and known, but that all possible rights are in fact recognized by positive law. Either that, or we must hold that only those rights recognized by positive law are relevant to the determination of the limits of obligation. That is very like saying that one may rightly be obligated to obey a law which can no longer be justified as binding. In addition to obliterating the very idea of rights as determinants of obligation, such a theory makes discussion of obligation irrelevant for it tells us that we must regard as the standard by which we judge the justifiability of obligation, the obligations actually encased in law. But how is it conceivable that we may test the legitimacy of obligations without being free in principle to criticize the way obligations are framed up in law and hence to assert the inadequacy of positive rights? The inability to do this renders discussion of obligation self-contradictory, trivial, or superfluous. For to say that our obligation to obey the law is to be tested by the law itself is to abandon all pretense to judge the worth of the law. It is to take the principle of legality to be the highest of all social ideals, to reduce challenges to the legal system to arguments over the hierarchy of existing legal rules. But the whole point of valuing rights is to be able to test the validity of legal rules. Rights can be justified and legal rules tested not by reference to positive law, but to principles which transcend that law and which provide standards by which it is judged. Rights help to

set the justifiable boundaries of legal rules. But restricting the justification of disobedience to positive rights in effect allows legal rules
to set the boundaries of rights.

Why is all of this relevant to disobedience? It is almost embar-
rassing to ask the question and to state the obvious fact that disobedience in the name of unrecognized rights has so often begun the
process which ended in their recognition. How many indispensable
human rights were not first asserted in the teeth of authority? To
affirm that we should always be ready to enlarge the scope of
human rights and to deny the justifiability of one of the most productive ways of asserting them is disingenuous at best, hypocritical
at worst.

It is sometimes said that this type of disobedience is, in principle
or in practice, too open-ended and subject to abuse. After all, who
is to say what is intimated by the conditions of the common life?
Clearly the disobedient and the prosecutor are unlikely to agree
and each will try to manipulate the meaning of 'common life' to
suit his own purpose. But argument over new rights is no more
ambiguous and subject to partisan interpretation than argument
over the meaning and applicability of positive rights. Nearly twenty
decades have passed since the American bill of rights was enacted,
but argument over the meaning of free speech or due process of
law is not exactly unknown. To search for acceptable authoritative
answers in this area is to search for what never has existed and
never will. Indeed, three hundred years after the development of the
concept of rights as a central concern of political theory, we are far
from any agreement – except in the most general and ambiguous
terms – of the basis or rationale for rights themselves. There is, in
this area, no island of certainty, no immunity from flux and doubt.
What I would suggest is that, if my notions of a common life and
of obligation are defensible, they impose boundaries on the indeterminacy of argument over rights and provide standards whereby
reasonable persons can test competing claims. In principle and
practice, the contention that a claim ought to be regarded as a
right is not an unresolvable matter of opinion, however the con-
tenders may disagree. Nor, I repeat, does it involve greater uncertainty and possibility of abuse than arguments about existing positive rights.

Burning the flag. The second type of disobedience of right involves the assertion of a private or conscientious commitment. Since the inclusion of such an assertion seems to contradict the distinction between conscience and rights drawn in chapter 5, a justificatory explanation is in order.

It is true that when we deal with conscience we deal with a vision that is private and subjective rather than – as with rights – public and testable by rational argument. It is obvious, of course, that conscience reflects in part the norms of society which nourish its development. But it is a peculiar type of moral expression in which the individual is ultimately answerable to himself rather than to others and where he is obligated to give no reasons for his decisions other than those he demands of himself. Where consciences conflict, there is no possibility of appealing to standards which rational men might find convincing. Indeed, there is no compelling reason to invoke standards at all. While there is nothing inherently absurd in my acting on the basis of such a private vision, it is hardly reasonable that that vision should be held binding on the rest of society. An act of disobedience based on conscience ought then to confer no immunity against punishment unless it can be shown that it is at the same time a right.

On the other hand, one of the hallmarks of a free society is its willingness to honor commitments of conscience. Man is a private as well as a public creature and his private self is as real and significant as his public. We can demonstrate our recognition of this only by showing a genuine concern for the expressions of his private self, by regarding one of the most significant of those expressions – the expression of conscience – as legitimate and worthy of respect. Such a recognition, however difficult to state precisely, makes good sense. A politics which destroys or unduly inhibits the private self is not likely to create a common life to which men may contribute, but a political order to which they must submit. The recognition of the private self underwrites a person's status as a member of a community rather than as a subject of a regime. It creates the possibility of individuality and invests human political life with a degree of dignity which men could otherwise not attain. Private man is the other half of juridical man – the half unknown to the regime and free to act within the limits imposed by the needs of the common life.

The political integrity and legitimacy of the private self are basic props supporting things like freedom of the mind and freedom of thought. For while the freedom to hold conscientious convictions does not require that men be always free to act on them, the capacity of men to cherish and develop convictions of conscience is not unrelated to the freedom with which they may be expressed. There is no need to labor this obvious point. Conscience is not immune to the pressures of fear, social conformity, self-interest and respectability. The proper manipulation of such factors as these has allowed regime after regime to alter private ideals and aspirations. The history of the totalitarian states provides the most revealing evidence of this. But even in the absence of the attempt to obliterate conscience, to politicize the private self and mobilize it in the service of the regime, the purposeful inhibition of conscientious expression has affected the depth and kinds of commitments people hold. The function of tolerance as a firm support of the phenomenon of private man cannot, however unpopular that concept may become, be underestimated. It is a necessary if undramatic element of liberty.

Yet in wishing to extend to expressions of conscience some of the protection of rights, we find ourselves in a dilemma. Most rights concern actions and they are stated and defined in terms of action. They may, in principle, be thought of in relatively clear, even categorical terms. But conscience concerns the inner self. Unlike other rights, rights involving conscience – if there are any – must be translated from rules regarding thought into rules regarding action. But as what we wish to protect is thought rather than action, we cannot make the protection of these translated rules as categorical as the protection of thought. We must be wary lest the limits imposed upon action affect the integrity of conviction; at the same time it would be gross to suggest a social order in which persons were free to act on their own standards.

The resolution of this difficulty is, I believe, quite obvious. While an act is not entitled to categorical protection merely because it is an expression of conscience, it is entitled to a degree of protection other acts do not deserve. What does this suggest but that we construct a balance in which we weigh the significance of the expression of conscience against the injury or inconvenience to the public that it involves, with the understanding that the balance weighs more heavily on the side of individual expression than on the side of public convenience? Not only should we resolve doubts in favor of conscientious expression, but we should take care that significant expressions be restricted only where serious public inconvenience or real injury will take place. Hypothetical evils or logical possibilities should be ignored. Expressions of conscience may be restricted not because uncertainty and instability may develop, but only where they actually do. If this seems to involve us in an uncomely process of judging the comparative significance or importance of particular expressions of conscience and public inconveniences, I can only express my regrets and maintain that that judgment is unavoidable. How else may we decide that a religious commitment which prevents me from saluting the flag may be protected while a similar commitment which requires me to take three wives may not? Must we necessarily choose between the categorical exemption of all acts of conscience from public control and a degree of protection of conscience which amounts to fair but otherwise uncontrolled regime discretion? What I am suggesting is that expressions of conscience may not be limited unless there is a clear and overriding public purpose in preventing real injury which justifies it. Mild public inconvenience or general moral outrage ought not to be enough to restrict significant expressions of conscience. Trivial commitments ought not to bind public purposes.

If there is no way cognitively to classify public injuries and conscientious commitments in terms of comparative importance, we can at least rely upon a developing tradition of comparative evaluation to guide us. The conscientious aspirations and commitments most clearly identified with the liberty of free men – commitments concerning public life, religious affirmation, moral aspiration – have persistently found protection in liberal societies. It is not too much to suggest that these form the basis of any inquiry into the significance of convictions and that the evidence of their impact on public purposes be used to estimate the degree of injury or inconvenience their protection might involve. H. L. A. Hart has shown us, in *Law, Liberty and Morality,* that such a balance may fruitfully be employed in the critical area of human sexual relations and that the protection of private moral visions – however immoral or trivial they may seem to some – may reasonably be accounted for. Clearly, it is possible to say that a law making homosexuality a crime, while not necessarily violating a right, restricts a form of private expression for no justifiable public purpose or reason. While it is in principle conceivable that such a law may be justified by evidence of injury to all or some of the public, where the evidence points to its enactment being the result of mere moral or conventional outrage, it violates the respect one must have for expressions of the private self.

The clearest example of a justifiable freedom of conscientious expression would occur where the regime has no interest in the expression save for restricting the beliefs behind it: where, in other words, nothing we are entitled to take account of as a public injury takes place. Consider a simple example: desecration of the flag.

Whatever the mythology, I think it is apparent that the laws against flag desecration serve only ideological purposes – that is, by deifying the national symbol, they protect and promote allegiance to that collection of patriotic myths and rituals which, when interwoven with an idealization of a nation's values and history, compose its civic religion. There are various arguments which justify protection of the civic religion, but they all necessarily serve to aid a sometimes subtle and sometimes overt coercion of opinion. For the civic religion is a set of beliefs supporting loyalty to the nation and laws designed to protect it against attack operate to restrict opinions of it. It is no help to argue, as it is sometimes done, that flag desecration laws contribute to the stability of society since such stability depends in part upon wide acceptance of common symbols. That may be true. But as protecting these symbols from publicly expressed contempt is simply protecting one belief against another, that argument is a confession that flag desecration laws are attempts to coerce thought. There may be occasions where displays of public devotion or reverence for authorities might be thought necessary for the carrying on of public business – in courts for example. In such cases, laws restricting flag desecration are justifiable for the same reason that restrictions on rowdy conduct or uncouth behavior are justifiable: to expedite the carrying on of legitimate and important public business.

It may be thought that a government has the right to suppress desecration of the flag for the same reason that it may prohibit sexual behavior in public: as an outrage to public decency. But this comparison is not apt. Sexual acts are not done primarily to communicate public opinion and their restriction to the privacy of the bedroom is not an unusual or unfair burden. But flag desecration is a form of communication whose point would be lost if it had to be done in private. Again, the protection of liberty requires a conscientious protection of expressions of opinion especially on public matters. By being denied the right to have intercourse in public, I lose little that is cherished by free or sane men. By being denied the right to express my opinions in public, by voice or symbol, I lose much. The interests, if you will, being infringed upon in the one case are far more important for liberty than those in the other.

The real question with regard to burning the flag is, of course, not its rationality. Flag desecration is an example of that too-common occurrence where an important public issue is raised by a trivial or juvenile act. The real question is what the purpose of the law forbidding such an act is. If it is designed to prevent the destruction of public property or to deter disruption of governmental processes, its validity could be admitted. But its purpose is not that. It is to insulate the national symbol from publicly expressed contempt: to restrict the expression of a certain opinion of it. In that case, I think it clear that disobedience of a flag desecration law is a private and conscientious expression against which no legitimate public interest can be asserted. It is done of right.

It might be supposed that the balancing process I propose is inconsistent with my argument that balancing endangers the concept of rights by converting them from moral standards into interests. But in the case of expressions of conscience, what is at stake is something which in any particular manifestion can only be regarded as a private interest. Expressions of conscience are not public rights, but private intuitions. We agree, however, that the process of defining and asserting such intuitions is of especial importance to us and deserves special protection: that we wish to secure to each person the right to engage in such an interest-defining process, but that its very nature makes it impossible to do this in the same way that we secure his right to vote or to speak. Where the expression of conscience is not by definition invalid – as it would be where it contradicted the values of the common life – it is legitimate to establish its validity by balancing it, with appropriate limitations, against public rights and interests.

Interdictive disobedience. It is too frequently assumed that the sole relationship between an act of disobedience and the law disobeyed must be a deductive one: that is, that justifiable disobedience is logically entailed by and flows from the defects in the law being disobeyed. Such a view stems, I think, from the unwarranted belief that I may disobey only those laws which directly violate rights – that I may never rightly disobey 'where the law being violated is not itself the focus or target of the protest.'[1]

But if I may disobey only those laws which directly violate rights, I leave many options open to the regime indirectly to support indefensible and wrongful policies. The enforcement of ends in a society is, after all, a product not only of laws directly proclaiming those ends, but of interrelated patterns of laws and administrative acts. Repression – whether mild or severe – is frequently a function of a complex interplay of laws, arbitrary enforcement patterns, improper use of tax monies, subtle subversion of standards of legality, and so forth. The restriction of disobedience to those laws which directly violate rights is thus both arbitrary and unrealistic. It leaves the citizen with no recourse to disobedience in that vast number of cases where he is unable directly to confront public authority. It obliges him to obey laws which operate in fact to repress rights if they are not formally objectionable. It forces him to participate in the process of repression or in the subversion of the common life. Such repression is not made less objectionable or oppressive because it is indirect rather than overt. If I cannot get a minimal education, vote, freely assemble, and so forth, it matters little that the laws which prevent me from doing so are not clear and direct prohibitions. What matters is that I cannot do what I ought to be able to do and that this is the result, however indirect, not of accident or unintended error, but of the purposeful action of public authority. The history of resistance to desegregation is in large part a history of indirect repression, of laws which appear to be fair while reinforcing discriminatory patterns, of laws so designed that they apply in fact only to a portion of the community, of biased administration and partial enforcement: in short of laws seemingly unobjectionable in themselves which lead to objectionable ends in fact. To invalidate disobedience to such laws is to make people unwilling accomplices to their own or their fellows' repression, to make it impossible for them to uphold a commitment to the basic conditions of political obligation. It is to proclaim to the world than an ostensibly free society may yet cleave to repression if it is artfully done, that lawfulness means little besides empty formalism, that freedom may be compromised by anyone clever enough to support his wrongdoing with disingenuousness.

We have traditionally interpreted disobedience to such laws as forms of protest, as attempts to dissociate oneself from injustice. Hence, we regard Thoreau's refusal to pay his poll tax as the paradigm case of indirect disobedience: it was not the poll tax that Thoreau objected to, but slavery and the Mexican war. His disobedience of the tax law was a way of refusing to participate in or lend support to those purposes. But an act of indirect disobedience may have deeper consequences than that. Disobedience may take the form of interdiction of a repressive law or process which cannot directly be disobeyed. Where the regime uses a law, valid and justifiable in its own right, to aid it to accomplish a wrongful purpose, it is right to disobey that law. It does not matter that the law being disobeyed is not in itself objectionable. It does not matter that it is not itself the source of the wrong or the act against which opposition is really directed. What matters is that the law is in fact being used in such a way that it supports or advances a forbidden deprivation of rights. Far from being a mere protest, disobedience of such a law has the same claim to rightness as direct disobedience. Interdiction is of right where the law being disobeyed, whatever its language or formal purpose, is functionally related to the deprivation of rights, where continued obedience to that law is equivalent to support of or participation in repression.

By functionally related I mean that the operation of the law or act being disobeyed in fact supports or advances a deprivation of rights which we have a right to contest. It is possible, although perhaps not helpful, to state it in terms of ends and means. Wicked ends may quite easily be produced not merely by laws which are designed directly to realize them, but by laws which serve in fact to promote them. The use of, e.g., trespass laws to restrict rights is the conversion of an ordinarily defensible law into an instrument of deprivation. Such conversions may be resisted: to insist on obedience to such uses is to defend the manipulation of legality to produce lawlessness. Unless law is looked upon as a set of formal and abstract categories with no relation to its application in society, obedience to a perversely used law is justified not by respect for law, but by respect for formalized tyranny. Such a view is insupportable. A prim legality is the tribute oppression pays to conscience.

It is, of course, nearly impossible to separate our evaluation of ends and means for the by-now obvious reason that ends, however posited, are defined in practice by the means used to attain them. We can no longer argue that the ends justify the means because we have learned that evil means produce their own wicked ends and corrupt good ones; and that a society which is unscrupulous about its means will shortly debase even the noblest ends it sets itself to serve. Now if means are thus inseparable from ends, then disobedience is not less justified when applied to means than to the end itself. Indeed, it makes little sense to see disobedience as legitimate when directed against a law directly enforcing an unjust end and wrong when directed against a means separable only grammatically from that same end. What counts is the actual relation of a law to a forbidden end, not its formal meaning. Interdictive disobedience of trespass laws used to deprive people of their rights is rightful.

Let us consider some common examples of interdictive disobedience. Suppose the police powers of a state are so exercised that blacks are systematically, but informally, denied the kind of police protection available to whites. Suppose also that no action is taken to correct this practice and that protest demonstrations have had no effect. Disobedience here may be the most powerful weapon blacks have to attain their right to equal protection. But how can such disobedience be exercised? Let us assume that we should not care to encourage riots, assaults upon the police, invasions of courtrooms and legislative chambers on the grounds that the employment of such violence is, however understandable, wrong. Police protection is made possible by tax monies which, in this case, are being wrongfully spent – used to deny equal liberty and the protection of rights. Is tax refusal not a mode of interdicting a repressive practice by disobeying a law functionally related to that repression?

Tax refusal, while the most obvious, is by no means the only type of interdictive disobedience. Let us consider some other examples. In the enlightened State of New York the commitment of a child to a state 'training school' is a comparatively simple matter. All that is necessary, under Section 711 of the Family Court Act, is that his parent claim that he is a 'person in need of supervision'.

The commitment may be ordered without a hearing and without the child being represented by counsel. I would submit that a person who secretly harbors a child whose commitment has been so ordered commits an act of interdictive disobedience. He is disobeying not the law which violates the child's rights, but the law which makes such harboring a crime or the law which makes the ignoring of a court order punishable. In neither case is the law being disobeyed objectionable in itself. But it may be disobeyed because it is functionally related to a gross deprivation of rights, a deprivation which might not take place but for it. Obedience to that law is necessarily participation in an indefensible destriction of rights.

No one would, I take it, argue that compulsory school attendance laws are themselves improper or wrongful. But suppose that certain children in a school are being segregated on the basis of race; or suppose that a school system arbitrarily disciplines children for an ostensibly legitimate expression of opinion. Resort to a school boycott or creation by the community of its own schools would be an act of interdictive disobedience.

Suppose blacks are systematically – if informally – kept off all juries in a certain county. Assuming his appeals are denied, may a black defendant refuse to pay a judgment granted by such a jury on the grounds that systematic exclusion of blacks deprives him of his rights and that payment of the judgment is tantamount to acquiescing in that deprivation? Here, too, we are faced with a form of disobedience that is clearly interdictive. The purpose of the defendant's disobedience is not to challenge the laws governing the execution of judgments, but the administration of an essential part of the judicial system.

Consider the consequences of permissive legislation. By 'permissive legislation' I mean the passing of laws or the making of rules which aid or permit deprivation of rights by private persons or groups. Permissive legislation need not *require* that anyone do anything and hence cannot ordinarily be directly disobeyed. Suppose a state gives to each town or community the right to enact its own zoning laws. Suppose also that many communities choose to prohibit the building of apartments and to zone residential property in such a way that only relatively affluent persons can afford to buy houses there. The poor, the black, the Chicano are thus confined by the facts of social life to crowded and badly-served central city ghettoes, cut off from adequate schools, deprived of jobs to which they cannot commute, and victimized in other ways common to those who live on the marches of society. Since even indirect or passive state support of the exploitation of a group's disabilities for the benefit of another group is a provision of something less than equal protection of the laws, we may conclude that the rights of these people have been compromised. But they have not been compromised by the imposition of a special duty: they have been compromised by a purely permissive law which, if it were not for the facts of social life, they would be free to take advantage of. Now suppose that such a scheme is immune from judicial veto. Would the people whose rights are compromised be right in violating the trespass laws by sitting in on new construction sites, or in refusing to pay taxes proportionate to the state's contribution to these communities? These acts are not intended to contest trespass laws or the principle of state grants-in-aid. Their purpose is to put an end to indirect state subsidization of racial and economic segregation and their attendant horrors. The laws being disobeyed are laws which are in themselves reasonable and common enough. But they are, in this instance, being used to support a wholly indefensible purpose. The act of disobedience is directed not at the laws themselves, but at the particular employment of these laws, an employment functionally related to a severe deprivation of rights. It is an attempt to outface a repressive process by interdicting it – by disobeying a law which is inseparably a part of that process.

A functional relationship between a nominally non-repressive law and actual repression is not determined by the language of the law, the logic of the situation, the interests in conflict, or the vague estimation of holy or nefarious purposes which is, alas, too frequently mistaken for principled debate. The functional relationship is determined by an evaluation of the use of the law in this precise circumstance, by an examination of how it relates in fact to the rights allegedly controverted. The question is always whether the law, whatever its language or ostensible purpose, is actually used to accomplish a forbidden end. If it is, it may be disobeyed. If it is not, then it must be obeyed, however it might have been used in the past or in other cases. Unlike a law which directly violates rights and which need never be obeyed, a law which is normally justifiable but is used in certain instances to support repression may be disobeyed only in those instances. It may be that, because of the facts of social life or the way a law is drafted or persistently enforced, there are presently no circumstances in which that law may rightly be enforced. In that case, it is always right to interdict it. But disobedience is justified only because the law is used in fact to violate rights; should it be applied in a case where no rights are violated, disobedience would not be justified.

Most people believe that disobedience is always a serious step and draw the conclusion that it ought to be restricted to clear and obvious violations of rights. Indirect (or interdictive) disobedience multiplies the instances where disobedience may be employed. Interdiction involves us in situations where the possibility of unjustifiable disobedience appears to be greater. If we limit rightful disobedience to direct disobedience, we would seem to reduce the possibility of unjustifiable lawbreaking. Moreover, interdictive disobedience increases the number of instances where disobedience may be employed and thus increases the possibility that the harmful consequences of disobedience will be multiplied. Consequently, it might seem that, even if principled objections to interdictive disobedience can be met, it is still possible to object to it on prudential grounds. As I have already noted, such a prudential objection is not a negligible one and deserves careful consideration.

To begin with, we must distinguish the argument that interdictive disobedience increases the risk of arbitrary disobedience from the argument that it increases the risk of reasonable, but ultimately unjustifiable, disobedience. The former argument I hold to be invalid. The latter describes a risk worth taking.

It is true that disobedience is a serious matter. But obedience is also a serious matter. For if disobedience is a mechanism by which society can be destablished and the authority of law attacked, obedience is a mechanism by which rights can be surrendered and liberties plundered. We must be satisfied that the laws we disobey are indeed wrongful and the circumstances of disobedience apt; but we must also be satisfied that the laws we obey are rightful and the threat of instability not a bogey. This forces us frequently to balance uncertainties. In balancing the uncertainties attendant upon disobedience, we must ask where the greater risk lies if we are wrong. It is interesting, although it is often forgotten, that zealous disobedience of laws thought wrongful normally results in less social dislocation, anarchy, or inconvenience than the proponents of persistent obedience claim. This holds even where the disobedience has ultimately been judged premature or unwarranted. The cry that disobedience leads to anarchy has not, in the stable societies of the western world, been borne out. Social compulsion, inertia, socialization, fear, conventionalism, patriotism are powerful forces working to restrain disobedience and reinforce the ever-present deterrent of punishment. The same cannot be said about the zealous defense of obedience. The loss of human rights that that defense has underwritten is neither negligible nor problematical. Consider the impact of what James Harvey Robinson called 'the philosophy of safety and sanity' upon the rights of dissenters during and after the first world war;[2] or the uses of the notions of lawfulness and stability during the expansion of capital enterprise in Britain. The incalculable destruction of liberty and human potential which is the history of the Indians and Negroes in America, and which accompanied their obedience to law and their employment of the traditional channels of reform, is much more evident and compelling than the disintegration of American social order supposedly resulting from their popularly exaggerated – and more productive – essays in disobedience. Can we seriously maintain that disobedience would not have been – and is not – preferable to this destruction, even if some of the laws disobeyed should appear to have been disobeyed wrongly?

The protection of rights often forces us to act without clear or certain knowledge of the outcomes of our actions. If we are required to wait until those outcomes are incontrovertibly clear, we should have to wait forever. But even if we must refuse to disobey until all reasonably grounded doubt disappears we may be lost; for in the process, social expectations might be altered so that a repressive process comes to be thought of as 'normal' and a deprivation of rights less than critical. What is clear is that the longer we acquiesce in the deprivation of rights, the harder it becomes to reclaim them; that rights can systematically and lawfully be claimed only by a people which already has rights; that the process of deprivation is incremental since the more rights we lose, the harder it is to protect the ones that remain and to reclaim what has been lost. Furthermore, the freedom protected by rights, once lost, cannot be regained, for the past cannot be reclaimed. The abrogation of my right to speak is not made acceptable by its being corrected a generation later. The condemnation of black children to disabling education is not excused by the promise that their grandchildren will have it better. The loss of rights condemns human beings to a life that is sub-human, that is qualitatively worse than is fit for men. In such a situation, we are entitled to ask where the greater risk lies: in the projection of the effects of a law which, because of the nature of our knowledge and motives may be faulty and may result in a wrongful denial of obligation, or in the acceptance of an obligation which will more likely than not result in a loss of rights? To a society committed to human liberty and dignity, that choice cannot be very hard. If we are able to distinguish between frivolous or superficial projections on the one hand and reasonable ones on the other, we can conclude that the risks of the latter course are greater than those of the former.

Any society truly committed to human freedom must be willing to tolerate reasonable but mistaken disobedience as a price which must be paid to preserve that freedom: not frivolously undertaken disobedience, not disobedience unjustifiable on its face, but disobedience which, although ultimately judged wrongful, has a basis in reason and principle. It must do this because it is unsafe to do otherwise, because the risk of wrongful but reasonable disobedience is less serious than the risk of a firm commitment to obedience which encourages us to postpone resistance to repressive laws and temporize on the question of rights.

The argument that the legitimation of interdictive disobedience will increase the risk of arbitrary disobedience is, I think, more rhetorical than real. We should have learned by now that the validation of a moral position does not by itself provide much of an immediate motive for action. As I have already noted, there are many factors working to restrain disobedient behavior. Disobedience is always a serious step for the disobedient, because he knows that, however he may ultimately be judged, he will probably be punished now. That knowledge may be offset by a conviction of rightness but it is hardly likely that that conviction will move him to act unless it is something more than an opinion of the abstract rightness of disobedience. Disobedience is chiefly produced by repression and the continued frustration of aspirations. Clearly, it may be arbitrary in some cases. On the whole, however, arbitrary disobedience is a blind thrashing out against that repression or frustration, an explosion of passion irrationally aimed at any available target but produced not by arguments justifying increased disobedience, but by conditions which make those arguments attractive in the first place. In a small number of cases, a conviction of the rightness of interdictive disobedience, combined with an irresponsible or ideological exaggeration of the evils of a society may appear to provoke acts of disobedience. But once again, this exaggerates the immediate causal value of theory. One so motivated is likely to use any theory as justification for what he wishes to do and if no theory is available it is easy enough to invent one. In this as in other cases, the wish is father to the thought, and convincing arguments against disobedience would hardly be a deterrent.

The fear of interdictive discipline is largely based on the fear of multiplying the instances where disobedience is employed. That is a rational fear. But the remedy is not to suppress or restrict the process of protecting rights, but to eliminate the justification for disobedience in the first place. Locke long ago recognized that responsibility for the disorders incident to resistance are not to be laid at the feet of the victims, but of the perpetrators of repression. There are times, of course, where disobedience ought to be avoided for the sake of social peace or civil order. But these occasions, rare enough in practice, are not the stuff of a principled argument against disobedience. The persistent perversion of laws in order to repress rights justifies persistent disobedience except in the most limiting of cases and if restraint is necessary for the protection of social order it is proper to insist that that restraint be employed by those who repress and not by their victims.

Let us finally consider the widely-held fear of tax refusal as a form of interdictive disobedience. The mention of tax refusal frequently causes special concern even among those who are otherwise relatively tolerant of disobedience. Almost every deprivation of rights is, after all, related to the tax laws and the justification of tax refusal as a form of interdictive disobedience might seem to be a blanket justification to withhold taxes for every sort of reason. The train of imaginary horrors then begins to unfold. We are left with a specter of chaos and confusion caused by the phenomenon of millions of citizens withholding taxes for every conceivable reason, or attempting to earmark the purposes for which their monies may be used. We foresee a nightmare of anarchic public finances. We conceive of a government being unable to govern, of a legislature frustrated by the arbitrary behavior of its constituency.

In our more reflective moments, we might realize that these fears are greatly exaggerated. Whatever the theoretical possibilities, tax refusal is an alternative rarely resorted to – and for good reason. Most people understand that the person who refuses to pay his taxes is more easily known to the regime than the person who engages in other kinds of disobedience. They know that governments are jealous of their tax prerogatives and are unlikely to ignore a potentially dangerous refusal to pay them. Thus, legal sanction is a more effective deterrent here than it is in those cases where disobedience can be anonymous or nearly so, or where the regime can be expected to take a more permissive attitude toward it. Second, tax refusal is frequently ineffective. Even if I refuse to pay my taxes, the regime may satisfy its tax claims – with interest – by taking and selling my property or by securing a judgment against me. In many cases, I cannot even resort to tax refusal because the government satisfies much – if not all – of its tax claims through the withholding technique. Thus tax refusal is at best a mode of postponing payment, an annoyance to a bureaucracy rather than a dramatic confrontation with an unjust government. This consequence, taken together with the greater certainty of punishment, does not provide an attractive motive for disobedience.

Shaw once suggested that the scandal of the suggestion that one should be free to marry one's sister was absurdly exaggerated. Who, he asked, would want to? And if a brother and sister wanted to, is it likely that they would be much deterred by law? Most people do not want to engage in tax refusal for the reasons I have suggested and for the further reason that they, too, fear the anarchic possibilities inherent in its widespread use. Besides, widespread tax refusal, like any form of widespread disobedience, is a sympton of deep dissatisfaction with a society or government – a condition bound to breed instability whether any particular form of disobedience is resorted to or not.

Despite these apparently common sense reflections, the idea of tax refusal is still seen by many as a particularly radical and potentially volatile form of disobedience. To some, disobedience of the tax laws is, unlike many other forms of disobedience, a type of rebellion because 'it is performing an act the nature of which is to deny to the government its capacity to govern, to administer and enforce any of its laws.'[3] If taxes are, as Hobbes claimed, the life blood of the commonwealth or, as Shaw's Caesar claimed, the chief interest of the world conqueror, such a contention seems at first blush plausible. But its plausibility is deceptive and is based on applying to tax refusal standards not applied to other forms of disobedience. For instance, later in the paragraph just quoted, Professor Bedau contrasts tax refusal with draft resistance. No one, he argues, 'is prohibited from volunteering for military service because other men refuse to be conscripted. No government totters simply because its jails are filled with men who won't go. But tax resistance undercuts the possibility of any government. . . ' Yet no one is prohibited from paying taxes because other men refuse to. In fact, tax refusal is rare and its impact, like some other forms of disobedience, is primarily symbolic. It undercuts the possibility of government only where it is sufficiently widespread. But a sufficiently widespread refusal to be conscripted undercuts the ability of the government to defend itself and is equally a threat to its continuance. By what rule of logic must we judge tax refusal on the assumption that it is universal, or nearly so, and draft resistance on the assumption that it is rare? This distinction cannot be justified empirically and is arbitrary as a matter of logic. If tax refusal is a form of revolution, so is draft resistance. Indeed, if we are to apply the Kantian test, so is every form of disobedience.

If governments cannot govern without money, neither can they govern without authority. Indeed, in small or primitive governments, the need for authority surpasses in importance the need for taxes. Unlike Bedau, Hobbes recognized this and quite consistently concluded that no form of disobedience was justifiable except where the preservation of one's life was at stake.

In principle, tax refusal is no more radical than any other refusal to obey a valid law. Each act of disobedience equally strikes at the right of the regime to do the thing it is doing, although, obviously, different types of disobedience have greater effects than others. But these effects result not from a logical relationship or a presumption that the conduct must be judged as though it were universal, but from the extent and intensity of the confrontation with authority. The point is that tax refusal is a not-very-intense mode of confronting authority. Its ostensible purpose – to withdraw the economic power of the government to act – is largely symbolic. Equally symbolic is the use of tax refusal to withhold from a government the money for a particular act (such as prosecuting an unjust war). The tax refuser knows, if he is sane, that if he successfully withholds one thousand dollars in taxes, the government is not going to spend one thousand dollars less on the purposes he holds to be wrongful. It is simply going to have one thousand dollars less to spend on the funding of all of its programs, including any good ones in its stock. Thus, it is wholly beside the point to argue the irrationality of tax refusal on the ground that the revenue lost will not be withdrawn solely from the wrongful program; or on the ground that, in a repressive society, welfare programs are most likely to suffer from a loss in revenue; or on the ground that only a Mikado would believe himself able to determine what proportion of tax money is spent on wrongful programs. It is beside the point because the purpose of withholding tax monies is not to achieve one's goals, but to persuade the government that it is too costly to achieve its. It is an attempt to say that, while I know I shall have to pay eventually and that I cannot – even if I should have the right to – control the purposes for which my tax money is spent, I am going to do what I can to oppose the official financing of repression. If I am not required to violate human rights with my body – say, by refraining from entering a white school if I am a segregated black – by what token of rationality am I compelled to support it with my pocketbook? Tax refusal is an attempt to interdict a wrong. To treat it as an attempt at personal legislation is absurd.

Opposition to tax refusal, however profoundly couched, normally concerns nothing more than the administrative convenience of government. It is prudent, of course, that that convenience be respected. It is absurd to suggest that a government may govern without granting to it the capacity to spend and tax according to its reasonable discretion. But there is a point where that discretion becomes unreasonable, where the argument that tax refusal undercuts the government's capacity to protect rights is hypocritical precisely because it is the government that is denying that protection. At these junctures, resort to tax refusal, however futile, is right and the primary responsibility for the consequent instability – supposing for the sake of argument that it occurs – must once more lie with the oppressor rather than with its victim.

But even if these arguments are denied, even if we believe that tax refusal is an extraordinarily dangerous form of disobedience, we are not helpless in face of it. For we can, under such conditions, properly limit its use. In discussing, as I shortly shall, the prerequisites necessary to justify disobedience by a claim of right, I shall abide by the common argument that, except in certain specific circumstances, interdictive disobedience should not take place until all other reasonable alternatives have been tried and have failed. These alternatives are normally thought to refer to traditional and lawful processes for the correction of wrongs: resort to disobedience is justifiable only when lawful alternatives have proven unsuccessful or unavailing. But this principle must also be applied to the choice of forms of disobedience: the less drastic must be tried before the more drastic can justifiably be employed If tax refusal is thought to be a more drastic type of disobedience than any other relevant to the deprivation, it should be employed only after these others have failed. Indeed, the validity of any type of interdictive disobedience is a function of one's inability directly to confront an oppressive law. The direct assertion of one's right is always preferable to its indirect assertion because direct assertion raises the question of right in its clearest form, mobilizes the moral arguments in the most cogent way, and gives the regime the best opportunity to correct the injustice. The charge that interdictive disobedience in general and tax refusal in particular invite indiscriminate or overly drastic disobedience on the mere showing that rights have been invaded is unjustifiable.

Resistance. I have thus far been talking about disobedience of a law or authoritative communication. But we must also consider disobedience directed at the regime itself. That kind of disobedience is normally called resistance or revolution and is usually defended by the claim that the regime is illegitimate.

The use of the word 'legitimate' to describe a regime which retains a title to be obeyed is at best unfortunate. That is not so much because of the ambiguity of the word itself as because of the confusion spread by those who theorize about it. Some writers hold a legitimate state or regime to be one which is in fact habitually obeyed by its citizenry; others hold it to be one which deserves to be obeyed. For some, legitimacy is a description of fact; for others it is a legal or moral category. These approaches have been fought over with all the passion of medieval doctors defending conflicting views of divine revelation, with each party enlisting science, logic, morality, and sanity on its side. It is tempting to enter the battle, to cast one's scorn, raise one's favorite objections, display one's polemical virtuosity. I would willingly do this – if I understood what all the shouting is about. But I do not. I do not know why the fact that a regime is habitually obeyed makes inquiry into whether it deserves to be obeyed irrelevant or why the reasons given to justify obedience foreclose inquiry into the reasons why obedience habitually takes place. Nor do I understand why the word 'legitimacy' may not describe the conclusions of either inquiry. It is perfectly reasonable to conclude that the word 'legitimacy' has several meanings, each dependent upon the nature of the inquiry taking place. The view of legitimacy I shall take is dictated solely by the approach of this book. In dealing with legitimacy as a moral category – as a conclusion that a regime ought to be obeyed – I hope I shall not be taken to assert that any other approach is invalid.

When we say that a regime ought to be obeyed, we cannot mean that all of its laws are entitled to be observed. As I have tried to show, the judgment that a law ought to be obeyed is a judgment which can be made by considering the law alone and apart from its source. A law which violates rights cannot bind us to obey it, whatever might be said about the regime which passed it. The statement that a regime ought to be obeyed is a statement about how its citizens ought to regard not its laws but the source of those laws. It is a statement that the source of an ostensibly authoritative command should be regarded as authoritative, and that the regime is entitled to claim our loyalty.

The fact that the source of a law ought to be taken as authoritative tells us that we are right in presuming that the communications directed at us by that source deserve to be regarded in a special way – different from the way we regard communications from parents, friends, pretenders to authority, and so forth. In considering whether to obey or disobey such communications, we must raise questions we might otherwise not have to raise. These questions basically concern the kinds of reasons we must give for obedience or disobedience: whether disobedience may be justified by our being right or only by our having a right; whether the source of the communication is entitled to any benefit of doubt in case of the disputed rightness of the communication; whether, and how, we ought to weigh the possibilities of destabilization; and so forth.

Where legitimacy means that the regime is entitled to claim our loyalty, different considerations intrude. Loyalty, as I shall use it, implies no worship of or dedicated obedience to the regime. By loyalty I mean only that there is no reason for us to regard the state or regime as lacking in authority. The function of this conclusion is basically negative: it means that resistance or revolution is not justified. Put another way, to be justifiably loyal is to be obligated to refrain from resistance or revolution. That conclusion has, as I have indicated, no necessary relevance to particular laws passed by the regime: if we are loyal, we may still be right in disobeying laws which violate those values of the common life and culture of civility which we may call rights.

Although I am sure that it is in general bad practice, I should like to deal with resistance and revolution together, seeing them both as denials of loyalty and hence as initially justified by the claim of illegitimacy. We may certainly draw distinctions between resistance and revolution, based perhaps on the claim that while both involve unlimited opposition to a given regime, only revolution requires the purposive use of violence in pursuit of fundamental change. But I am now concerned with the justification of total opposition, with the reasons for the denial of loyalty and the imputation of illegitimacy, rather than with the mode of expressing this opposition or weighing the consequences of different modes. I believe that both resistance and revolution share this justification, however much they may differ on other points. Accordingly, I shall deal with them both under the head of resistance.

Loyalty to a regime is justified, as all political obligation is justified, by the extent to which the values of civility and the common life are supported. A regime may claim our loyalty when and as it upholds these values. The argument that a regime ought not to be obeyed can be sustained only where we can show that the conditions of obligation have been violated.

But the mere violation of a condition of obligation normally justifies only disobedience. It can justify resistance only where something else appears: where it appears that violation of the values of the common life is the condition of the existence of the regime. Legitimacy is called into question not merely when rights are violated, but where it appears that there is no way to correct that violation within the existing political processes. To justify resistance, repression must be systemic.

Clearly, one element of such repression is its persistence. By persistence, I refer not merely to an arbitrary length of time but, as I shall argue in the next section, to that length of time necessary for the particular repression to become part of the political process and identifiable with the normal order of society. A widespread but ephemeral suppression of rights – such as we are likely to experience during wartime or times of grave national emergency – should not be held to be grounds for resistance provided that the event which serves as an excuse for that suppression is on the whole authentic and defensible. There must be good evidence that the repression of rights is built or is being built into the political life of the society or the structure or traditions of the regime.

Again, the scope of the suppression of rights ought to be widespread. If it is not, it is still possible to hold a regime illegitimate if the repression is systematically directed at a defined group singled out for discriminatory treatment for reasons justifiably held to be arbitrary (e.g., race, sex, class, status, etc.). Such repression, even if it does not touch all members of society, destroys the very nature of a common life by negating its juridical and egalitarian elements.

Third, the rights denied ought to be serious. If the regime need not invade the whole spectrum of rights, it must at least suppress those which seriously impair the common life and civility. Behind all of these qualifications is the supposition that the regime is so constructed or acts in such a way that it attempts to prevent any alteration in its political processes which would alleviate repression. That is what I mean by saying that repression must be systemic. To justify resistance, the repression must spring out of the exercise of authority and must be identifiable with the political processes of the regime. Resistance is the assertion that the regime does not merely deny rights, but is incapable of adequately redressing the evil once it is brought to its attention. The question is always whether the society is open enough to allow corrective action to be taken, whether its political processes can be employed to alleviate the conditions which otherwise justify resistance. And these questions must be answered by consulting something besides the formal or constitutional processes to which the regime is ostensibly committed. They must be answered by evaluating the probability that those processes can or will be employed in fact – that redress of wrongs is more than a theoretical or formal possibility.

The relevance of the possibilities of regime action thus means that we must frequently distinguish between widespread disobedience and resistance. If a regime is embarked on a wrongful course which touches many aspects of life, if it passes a variety of laws which may rightly be disobeyed, disobedience may yet fall short of resistance where it is reasonably possible that the political processes may still be employed to correct this. It is only – I repeat – when these processes become closed that we may turn to resistance. Yet the line is often hard to draw since the widespread denial of rights frequently leads to the closure of processes as the regime strives to protect its authority and defend the rightness of its actions. If it is true that disobedients often exaggerate the evil of the regime whose laws they disobey, it is also true that the denial of rights is an incremental process; that that process, once embarked on, is difficult to reverse; that it may lead to a corruption of the political processes themselves; and that the reclamation of rights may be foreclosed by the denial of rights as well as by a conscious effort to close off channels of reform. In principle, therefore, it is difficult to avoid raising questions of illegitimacy once rights are denied with any regularity.

Prerequisites to disobedience of right

Disobedience as direct assertion of a right. What steps ought to be taken before we engage in disobedience ? The question is posed by nearly every writer on the subject and is answered pretty generally the same way: we ought not to disobey before we have satisfied ourselves that no alternatives to disobedience actually exist. We do this to demonstrate our commitment to lawfulness and, in a defensible society, to the essentially just political processes of that society. Disobedience may then take place where appeals to judicial and political authority have been rebuffed or may fairly be called futile.

But where the law or rule in question directly violates a right and the act of disobedience is at the same time the assertion of that right, this argument is somewhat less than convincing. We may be called upon to pursue alternatives where we are contesting the wisdom or virtue of a law, not its capacity to bind us. If a law cannot bind us, it cannot bind us. It is nonsensical to say that we are not obligated to obey a law but may disobey it only after we pursue alternatives; for this would mean that we are obligated to obey a non-obligatory law during the interval in which alternatives are being pursued. Such a course of action may, in certain circumstances, be prudent or wise – as I shall shortly point out – but it cannot be a principled prerequisite applicable to all cases.

Furthermore, the assertion of a right in the face of a repressive law is not lawlessness, but lawfulness in its profoundest sense. Unless we are to equate lawfulness with mere formal legality and orderliness, the enforcement of a repressive law is itself an act of lawlessness, being an attempt to obligate us by force. Acquiescence in rule by force is participation in lawlessness, however legal-in-form that force may be made to appear. Positivist objections to this point are irrelevant: the argument that we must pursue alternatives is compelling only where the word 'lawful' is given a moral dimension. If 'lawful' means only 'legal-in-form' the requirement that we pursue alternatives comes down to a requirement that we not disturb the stability of the legal process. Such an argument, although not insignificant, is limited; for we cannot rightly be required to uphold the stability of a legal system by sacrificing our rights unless that system is basically defensible, the sacrifice minor, and the consequences of destabilization great.

Now in certain situations the requirement that we pursue alternatives is not absurd. In a basically defensible society, a prudent regard for legality and order might be invoked in appropriate cases to limit disobedience. Where, for example, I am wrongfully deprived of my right to vote, but where the next election is a year off, there is nothing unreasonable in suggesting that I attempt to invoke lawful means to vindicate my right during this interval. Where my disobedience could have serious repercussions and where my testing of alternatives would not prejudice my rights in any material way, it is no violation of principle to say that I ought to test them.

The pursuit of alternatives may be required, then, when such

pursuit is justifiable on prudential grounds and would not be tantamount to a material waiver of my rights. I say 'material waiver' to
keep the problem within a reasonable perspective. For there are
times when it may be wise or right to forego disobedience even at
the cost of waiving my rights for a brief period of time: where, for
instance, public order or judicial processes may seriously be
impaired by disobedience and where there is a real prospect of a
quick and orderly vindication of my rights. The decision here
requires that we balance many factors. What kinds of rights are
involved? What is the nature of their repression? What is the real
threat to public order? How long will the testing of alternatives
take? I am certainly not required to forego crucial rights for long
enough seriously to deprive me of their benefits. The demands
of prudence are legitimate when a satisfactory balance can be
attained, when the loss of choices and liberties for which rights
stand is not serious and when imprudent disobedience might be.

Disobedience as an expression of conscience. As I have indicated,
this type of disobedience is close to the traditional idea of protest
because it is the assertion of a private intuition rather than a public
right. We are required, in judging the validity of this form of disobedience, to balance the expression against the public injury it may
be expected to cause. Clearly, where there is no public injury – as
where the regime's interest is only in repressing the idea behind the
act – this form of disobedience is to all intents and purposes similar
to the first type and shares its immunities. In other cases, however,
it is less protected. Here it is reasonable, because of the private
nature of the expression, to demand that acts of disobedience
which are conscientious expressions take place only after all available legal alternatives have been tried or are unavailing. The disobedients in this instance do not claim that a public and articulable
right has been broken, that the law or rule in question does not bind
them. They call into question the wisdom or virtue of a rule or policy
which forbids them from doing something they believe they ought
to be able to do. Their act – if it is not an act of resistance – does
not challenge the lawfulness of the rule. To uphold their commitment to lawfulness – which by their action they accept – they must
at least satisfy themselves that every reasonable appeal to lawfulness has been made. Further, since their claim is certainly

weaker than those who deny the obligatoriness of a law, they may be required to fulfill all the prerequisites which must be fulfilled where an act of disobedience is itself the assertion of a right.

Interdictive disobedience. A functional relationship is harder to establish than direct repression and, therefore, the justification of interdictive disobedience is often somewhat problematical. In addition, the effects of interdictive disobedience are more varied and less predictable. For these reasons we may reasonably require that greater care be exercised when engaging in interdictive disobedience than in the direct assertion of a right. Among other things, we may ask that – without going so far as, in effect, to acquiesce in the repression for a long time – the disobedient resort to interdictive disobedience only where available legal alternatives have been tried and direct disobedience, if relevant, has also been tried. It may be true that, in particular circumstances, the ambit of alternatives has already been tried and found unhelpful. This is frequently the case with regard to systematic repression of the rights of a group or class. In such a situation, the individual disobedient may be justified in engaging in interdictive disobedience without personally testing the alternatives.

For the same reasons (i.e., the difficulty of establishing functional relationships and the greater danger of unintended and unwanted consequences), interdictive disobedience should be considered only where the repression seems likely to be relatively persistent. In one sense, the requirement that the repression be persistent is academic: a repression that lasts long enough for disobedients to test alternatives to interdictive disobedience is normally sufficiently persistent. Put another way, a repression which may be quickly reversed is likely to be weak enough to respond to alternative means of reversing it. Under some conditions, however, repressive measures may be so intense or have such widespread repercussions that we may be entitled to infer that if they remain unchallenged for any substantial length of time, they will become so deeply ingrained into the political order that vindication will become nearly impossible. The results of the internment of the Japanese-Americans during the second world war spring quickly to mind. In such a situation, the gravity of the evil may entitle us to act with less deliberation and to forego certain less promising alternatives. (While in the case of the Japanese, disobedience would have been futile and indeed would have confirmed the hysterical fears about their loyalty, it is hard to see how, in the absence of genocide, they could have suffered more.) We are justified in doing this by reflecting, for a moment, on the meaning of the word 'persistence' in this context. It would be arbitrary, or at least unreal, to define persistence in terms of a measurable period of time. In the history of a nation, a repression which – like the security investigations of the Fifties – persists for five or six years appears temporary and may even permit later generations to applaud the efficacy of the alternatives to disobedience their system provides. In terms of human suffering and unwarranted hardship, however, a repression which lasts for five months may prove intolerably costly. What then may persistence mean? It must refer to the length of time it takes for a repressive measure to become part of the habitual political behavior of a system or the length of time it takes for it to begin to have its intended effects. A more expansive notion of persistence, which might be justifiable in other contexts, poses too great a danger to rights and liberties in this one. The purpose of setting down prerequisites for disobedient behavior is to insure that disobedience will not be carelessly undertaken, to insure that legal means for vindicating rights will be used where relevant. It is not to hold rights hostage to the punctilious fulfillment of logical requirements.

Resistance. Resistance is justified by persistent repression and by the closure of political processes. By its very nature, justified resistance can take place where there are no realistic alternatives to pursue, where the redemption of rights and the re-creation of a common life are hopeless. This makes the discussion of prerequisites redundant. By saying this, I do not mean to deal cavalierly with the question of resistance. No one has to be told that resistance may have the greatest consequences for society and for the future. But I am not concerned, in this book, with evaluating the conditions which might justify resistance. I have included it only to complete my categorization of the types of rightful disobedience, being mindful that a proper discussion of it would require a second volume. Having stated when resistance may be conceived to be rightful, and how this forecloses the question of prerequisites, I have done all I intended to do.

7. *Stability revisited*

No argument against disobedience is advanced more frequently than the claim that it leads to instability or chaos. This argument appears in many versions. The simplest, and most simple-minded, version is the one which sees in every act of disobedience a serious blow struck at the stability of the body politic. In somewhat more sophisticated versions, we are warned that every act of disobedience is a potential cause of instability or that acts of disobedience encourage further disobedience and, hence, lead to increasing disorder. We may also be told that law is a necessary prerequisite of social life and that disobedience threatens the sanctity of law and leads to lawlessness and thus to chaos. And since law is necessary for the protection of rights, disobedience is also held to be self-contradictory, endangering the very security of rights that the disobedient strives to promote. Consequently, the good motives of the disobedient are irrelevant. What is necessary is to preserve the rule of law; and the rule of law requires, among other things, that every judicially-determined breaking of the law be punished, regardless of the moral worth of the law-breaking. Thus, to protect the rule of law and to prevent anarchy, we are justified in taking measures to contain disobedience and assure that dissent is largely channeled into conventional legal and political processes.

The difficulty with these arguments is not that they are wrong, but that they prove too much. It is true that anarchy is not pleasant to contemplate and that laws cannot be disobeyed with splendid abandon. But if taken literally, this position becomes the handmaiden of authoritarianism where even the most iniquitous law becomes binding to preserve us from the greater evil of anarchy. As to the rule of law, we must be wary of turning that into a veneration of a predictability in law which is, on liberal terms, insupportable. Some relationship between instability and disobedience does exist, but the impetuous association of the two at every turn does little to clarify it.

Disobedience and stability

Of the three most frequent appeals to the dangers of instability, the

201

one which equates disobedience with the actual and inevitable spread of chaos is clearly the weakest. The relation between obedience and social order is at once obvious and limited by the fact that, in many cases, there is no more than a rhetorical connection between an act of disobedience and the fragmentation of social order.

The appeal to stability, far from being a conclusive argument against disobedience, actually adds little to what I have already said. Obviously the preservation of social stability cannot be used to justify condemning all acts of disobedience in the absence of a showing that every act of disobedience causes instability. The major premise of this argument must be that all acts subversive of social order ought to be prohibited. In order to conclude that all acts of disobedience ought to be prohibited, the minor premise must state that all acts of disobedience are subversive of social order. Clearly, there is no empirical evidence to justify such an assertion unless we assume that by 'order' we mean a utopian state of stability and repose. Yet that would be a rather unrealistic assumption and we would be hard put to justify reliance on it. There have been no perfectly ordered complex societies so far as we know, but we do not for that reason refuse to call certain relatively stable societies orderly. Again, such a definition of order encourages a vision of a society without conflict – an order which may be the product of the destruction of human personality and its replacement by controlled and manipulated response as well as the result of a voluntary harmony. The former alternative is repulsive while the latter, assuming that it is conceivable, must also entail universal voluntary obedience to laws perfect in themselves, in which case the question of legal coercion is irrelevant. If we define order in terms of relative and reasonable stability, we shall have to admit that stable social systems are not subverted by all – even by most – acts of disobedience.

The minor premise of this argument, then, must be that some acts of disobedience are subversive of social order. Hence, all we can conclude from the use of this premise is that some acts of disobedience ought to be prohibited, i.e., only those subversive of social order. Thus, use of the stability argument tells us nothing about disobedience in general. It does not relieve us of the need to consider the consequences of each individual act of disobedience and – even if we are bent on preventing instability at all costs – to prohibit only those in fact subversive of order.

We may rightly suspect that, if disobedience were widespread, social stability might be subverted. Widespread disobedience may create, in appropriate circumstances, a weakening of authoritative ties and, hence, of authority itself. This, as we know, may create a social dislocation favorable to the growth of authoritarianism. In such a case, it might be reasonable to conclude that a basically just society could prohibit all acts of disobedience. But it is wrong to use that conclusion, which is valid only where disobedience *is* widespread and destabilizing, in a wholly different context – in a context, for example, where disobedience is infrequent enough not to be destabilizing or where instability is actually the result of repressive laws. Indeed, in the latter case, disobedience may be the first step toward stabilizing society.

When people equate disobedience with instability, they seem to envision a society in which there is a general refusal to obey all or most laws. They think not about people disobeying a particular law, but about them disobeying *the* law. But no one committed to disobeying *unjust* or *repressive* laws need commit himself to disobeying *all* laws. If I believe that a law which discriminates, say, against black persons cannot bind me, I do not, explicitly or implicitly, agree to disobey all other laws. The conclusion that disobedience means that I may disobey *the* law derives from the confusion created by associating disobedience to law with resistance to the regime. If a regime is illegitimate and its communications no longer binding I may clearly disobey *the* law. Widespread disobedience of *the* law would certainly create instability: we are indebted to the advocates of stability for the startling revelation that resistance and revolution create instability. But, except where the society is itself extremely unstable, widespread disobedience of a single law does not threaten grave instability, especially if by 'instability' we have in mind the chaos and anarchy which figure so prominently in the rhetoric.

The association of disobedience with instability is built upon suppositions which only rarely come about. But the argument is based upon the presumption that they do come about quite easily. That incoherence is what makes this version of the stability argument unconvincing.

Finally, it is painfully obvious that the proposition that stability is the only, or the chief, consideration relative to disobedience is insupportable. The stability of a society is not a value independent of the worth of that society: the rightful defense of social order hinges upon the proposition that the society whose order is being preserved is morally defensible and that the means it employs to preserve itself are acceptable. The preservation of stability depends upon the extent to which that stability need not be purchased by repression or destruction of rights. Hence, as I argued earlier, stability is a factor to be weighed along with other factors in the decision whether or not to disobey. A significant vindication of rights is worth some instability.

The second type of appeal to the dangers of instability derives from the question, 'What if everyone disobeyed the law?' If you assert that you have a right to disobey, you must surely affirm that everyone else has a similar right. But if everyone disobeyed, the result would be chaos or at least a genuine injury to the sanctity of law and the security of legally guaranteed rights. Hence, disobedience in the name of rights is self-contradictory. Once we understand what the result would be if everyone disobeyed, we can understand why it is never right to disobey.

This form of argument is somewhat confusing. Its source is in the demand that a moral principle must be capable of being generalized, but the reasons advanced for never disobeying have nothing to do with the logic of disobedience or with the right at the root of it, but rather with the *consequences* of disobedience: the contention that, if everyone disobeyed the law, chaos would result is an attempt to assess the consequences of a certain type of conduct. In other words, the force of the conclusion depends not upon a logical inconsistency in the argument for disobedience, but upon a presumption of the disagreeable consequences of it. Such a presumption is actually a prediction to which empirical evidence is relevant. It is then always reasonable to argue, as I already have, that advocating disobedience of a particular law is not the same thing as advocating disobedience of all laws. We may surely distinguish, with Richard Wasserstrom, between discriminate and indiscriminate disobedience.[1] If we do this, we may see that the objection, 'What if everyone disobeyed the law?' refers not to discriminate disobedience of a particular law, but to indiscriminate disobedience of all laws. There is all the difference in the world between asking, 'What if everyone disobeyed *this* law?' and asking, 'What if everyone disobeyed *the* law?' There is no evidence to suggest that there is a necessary relation, causal or otherwise, between disobedience of a particular law on carefully thought out grounds of right and disobedience of all law. But it is this type of disobedience that may create chaos. Again, the question, 'What if everyone disobeyed this law?' can never be answered by presuming the consequences, but must be answered by evaluating the evidence relating to the effects of disobedience. And this evidence hardly supports the predictions of doom which advocates of stability make.

It is also true that, in this context, a proper answer to the question, 'What if everyone disobeyed?' is 'Not everyone will disobey.' We are entitled to say this on the basis of quite convincing evidence that disobedience is the exception rather than the rule. Now some philosophers contend that we cannot answer 'Not everyone will disobey' where the purpose of the question, 'What if everyone disobeyed?' is to compel us to justify the moral principle we wish to affirm by showing that it is generalizable. In that case, we may be precluded from considering the consequences of our act on the supposition that a principle which permitted such an appeal must be incoherent.[2] However valid that argument may be, it is irrelevant in this context where objection to disobedience is made on the basis of stability. For here the question, 'What if everyone disobeyed?' asks us to generalize not a moral principle, but the consequences of an act to which evidence is relevant. In this context, therefore, the reply, 'Not everyone will disobey' is, if justified by the evidence, permissible. On Singer's terms, the objection to disobedience on grounds of stability is itself incoherent, being an attempt to justify a moral principle by appeal to consequences.

Finally, if I ask 'What if everyone disobeyed?' in order to elicit the intelligence that chaos would result, I may have one of two purposes in mind. I may merely wish to remind the disobedient that he must carefully weigh the consequences of his act or I may wish to show that it is never right to disobey.[3] But is it never right to disobey? What if everyone always obeyed? Are the authoritarian or totalitarian consequences of such conduct more commendable than instability? If the conclusion is amended to read that it is never right to disobey in a democratic society, is that conclusion meant to apply to laws undemocratic in character or to laws which reduce the democratic nature of that society? Or are we to assume that a democratic society never promulgates undemocratic laws? It is instructive that, in societies we call democratic, those who consistently argue that it is never right to disobey always presume the existence of alternative and meaningful strategies of change and reform. But the existence of alternative strategies is a matter of evidence rather than a presumption which can always be made. Can the principle that it is never right to disobey be defended on the supposition (supported by evidence) that no alternative meaningful strategy actually exists?

If the question, 'What if everyone disobeyed?' is an appeal to the chaos that might result from disobedience, it can mean no more than that, before one decides to commit an act of disobedience, one should attempt to take into account the probable behavior of others and balance the probable benefits of disobedience against the instability it might cause. But, as I have said before, one ought to do that in any case. Raising the question, 'What if everyone disobeyed?' does not help us to resolve the problems of that balancing process or to evaluate the consequences of our action. Nor does it alter the obligation of those who oppose disobedience on grounds of stability to show that it is reasonable to expect that the rights in question can be realized within the existing order.

Disobedience and the rule of law

The third common type of appeal to the dangers of instability cites the need to preserve lawfulness in general and the rule of law in particular. The rule of law, according to this argument, is the only way a society can combine stability with fairness and civility. Disobedience, in striking a blow against the law subverts, or tends to subvert, the rule of law and thus endangers the best and truest foundation of stability.

Let us reflect upon such evidence as we have. If by lawlessness we mean a general condition of lawless social behavior, a conditon in which law is generally subverted, we shall be hard pressed to show that disobedience of right produces such an end. If by lawlessness we mean not a condition of general lawlessness, but the existence of occasional lawless behavior, we shall have to admit that regime lawlessness, which is usually tantamount to the suppression of rights, is at least as prevalent as the lawlessness of disobedients. And if regime lawlessness leads to disobedience of right, is it just to blame the resulting weakening of law upon those who, because they see in their own lawless behavior the only route to redress of substantial grievances or realization of justifiable demands, act to defend their rights?

I have also suggested (in chapter 5) that lawlessness includes the forceful imposition of arbitrary social rules. Principled disobedience, to the extent that it is directed against arbitrary rules, may actually promote lawfulness. Those who wax eloquent over the rule of law must do so not because adherence to formal rules is good in itself, but because adherence to formal rules creates the possibility of a fair and stable social order. But arbitrary rules cannot create the possibility of a fair and stable order and disobedience of such rules is often the highest service that we can pay to the ideal of the rule of law.

This means that the rule of law can be realized only where the law itself is neither arbitrary nor unprincipled. Thus, the appeal to the rule of law is an appeal transcending the need for mere stability. Yet it is not uncommon – at least among lawyers and judges – to hear it interpreted only in terms of stability. Consider, for example, the argument advanced by Justice Fortas. Suppose, Fortas suggests, a Negro disobeys a law mandating segregation and that law is upheld as constitutional by the Supreme Court. Despite the moral validity of his views, the Negro would be punished and this punishment, however unjust, would be congruent with the rule of law.

This is the rule of law. The state, the courts, and the individual citizen are bound by a set of laws which have been adopted in a prescribed manner, and the state and the individual must accept the courts' determinations of what those rules are and mean in specific instances. *This is the rule of law,* even if the ultimate judicial decision is by the narrow margin of five to four![4]

Even if we pass over Fortas' naive assumption that the courts are somehow thoroughly independent of 'the state', his argument is still badly taken. He seems to be equating the rule of law with mere obedience, whether by state or citizen. But surely the rule of law means more than obedience to the courts. Such obedience is implied in the notions of right law and the citizen's justifiable obligation to accept right law as binding. The rule of law describes a situation whereby a regime endeavors to control behavior not by means of arbitrary fiat or whim, but by formal, known rules under which variable treatment is discouraged. The rule of law provides a standard whereby we judge the actions of the regime and implies that such things as bills of attainder, *ex post facto* laws, or the exemption of certain classes from the duty to obey the law violate its mandate. The rule of law is thus a limitation placed on the justifiable actions of regimes, rather than a general obligation to obey the courts.

Further, the realization of the rule of law cannot reside in the opinion of a 'state' or its courts – however independent – that a law is consistent with the state's constitution or that it has been enacted in the prescribed manner. American history is replete with examples of laws which have violated the very basis of the rule of law, yet which were held constitutional and enforceable: the segregation laws, which prescribed different rights and duties for blacks and whites, to the clear detriment of the disenfranchised blacks, are examples. Can we say that the enforcement of these laws and the punishment of those who disobeyed them was consistent with the rule of law? Was the internment of the Japanese during the Second World War – accepted by the Supreme Court – a triumph of the rule of law or a profound negation of it, constituting in effect a bill of attainder directed against a group of people who had violated no known law? Laws enacted in a prescribed manner and applied impartially by the courts may still violate the rule of law by their very terms.

Of course, not every injustice violates the rule of law. A decree which wrongfully restricts my liberty to speak may not violate the rule of law if it affects all people similarly, does not punish past speech, etc. But this merely illustrates the limited applicability of that standard. The rule of law may not be violated by the passage of particular types of revolting laws. Consequently, the fact that the application of a certain law is consistent with the rule of law does not entail my obligation to obey it. Many other things than the rule of law are relevant in determining this obligation. If liberty of speech is thought to be a right which, for one reason or other, may not justly be taken from me, I may quite cogently argue that punishment resulting from my disobedience of that law is unjustifiable. I do not see how that argument is affected by the notion of the rule of law.

It is possible to argue that, if a government is to rule by law, it can do so only on the condition that citizens obey the law. This is a perfectly reasonable assumption up to a point. It is clearly possible for a government to rule by law even where many citizens do not obey the law: otherwise crime could not exist in a society ruled by law. Thus, the requirement that citizens must obey the law in order for the rule of law to be operable is at best a general requirement: widespread disobedience tends to subvert the rule of law. But this general observation cannot be used to justify punishment of disobedience in a particular case where widespread disobedience is not present.

Furthermore, no one could contend that the rule of law applies to all actions of a regime. No society could exist so rigidly structured. For instance, some latitude is always given to administrative and executive discretion – to what used to be called the sovereign prerogative. Locke, who defined civil society in part as a society ruled by law, also saw the need to allow the executive to act without legislative authorization and even in express contradiction to the law in extraordinary circumstances for the good of the commonwealth. Such acts – which differ only conventionally from acts of disobedience – are always tolerable. No concept of the rule of law can be so iron-bound as to exclude them. If the rule of law is consistent with limited executive discretion to put the law aside, why is it not also consistent with disobedience in the name of a right – a claim which is equally limited and asserted in the name of the good of the commonwealth?

Perhaps Fortas' difficulties stem from his discussing disobedience from the standpoint of the American constitutional system without considering one of the critical assumptions of American constitutional theory. That assumption is that, because of the nature of the American constitution, the decision of an unbiased and independent court that a particular law is constitutionally valid answers not merely the question of formal validity, but the question of right. A constitutional determination of validity is, in other words, a determination that the rights in question have not been violated. It is reasonable to punish the disobedient precisely because the issue of right has been weighed in the course of decision, precisely because the disobedient has been determined to have no right. But this assumption is merely a legal fiction – a conventional presumption of constitutional law. A constitutional decision may, for the time being, foreclose legal controversy and bind us in fact. But can it be presumed to foreclose all rational controversy and bind us in principle as well as in law? If Justice Fortas believes it can, he is obliged to tell us why. Until a convincing answer is forthcoming, we are entitled to rely upon the ancient belief that reason alone – and not authority – may bind us on questions of right.

Disobedience and violence

On opening an old question. On first glance it appears that nothing both new and interesting can be said about violence. As Wolff has justly written: 'On a subject as ancient and much discussed . . . we may probably assume that a novel – and, hence, interesting – view of violence is likely to be false.'[5] The astonishing fact is, however, that the newly awakened interest in this subject has begun to generate approaches which might permissibly be called new. There are those who create heroic moral distinctions between violence used by the regime and violence against it; there are others who conclude, apparently soberly, that disobedience is synonymous with or always entails violence; and there are, as we know, many who see violence as a mode of personal or group self-realization. While none of these approaches is, strictly speaking, novel, the context in which they have appeared sometimes makes them seem so. At any event, these notions place in question the view I believe to be true: that violence is, and can only be, a technique of last resort – a strategy justified only when all other attempts to attain justice have failed. To justify what I had, in my innocence, believed to be the only rational view of violence possible, it becomes necessary to open up the topic and discuss the conflicting versions.

This discussion will, unfortunately, require me to repeat a good deal of worn knowledge and sensible people who resent being told what they conceive to be common coin may take it upon themselves to skip it altogether. That is perfectly satisfactory: I have not written this section for them. I have written it for those who romanticize violence or who are insensible to the violence of legally constituted governments or who see violence in every act of disobedience – in short, for those upon whose thinking good sense has not yet intruded.

It should be thoroughly clear, for example, that violence and disobedience are separable problems. Neither entails the other although they are occasionally found together. But this relation to violence is true of all social behavior. Violence becomes relevant to disobedience when we ask how disobedience may be manifested rather than when we ask whether resistance to authority is justifiable or not. Furthermore, the mode in which disobedience is expressed may itself be subdivided into two aspects. The first aspect is the systemic: it concerns the actual or intended scope and range of the disobedience. We ask here, how much of the political system does the disobedience affect or seek to affect? Put another way, we are here concerned with the amount of conceptual space in the political order challenged by the disobedience. The disobedience may be directed at the enforcement of a single law held to be immoral and not rightly binding, or it may be directed at the political system itself and a challenge to its legitimacy.

The second aspect of disobedience may be called the intensity aspect. This aspect concerns not the scope of disobedience, but the forms of action employed by the disobedients – for instance, individual refusal to obey a law, cooperative or organized passive resistance, mass demonstration, armed insurrection, etc. It is to this aspect of disobedience that the question of violence is related. Violence comes into existence at some point in the scale of intensity. The precise point where violence begins cannot be specified *a priori* but must be inferred from an analysis of the dynamics of every act. Because of this, it seems to me to be more fruitful to consider the intensity level of a particular act of disobedience as controlling, rather than its classification as violence. For the more intense forms of disobedience clearly require justifications that less intense forms do not.

Much confusion results from the refusal to separate discussion of the systemic aspect of disobedience from the intensity aspect, since it is not true that the intensity of the disobedience varies directly with its scope. Clearly, I may challenge the legitimacy of a regime in many ways. Disobedience having high systemic value need not have high intensity value: individual passive resistance may entail a rejection of a regime's claim to legitimacy. Just as clearly, disobedience having very low systemic value may have high intensity value, as in the case of the political assassination of a policeman.

Clearly, then, violence must be considered in itself and justified or condemned on principles different from those used to justify or condemn disobedience. Rather than treating, e.g., the assassination of a policeman as an act of violent disobedience and condemning both violence and disobedience, it is both clearer and more honest to condemn it solely as an act of violence, or murder. For it is not the disobedience of law that we most object to, but the manner in which that disobedience was manifested.

Violence as anti-politics. The profoundest treatment of violence, in my opinion, is to be found in the work of the seventeenth-century social contract thinkers. These theorists held violence to be the antithesis of politics – a form of action characteristic of the anarchic realm of the state of nature. Hence, the seventeenth-century thinkers could conceive of violence not simply as force, but as non-political or pre-political force, as force used against rather than in conformity with the dictates of natural law or the logic of political association.

Now this does not mean that the seventeenth-century contract theorists thought of violence as the illegitimate use of force where the word 'illegitimate' means 'not authorized by the regime'. Nor does it mean that they were blind to the obvious fact that violence can exist in civil societies whose order exhibits traditional characteristics of authority, rule, formal offices, and so forth. Locke's belief that the wrongful use of force is an act of war while the lawful use of force in civil society is not; Hobbes' differentiation between the violence of a state of nature (the war of all against all and each against each) and the use of force by the sovereign, cannot be taken as mere conventional identifications of violence with anti-state or anti-regime behavior. Locke certainly thought that *de facto* regimes could employ violence against their subjects and thus convert civil society into a state of war. Hobbes believed that a sovereign incapable of maintaining order lost his title to be obeyed and could use force only where he was entitled to do so as a private person.

These beliefs were based on the assumption that the word 'politics' is not an analytical word or a word which describes a factual state of affairs, but a word with substantive moral connotations. Politics is an attempt to do more than regularize a community. It is an attempt to create a tool to avoid barbarism amd make civilization possible. Nowhere is this set out more dramatically than in that most famous of Hobbesian perorations:

Hereby it is manifest, that during the time men live without a common power to keep them all in awe, they are in that condition which is called war. . . In such a condition, there is no place for industry; because the fruit thereof is uncertain: and consequently no culture of the earth; no navigation, nor use of the commodities that may be imported by sea; no commodious building; no instruments of moving, and removing, such things as require much force; no knowledge of the face of the earth; no account of time; no arts; no letters; no society; and which is worst of all, continual fear, and danger of violent death; and the life of man, solitary, poor, nasty, brutish, and short.[6]

But politics has more than this instrumental relationship to civilization. The very notion of obligation is a step toward civility, toward the discovery that civilization is possible only on the condition of a common life and culture. Moreover, the realization of human dignity is largely a function of politics and, at the same time, an indispensible factor in developing civility.

Civilization is possible when men come to realize that the meeting of threats and the resolution of conflict can be used on something other than brute force — that some notion of rational authority combined with a willingness to appeal to that authority is present. It is a process which requires continual appeal to standards (hence, to something external to man) which are capable of forming the basis of a common life – to standards which can be shared and determined publicly, in common. Such standards are most civil when they are justifiable by reason. But violence is the antithesis of reason and the condition not of common life but of dissociation. It creates a lust for further violence, a desire for vengeance. It tends to diffuse easily throughout a community and hence to corrupt and debase it. It precludes sane resolution of conflicts: positions are more likely to harden, philosophies to degenerate into ideologies, opponents to be conceived of as criminals, solutions to be judged by the parties they serve rather than by the justice they do.

Civilization is possible only on the condition that an alternative to violence can be found: that there come into being means which make appeal to rational standards of a common life in principle possible and in practice likely. Politics is this means: the alternative to violence produced by the creation of a common life. Of course, politics frequently degenerates into violence. In many cases, this degeneration does not totally affect the phenomena of rule or power. In principle, then, violence may be an alternative mode of rule – a decivilizing mode, but one capable of creating persistent patterns of social power. It is only apparently paradoxical to state that violence may be consistent with regime stability. States were governed during barbarous wars while the organized and controlled terror of modern totalitarianism has shown us that a specific type of organized violence may not only coexist with order, but be the condition of its survival.

I am not now interested in pursuing the question whether the word 'politics' is a moral or a neutrally descriptive word, although I conceive that many readers would wish to raise it. My point is that we may understand the tensions of the political process and the relationship of violence to social order better if we think of it as a moral word. Moreover, thinking of politics as a moral word forces to the front of our minds the realization – which should be there in any case – that, if violence is an attempt to by-pass standards which create civility, it is true in principle that regimes can be violent. Now there are undoubtedly some people who would argue that violence is an illegitimate use of force and that this means that legitimate regimes employ not violence but lawful force. It would be simple to demonstrate that such an argument is either incoherent – depending upon an erratic application of the word 'legitimate' – or else trivial. For what matters is not the name we give to force, but the justifiability of using it. It is probably true that thoughtless persons may be emotionally affected by the word 'violence' and not by the word 'force', but such persons cannot be counted upon to deal with the problem reasonably and without bias in the first place. The real issue, in dealing with violence as the illegitimate use of force, is whether we conceive that the regime is more entitled to use force than private persons.

To uphold such a contention requires us to show that the regime may use force because of some general and *prima facie* legal entitlement to do so (in order to preserve stability, uphold laws, and so forth) which does not apply to individuals. But such an entitlement, which undoubtedly can be shown, can only refer to the enforcement of valid laws, whose observance is necessary for justice or public order and when other means have failed; or to acts done for a justifiable public good in extraordinary circumstances. Making law enforcement a prerogative of the regime does not relieve it of the need to justify its use of force by referring to standards which are generally applicable. That prerogative confers no added validity on arbitrary force merely because it is used by the regime.

The question may arise whether a private person may use force to enforce a law the regime does not. Here too the issue is not the justifiability of using force, for neither the regime nor the private person is entitled to use force to enforce an unjust law or where other methods would suffice. The issue is merely how much discretion we must allow to the regime to determine when force may be used.

It may also be argued that the regime has a *prima facie* right to use force to uphold *any* law because the breaking of a law is a form of violence to which regime action is a defensive response. To this, two objections may be raised. The first is that the breaking of a law which violates a right confers no grounds for reprisal. The second is that it is arbitrary to call the mere breaking of a law an act of violence if no force is used or threatened. It is of course true that the end result might be the same whether force is used or not. This is not a unique circumstance. Whether I rob you or embezzle your money, you end up poorer. If I forcibly imprison you in a ghetto or create informal conventional barriers which make it impossible for you to leave, the end result is the same. But we are not dealing with ends when we deal with violence: we are dealing with processes. The examples I have just given merely indicate that repressive or wicked things may be done non-violently and, therefore, that the mere absence of violence does not make what is done justifiable. But they do not show that robbery and embezzlement are identical.

Every act of violence poses a threat to civility, no matter who does it. Hence, no act of violence is *prima facie* legitimate or right. The obligation to refrain from violence applies equally to regimes and private persons and all justifications offered for the use of violence must meet the same standards. At the same time, the obligation to refrain from violence cannot be absolute. The persistent repression of persons or classes may sometimes be remedied only through the use of violence just as the justifiable maintenance of order may require the use of force. Violence may be justifiable in self-defense. Indeed, since persistent repression can normally be accomplished only where there exists a credible threat of imminent violence in the event of efforts to remove that repression, violent resistance to persistent repression may often be justified as a form of self-defense. Violence may be the only way to remove a tyrant who imposes his will by force, to outface his threat to civility. No one can be asked to purchase peace by accepting slavery and degradation, especially where that peace is the turgid slumber of barbarism. How, in the name of civility, can we argue that, if the question is one of submission to tyranny or revolution, that submission is the better policy; or deny that an enslaved population may resort to violence when all other means to eradicate that slavery have failed? There is always a presumption against violence, but that presumption is rebuttable.

The limits of violence. The justifiable limits of violence in cases of disobedience are no different from the justifiable limits of violence in general. The obligation to refrain from violence demands that, even where one's cause is just, recourse to violence must always be an exceptional political strategy, adopted only where all other means of attaining one's goals fail. As a corollary, where violence is justifiable, the least intense form of it ought always to be chosen. Against a weak and vacillating government, massive demonstrations to attain rights may be justifiable and armed attacks wrong. Against passive hunger strikers, the use of tanks may seem somewhat out of place.

It is equally obvious that not every claim, however just, may serve as an excuse for intense violence. It is true that differences in policy may justify action which is violent in rhetoric rather than in fact and whose intensity is extremely low: the 1967 march on the Pentagon is an instance. But recourse to intense violence demands causes which transcend policy differences and involve serious questions of right. From the point of view of the disobedient, the rights involved must be important rather than trivial and denial of them systematic and intentional. From the point of view of the regime, the challenge to its rightful authority must be serious and the force real rather than speculative.

Violence justified as a form of self-defense also presumes the rightness of one's cause. An evil and debased regime or a disobedient whose claims border on the legitimation of privateering cannot be said to have a right to defend themselves. In addition, serious questions of self-defense arise from the fact that violence must include the plausible and imminent threat of force as well as the overt use of force. This is an especially difficult question where that threat is implied rather than expressed. Clearly, violence may be implied from certain actions. Suppose demands are made on a regime in a situation where resistance to them cannot conceivably be effective without ultimate recourse to violence. Resistance by the regime certainly indicates a willingness to use force if the demands continue. The use of certain kinds of violence sometimes implies a willingness to use greater force. Exceptionally harsh penalties for disobedience coupled with threats of widespread prosecution raise similar implications. But these implications are difficult to evaluate. For instance, what kinds of threatened violence are implied by the substitution of political for legal justice? Logically, the notion of violence as self-defensive does not preclude the ostensible initiation of violence, but one is hard put to determine just when an ostensible initiation of violence is in reality a response to threatened violence and whether the intensity of the violence employed as defensive is commensurate with that threatened.

Problems such as these indicate that the conditions in which violence may be used are difficult to specify and evaluate. In the end, it may be possible to say with certainty no more than that violence remains, as always, a political technique of the last resort, to be used when other means will not avail. Ortega put the matter simply:

Man has always had recourse to violence; sometimes this recourse was a mere crime, and does not interest us here. But at other times violence was the means resorted to by him who had previously exhausted all others in defense of the rights of justice which he thought he possessed. It may be regrettable that human nature tends on occasion to this form of violence, but it is undeniable that it implies the greatest tribute to reason and justice. For this form of violence is none other than reason exasperated. Force was, in fact, the *ultima ratio*. Rather stupidly it has been the custom to take ironically this expression, which clearly indicates the previous submission of force to methods of reason. Civilization is nothing less than the attempt to reduce force to being the *ultima ratio*.[7]

Violence is defensive because the last resort is always a response to violence: one does not reach the point of last resort unless alternatives have been closed by force or threat of force. The last resort speaks to a situation where there is no hope for justice except in violence, a situation that can never exist in the absence of force used against those deprived of justice.

Admittedly, Ortega's argument is vague, the standards are inconclusive, the principle seemingly devoid of content. That is in the nature of the case unavoidable. But it does not leave us helpless. The standard of the *ultima ratio* is not entirely relative or arbitrary. If it does not create a set of lines already drawn and easily applied, it does create a stern imperative to be cautious in the use of violence. It demands that those who advocate violence bear the burden of producing convincing arguments, aimed at reasonable men, to justify their conduct. Moreover, it may lead us to accept certain rules concerning violence:

Rule 1. Violence ought never to be arbitrary. Thus, for example, it must be directed only against those plausibly guilty of actually violating rights or of materially and knowingly aiding in such violation. Violence directed against people not guilty of these things is unjustifiable. Bombing the physical property of an offensive institution in circumstances where non-guilty people may be injured is wrong. Violence directed against a social class or group defined by criteria other than reasonably ascertainable guilt is insupportable, whether this group be blacks, whites, Jews, radicals, hippies, or policemen. Again, the violence must be capable of producing substantial benefits to those deprived. Violence which is capable only of releasing group tensions is, however understandable, justifiable only if continued forbearance would eventuate in worse violence.

Rule 2. Violence is justifiable only where the rights in question are important and are systematically violated – where, in other words, serious doubt can be cast on the moral legitimacy of the regime, or where important public rights are being undermined by resisters or rebels.

Rule 3. One's first duty is to retreat from any course of conduct promising violence, if at all possible. That is to say, the interpretation of available alternatives to violence must be the widest possible consistent with political reality. The notion of alternatives very much includes compromises, where reasonable.

Rule 4. No act of violence ought to be advocated which one would not willingly advocate publicly.

Rule 5. Violence whose goal is preserving public order or law must be consistent with the law. The degree of violence here ought not to go beyond what the law allows.

Rule 6. The minimum degree of violence necessary to accomplish one's purpose is the limit of violent action.

Rule 7. It must be reasonable to expect that the violence will do greater good than harm.

These seven rules do not exhaust the implications of the *ultima ratio*, but seven suffice to illustrate my point: something substantive and compelling can be said. If it is true that people will differ over the application of these rules – if some are led to justify Watts or Columbia and others to condemn them – it is not true that these rules differ in this respect from other rules. By articulating the principles governing a certain kind of behavior, one does not foreclose argument on the application and meaning of those principles. To mobilize a few more platitudes, conflicting evaluations of a situation to which certain principles apply cannot be resolved by consulting those principles. As Kant said, there are no rules teaching us how to apply rules. We may then disagree on whether a regime is illegitimate, whether rights are being systematically violated, whether realistic alternatives do exist, and so forth. But the purpose of principled argument is not to answer such questions but to enable us to agree that they are the right questions to ask.

Oddly, modern philosophers have often to be reminded that reason is not powerless to deal with conflicting arguments over the application of principles, even if it is powerless to convince participants that they are wrong. But the appeal of reason is, unfortunately, not to participants – though we may hope that they listen to it – but to non-participants, to those whose egos, passions, and interests are not involved. The evaluation of justifications for violence is best done by (hopefully) independent, reasonable, disinterested persons. It is not at all obvious that the *ultima ratio* standard is insufficient to allow such persons to evaluate the justness or appropriateness of violence.

8. *Permissiveness and restraint*

Restraint

Conservatives such as Michael Oakeshott constantly remind us of the dangers of building a rationalist picture of political right and demanding action in accordance with it. Whatever reservations we have about such theories – and I have many – we are bound to respect the warning implicit in them. We cannot build a common life on a foundation of abstract or esoteric declarations of right unrelated to reasonable expectations of human nature or to the social culture of a particular society. It is for this reason that I have attempted to describe the common life in terms that are relevant to developing political traditions. The conditions of obligation are, I believe, derived from existing elements of the liberal political tradition or they are extensions of that tradition, readings-out of the social and political ideals of liberalism, extensions of things we now do or consider worth doing. They are framed so as to relate quite directly to the political traditions of western liberal democracy because I believe this democracy to be the best existing foundation for the creation of adequate common lives. If anything, my conception of the conditions of obligation may be too traditional. The fact that some of them demand what are perhaps radical revisions in the practice of liberal societies proves nothing. There are great inconsistencies in any tradition: practices may exist side-by-side with values or other practices which overtly contradict them, as the development of the corporation in liberal society contradicts the liberal values of accountability and control of arbitrary power. In that case, the job of the philosopher who works within a specific tradition is to recommend the solution most consistent with what he takes the fundamental intimations of that tradition to be. For example, Oakeshott, who is more fully concerned with adhering to tradition than most of us, accepted as valid the argument that giant corporations be reduced in size in order to preserve economic freedom.[1] Such decisions are unavoidable, however radical may be the institutional changes they require. To condemn them as overly-rationalistic or esoteric is to assume either that a political tradition contains no conflicting intimations or that the resolution of such conflicts as exist can be made simply by consulting the admittedly contradictory tradition itself. I do not know of anyone who has successfully maintained either of these propositions and that is not surprising, for I believe that they are either trivial or absurd.

But a conception of political right, however reasonable and restrained, may yet be combined with a too-radical demand for its immediate realization. In appropriate circumstances, this is at least understandable. Impatience in the face of clear and indefensible wrongs may be impolitic, but it is hardly the greatest of political vices. Nevertheless, the degree of impatience that is justified is a function not merely of the wrongs that are perceived, but of the reforms that are proposed.

The conditions of obligation, however much they are derived from existing elements of the liberal tradition, demand, in some cases, radical developments in political practice. They are mostly not direct prohibitions on regimes, but calls for performance, for the realization of things like the attainment of equality, the nourishment of the private self, the imposition of accountability upon corporations. Such steps are not things of a moment and it would be a childish form of radicalism to demand their total realization before obligation can be justified. But we are entitled to demand more than a formal statement of intentions. We are entitled to demand, at the very least, a commitment to the values of the common life evidenced by actual steps taken in that direction. We may be asked to refrain from resistance or from intense forms of disobedience where discernible progress toward realizing the conditions of obligation is present.

But this is not the same thing as saying that discernible progress entails our forgoing all disobedience. Disobedience is, after all, an attempt to put forward in action the values of the common life. Regimes are not normally committed, in any deliberate way, to the realization of these values. They may be so constituted that some of the values of the common life are, for one reason or other, protected. This protection, however inadvertent, may nevertheless be real; but it would be naive to think of it as a persistent and operative commitment. Even the best of regimes will act in some ways to realize the values of the common life and in others to retard or subvert them. Disobedience is always relevant in those instances where the regime acts to subvert the values of the common life or where it unreasonably tolerates the perpetuation of conditions which subvert it. An operative commitment to the values of the common life can only require that we exercise restraint in our actions, that we forbear from doing those things which would, by causing undue social upheaval, in effect retard such progress as has been made. It can caution us to exercise sobriety in our evaluation of the potential of the regime's political processes. It cannot require us to forgo claiming our rights, for that would be to make the shortcomings of man the measure of all political things.

In general, disobedience is a moderate way of facing society with the need to render a verdict on its own wrongdoing. It is unfortunately true that the regime is ordinarily the judge of its own behavior. But by demanding that he be judged right, that he not be punished, the disobedient raises for the regime and the community claims which otherwise might never be raised and engages them in the consideration of values which lie at the heart of the obligations they impose. This is crucial, for argument over which values ought to be chosen is indispensible in discussion of obligation. We deceive ourselves if we think that we can resolve the dilemmas raised by political obligation merely by invoking virtues such as toleration and compromise. These concern only the way in which conflict ordinarily ought to be resolved. They say nothing about which values ought to be chosen, unless they mean that the values of the majority or most powerful minority ought to be chosen, in which case they stand for a moral theory somewhat more debased than their advocates pretend. It is also necessary to remind ourselves that the assertion of a conception of political right is not inconsistent with the tolerance and openness which ought to characterize civil societies. One may believe that certain values are right and also recognize that that belief is not the same thing as divine verification. One may then believe that these values must be brought into being not by forceful imposition upon an unwilling populace, but by the processes of self-government and persuasion. In advocating conceptions of political right we may speak the language of fanatical absolutism; but we need not do so. We may present visions of political right not as the tables of the law, but as subjects to be placed on the public agenda.

Permissiveness

Who decides? Few questions arise as persistently as this one in argument over disobedience. Disagreement over the justifiability of an act of disobedience is inevitable: who decides who is right?

I have not dealt with this question up to now because it is irrelevant to most of my argument. To the extent that the analysis of obligation and disobedience is undertaken to determine which standards and principles ought to govern our judgments, to the extent that the purpose of such an analysis is to enlighten our thinking rather than to set up a mechanism for resolving conflicts, each person must be free to decide for himself. On such an issue there can be no final word, no morally binding authoritative answer. The question, 'Who decides?' is irrelevant to moral argument over disobedience. Determining the morally binding nature of a law cannot be – in the absence of a belief in something like divine governance – a function of authoritative status, but only of moral argument. Now if moral argument is nothing but a rationalization of habits and preferences, of emotive reactions, arbitrary affirmations, and the like, nothing can be said by anyone. In that case, disobedience can only be judged arbitrarily, it being impossible even to justify giving the say to an impartial public tribunal in order to preserve stability. If, however, it is possible to import a degree of rigor into moral discourse, to limit indeterminacy, or to create binding moral principles, then the disobedient may be judged. But there is no reason to assume that the best or most justifiable judgment will be rendered by a public tribunal into whose hands the problem is consigned. Each has his own say. The best answer is the one with the most persuasive and coherent reasons supporting it or, perhaps, the one which is right.

But this answer may seem unsatisfactory. There are those who interpret any attempt to justify disobedience as a move which would logically preclude judgments from being taken. If the legitimacy of disobedience turns on questions of right and if these questions cannot be resolved with finality or certainty, is it possible to judge acts of disobedience at all? Who is to say who is right?

To begin with, there is an air of unreality and disingenuousness about the question, 'Who decides?' Stated baldly, it conjures up a situation where the contentions of the disobedient and the regime remain suspended in a relativist limbo; where, therefore, no decision can be made, no tribunal may act, and there is a consequent possibility of anarchy. Yet the reality is precisely the opposite: the fact is that the disobedient *will* be judged, anarchy *will* be prevented, and those who worry most about who is to decide will, as usual, succeed in rendering that question academic. Who will decide? Public tribunals will decide and they will not be much troubled by doubts about their right to make the decision. Nor are those who man the tribunals likely to be predisposed toward the disobedient. The real problem is not that a moral defense of disobedience will foreclose action and prevent judgment, but, on the contrary, that it will be ignored. It is that traditional views of rights will automatically be upheld, that the challenge raised by the disobedient will be dismissed on conventionalist grounds, that the dilemma of disobedience will be glossed over. The real question is not, 'Who decides?' but, 'How may the inevitable decisions be made fair and just?'

I do not wish to convey the impression that judgment by public tribunal is arbitrary. It may be far from an ideal solution but there is no need to assume that a defense of disobedience entails a blueprint for utopia or that we suspend judgment until a final truth is discovered or a universal consensus reached. Conflict over rights will likely persist and societies are not so organized that conclusions regarding obligations can always be left to individual decision. Therefore, where a society is basically defensible, a prudent regard for preserving both the social tie and the traditions of orderly political discourse make the assignment of the judging function to a relevant public tribunal an adequate response to necessity. The right of the tribunal to judge exists, but conditionally, and is justifiable not in the abstract, but where it is exercised properly.

What are the conditions of its exercise? Some traditional answers spring instantly to mind. The tribunal ought to be independent of those charged with the making and enforcement of laws. Its decisions ought to be guided, insofar as possible, by a set of actually operative legal or constitutional provisions safeguarding basic rights. Clearly, the adequacy of the conception of rights upon which decisions are based is critical. In the absence of an adequate constitutional conception of rights, the fairest and most independent body could not for a moment be counted upon to render defensible judgments. Third, the tribunal must be one which habitually avoids deciding any but the narrow questions put before it. Fourth, the decision should as far as possible be rational: that is, based upon reasons. Fifth, the decisionmaking process should be public and the disobedient's right to argue and defend his conduct fairly guaranteed.

But these requirements, although valid, are not enough. To make decisions about disobedience functions of a public tribunal is in a real sense to make the regime a judge of its own performance. Such a situation is hardly ideal and its justification by prudence and necessity gives the public tribunal something less than a clear moral title to judge. To make good that title, the tribunal must recognize the conditional nature of its right to judge and act on that recognition. That is, it may exercise its right to judge and evaluate the claims of the disobedient, but it must exercise that right with restraint and modesty. It must recognize the profound moral dilemmas raised by an act of disobedience and the tenuous nature of its own authority to resolve them. It must assume that the questions of right are not closed, that, as a public tribunal, it bears as serious a responsibility to the disobedient as to the regime and its laws. Its judgment ought to reflect the perplexities and uncertainties of the situation.

That there are serious uncertainties in this situation must by now be clear. Argument over disobedience is frequently argument over obligations whose validity is not exactly beyond contravention. Quite often, they are the subject of widespread and profound dispute. The obligations formally to proclaim one's loyalty to the regime, to support practices which perpetuate the existence of gross inequalities, or to serve in an aggressive war, are examples of duties against which powerful rational arguments have been raised and which are or have been taken to be invalid by a significant portion of the population. Even if we would not agree that such obligations are invalid, it is possible to agree that they are the subject of more than ordinary dispute and that no tribunal can impose sanctions for their violation with the same degree of assurance it could with respect to, say, murder. Now the sanctions imposed for violation of law are justified not by the mere existence of a law, but by the validity of the obligation that law imposes. Where the validity of an obligation is unclear, ought a tribunal to impose sanctions? Perhaps it may where it considers the need to uphold the particular law so imperative that it overrides the doubts as to its validity. But such situations are uncommon. Given the tenuous nature of the tribunal's authority, the conversion of politics to bargaining, and the crude authoritarian biases that often color our understanding of politics, may a tribunal faced with a law whose validity is disputable not assume that its right to enforce that law is somewhat compromised? May it not assume that the doubts raised and the conditions in which they arise require it to exercise its authority with greater than normal restraint?

A tribunal acting on such assumptions will adopt a more permissive attitude toward disobedience. It will recognize that *it should impose sanctions for breach of an obligation only where it is abundantly clear that the obligation involved is justifiable.* Rather than assume that doubt is an inconvenience to be put aside as expeditiously as possible, it would welcome doubt as a factor in its decision and would consider what a doubtful obligation means when weighed against the act of disobedience.

Let us turn once again to the United States and ask what such a recommendation might mean. It should mean that the courts – the public tribunals in question – must be more willing than they are at present to review and invalidate laws imposing obligations. Courts tend not to overturn the actions of legislatures unless there are clear and compelling reasons for doing so. This, of course, creates a tendency to strike the balance, in cases of serious disputes over rights, in favor of the regime and against the individual disobedient. The burden of this book is that this balance should be struck the other way – that courts should be willing, in appropriate cases, to give the individual disobedient the benefit of a substantial doubt and *to hold obligations invalid where serious questions regarding their validity appear, rather than holding them valid until convincing arguments against them can be put forward.* This permissiveness, this widening of the boundaries of legitimate disobedience, is nothing less than the consideration courts owe the citizens of a democracy.

No doubt this suggestion will perturb those advocates of judicial restraint who conceive that restraint to be merely a brake on court invalidation of legislation. They believe that, as the legislature is the chief representative authority and as it is charged with primary responsibility to resolve complex and difficult social problems, there should be limits on a court's control over legislative action. In cases where the legislature's action is of doubtful validity, a court ought not to arrogate to itself the sole right to decide what the constitution implies. Recognizing its limited role in a democratic society, it ought to defer to the judgment of the elected representatives of the people except where it is convinced that that judgment is clearly beyond their rightful capacity. Hence, whenever an issue is really doubtful, the benefit of the doubt goes to the legislature. To grant to the courts the right to invalidate legislation merely on grounds of doubt is to subvert the primary role of the legislature and to arrogate to the courts a function they cannot and ought not to fulfill.

Such a theory would be plausible where the question involved only the authority of court and legislature and where a reasonable balance had to be struck between them. But of course there are not only two parties involved, but three – the third being the body of citizens from whom the legislature derives its authority and whose passive role in the process of conflict resolution is defined by necessity, not principle. For the fact of the matter is that in a democracy public authority cannot be assumed to repose only in elected officials. One of the things that differentiates democracies from other forms of government is that, in a democracy, citizenship is not a private status but a public office. It is through an act of delegation from the citizenry that a legislature receives its authority in the first place. The democratic citizen is the author, if not of public right, then at least of the capacities of the legislature to deal with issues affecting public right. In consistently deferring to the judgment of the legislature, a court necessarily considers the views of only one segment of public authority. But should it not also consider the demands and opinions of the citizens of society whose agents the legislators are? There is a second side to judicial restraint. That side is the obligation the judge has, not merely to the legislature, but to the community to which he is ultimately responsible and to which he owes his final allegience. The capacity to consider the arguments against the legislature and to weigh them as the demands of another order of public authority; the capacity of the court to represent that other order when no one else is there to; the capacity of the judges to refuse to arrogate to themselves the power to make all final decisions, but to be willing at times to defer to the demands of a citizenry intent upon claiming its rights – these also are aspects of judicial restraint and adjudication in a democracy.

This deference to citizen demands is analogous to Learned Hand's belief that where a case requires the making of a moral judgment – such as whether one who performed euthenasia on his blind, deaf-mute, idiot son met the test of 'good moral character' required for naturalization[2] – the judge ought not to impose his own moral convictions but should apply those of the community. Of course this raises formidable questions. How are the moral convictions of the community to be determined? Are we concerned with the convictions of ordinary people, of a majority, of those 'whom the social mind would rank as intelligent and virtuous'?[3] I pass over these because it is not my purpose to recommend that courts test the views on the obligations before them at the bar of public opinion. I mention the point only to suggest that it is not unique in modern legal theory for courts to think themselves bound to defer to the convictions or demands of a community.

Where the legislature seeks to impose an obligation upon a community, and where the articulated demands of a significant portion of that community suggest widespread disagreement with legislative conclusions, and where the court is in doubt as to the validity of that obligation, the court owes no greater duty to defer to the judgment of the legislature than it does to the judgment of the community. There is simply no reason to suppose that democratic theory requires deference to one element of public authority rather than to another, especially where that other is, formally anyhow, higher. It is legitimate, in appropriate cases, for a court to rely on values widely held in the community, values which represent not the private vision of a single disobedient, but the public views of a citizenry.

In a deeper sense, a court may represent the citizenry even without consulting it and even acting against its will where it articulates and develops or protects rights which ultimately enlarge the scope of civility. As a court gives legitimacy to certain values, it may work to produce a more viable common life or to realize more fully the conditions of obligation. In the American system, this form of representation is justified when legitimizing a particular objection to an obligation or upholding a particular law will, in the long run, create a more civil and more democratic society. Obviously, I do not insist that courts always do this, that it is always wise, or that we can read the long run with precision. I am fully aware of the elitist and even authoritarian implications of this view. Yet, imbedded in a context of conflicting and representative institutions, alive to the pulls and pressures of the complex political process of which it is a part, a court may, in imposing its own values, formed under the guidance of constitutional traditions and representative experience, in fact promote ultimately democratic values. We have sound empirical evidence that this has, at times, happened (for example, under the Warren court). Naturally, we cannot be certain that a court's action will have this effect. We must occasionally take a chance, hedging that chance in with appropriate formal and informal restrictions. But a court speaks most truly for a community where it protects the rights of the common life.

But the issue of judicial restraint is a side issue and it should not deflect attention from my main point. That point is that a tribunal's authority to decide the validity of a contested obligation is contingent upon its exercising its authority with restraint and that one of the things this restraint implies is a more permissive attitude toward disobedience. In the end, we ought never to forget that disobedience in the name of rights is a fruitful and legitimate way of pursuing the values of the common life and, as such, requires greater protection than is customarily given it. To argue for a more permissive attitude in judging disobedience is only to remind ourselves that those who decide whether an act of disobedience is right or not are not infallible. Where serious questions of right are raised, a strict legalistic attitude toward disobedience may prejudice the realization of rights and expand the prerogatives of authority beyond their proper bounds. A more permissive attitude toward disobedience is neither a reflection of weakness nor an invitation to instability. It is a token of the regime's good faith in the pursuit of common goals, a reflection of its commitment seriously and conscientiously to explore the moral basis of our social life.

Notes to the text

Chapter 1: The setting, pages 3–21

1   I do not mean to imply that civility was the only argument relied upon or that there was (or is) universal agreement among liberals on this issue. But it seems to me to be a fair statement of an important and representative liberal position and it raises an important – to me, central – issue in modern liberal theory.

2   Here I follow the argument of C. B. MacPherson, *The Political Theory of Possessive Individualism* (Oxford: Oxford University Press, 1962), pp. 197–221.

3   Cf. John Hallowell, *The Moral Foundations of Democracy* (Chicago: University of Chicago Press, 1954), chap. 2.

4   Few writers have stated this point with greater certainty than Seymour Lipset. See *Political Man* (Garden City: Doubleday, 1963), p. 440 and chap. 13 *passim*.

5   Peter Townsend, *Observer* (24 Feb. 1963), p. 10; quoted in Brian Barry, *Political Argument* (New York: Humanities Press, 1965), p. 151.

6   Lipset, *Political Man*, p. 439.

7   Morris Cohen, 'Property and Sovereignty', *Cornell Law Quarterly*, XIII (Dec. 1927), 13.

8   An excellent discussion of these powers is found in Grant McConnell, *Private Power and American Democracy* (New York: Knopf, 1966), pp. 196–335, upon much of which I have obviously relied.

Chapter 2: Traditional justifications of obligation: a critique, pages 22–62

1   Joseph Tussman, *Obligation and the Body Politic* (New York: Oxford University Press, 1960), pp. 135–8.

2   H. L. A. Hart, *The Concept of Law* (Oxford: Oxford University Press, 1961), pp. 181–95.

3   Morris Ginsburg, *On Justice in Society* (Baltimore: Penguin, 1965), p. 43.

4   H. B. Acton, 'Political Justification', in H. D. Lewis (ed.), *Contemporary British Philosophy* (London: Allen & Unwin, 1956), sect. 4.

5   Locke, *Second Treatise*, par. 22.

6   *Ibid.* par. 131.

7   Hanna Pitkin, 'Obligation and Consent – I', *American Political Science Review*, LIX (Dec. 1965), 996.

8   Cambridge: Harvard University Press, 1971. For the sake of convenience, page references to this book will, in this discussion, appear in parentheses in the text rather than in notes.

9   See the excellent discussion of Rawls' 'capitalist economic rationality' in C. B. MacPherson, *Democratic Theory* (Oxford: Clarendon Press, 1973), pp. 87–94.

10   Tussman, *Obligation and the Body Politic*, p. 36.

11   Peter Laslett has challenged this conclusion but, I think, unsuccessfully. See his 'Market Society and Political Theory' (*Historical Journal* [1964], VII, i) and the rejoinder by MacPherson in *Democratic Theory*, pp. 207–23.

Chapter 3: Civility and obligation, pages 63–83

1   This paragraph and the next are based on arguments made by Ortega and Michael Polanyi. For extended treatment of this concept, see Ortega's *Revolt of the Masses* (New York: Norton, 1957), chap. 8; and Polanyi's *Personal Knowledge* (New York: Harper & Row, 1964), chap. 7.

2   Robert J. Pranger, *The Eclipse of Citizenship* (New York: Holt, Rinehart & Winston, 1968), pp. 42–6.

3   *Ibid.* p. 45.

4   Polanyi, *Personal Knowledge*, p. 219.

5   *Ibid.* p. 222.

6   I shall argue in the next chapter that these causes constitute the basic rights of the common life.

Chapter 4: The conditions of obligation, pages 84–142

1   Herbert McClosky, 'Consensus and Ideology in American Politics', *American Political Science Review*, LVIII (June 1964), 361-82; Berelson, *et al., Voting* (Chicago: University of Chicago Press, 1954), chap. 14; Lipset, *Political Man*, pp. 14–16. Truman, Key, and Dahl all stress the importance of a 'consensus of elites' or agreement among the activists or leaders. David Truman, 'The American System in Crisis', *Political Science Quarterly* (Dec. 1959), pp. 481–97; V. O. Key, Jr, *Public Opinion and the American Democracy* (New York: Knopf, 1961), p. 558; Robert A. Dahl, *Who Governs?* (New Haven: Yale University Press, 1961), pp. 311–25.

2   Dahl, *Who Governs?*, p. 225.

3   See Jack Walker, 'A Critique of the Elitist Theory of Democracy', *American Political Science Review*, LX (June 1966), 285, and the studies cited therein.

4   Lewis Lipsitz, 'Work-Life and Political Attitudes', *American Polit-*

ical Science Review, LVIII (Dec. 1964), 961–2.

5   Carole Pateman, *Participation and Democratic Theory* (Cambridge: Cambridge University Press, 1970), p. 53, citing Lipsitz; R. Blauner, *Freedom and Alienation* (Chicago: University of Chicago Press, 1964); C. Argyris, *Personality and Organization* (New York: Harper, 1957) and *Integrating the Individual and the Organization* (New York: John Wiley, 1964).

6   *The Civic Culture* (Boston and Toronto: Little Brown, 1965), pp. 294–7.

7   On this latter point, Beatrice Webb's comments are illuminating. She criticized the Guild Socialist movement on the grounds that it would lead to the 'the extension and strengthening of state bureaucracy – a form of government which the Syndicalists and Guild Socialists were intent on superceding' (Margaret I. Cole [ed.], *Beatrice Webb's Diaries, 1924–1932* [London: Longmans, Green, 1956], p. 91). Earlier, she noted acidly that syndicalism had 'taken the place of old-fashioned marxism. The angry youth, with bad complexion, frowning brow and weedy figure, is now always a Syndicalist . . .' (Margaret I. Cole [ed.], *Beatrice Webb's Diaries, 1912–1924* [London: Longmans, Green, 1952], p. 7).

8   On this point, see Pateman's discussion (pp. 67–102) and Roger Garaudy, *The Crisis in Communism* (tr. by Peter and Betty Ross; New York: Grove Press, 1972), pp. 140–87.

9   See R. H. Tawney, *The Acquisitive Society* (London: G. Bell, 1952), p. 122; Samuel Hobson, *Pilgrim to the Left* (London: Edward Arnold, 1938), pp. 226–30; Charles L. Mowat, *Britain Between the Wars, 1918–1940* (London: Methuen, 1955), pp. 508–12.

10 See, generally, Pateman, *Participation and Democratic Theory*, pp. 85–102.

11 H. L. A. Hart, 'Are There Any Natural Rights?' *Philosophical Review*, LXIV (April 1955), 175.

12 *Ibid.* p. 190.

13 Robert Paul Wolff, *In Defense of Anarchism* (New York: Harper & Row, 1970).

14 Kant, *Philosophy of Law* (tr. Hastie; Edinburgh: Clark, 1887), p. 56.

15 Kant rests his argument on the general impossibility of successful resistance to the state: 'For whoever would restrict the supreme power of the State must have more, or, at least, equal power, as compared with the power that is to be restricted; and if competent to command the subjects to resist, such a one would also have to be able to protect them, and if he is to be considered capable of judging what is right in every case he may also publicly order resistance. But such a one, and not the actual authority, would then be the supreme power; which is contradictory' (*Ibid.* p. 175).

16 Isaiah Berlin, 'Two Concepts of Liberty', *Four Essays on Liberty* (Oxford: Oxford University Press, 1969), p. 133.

17 *Ibid.* p. 124.

18 Hannah Arendt, *The Origins of Totalitarianism* (2nd ed.; Cleveland: World, 1958), p. 296.

19 Arendt, *The Human Condition* (Chicago: University of Chicago Press, 1958), pp. 198–9.

20 *Ibid.* p. 199.

21 Arendt, *Origins*, pp. 290–302.

22 See chapter 6.

23 Lipsitz, 'Work-Life and Political Attitudes', p. 961.

24 R. H. Tawney, *Equality* (4th ed.; London: Allen & Unwin, 1952), p. 67.

25 *Ibid.* p. 210.

26 R. H. Tawney, *Recent Thoughts on the Government of Industry* (Manchester: Manchester University Press, 1920), p. 8. The argument that investors are entitled to interest only is made in greater depth in *The Acquisitive Society*, pp. 123–6.

27 See Robert Heilbroner, *The Limits of American Capitalism* (New York: Harper & Row, 1967), Part I, esp. pp. 28–35.

28 A. A. Berle, Jr, 'Constitutional Limitations on Corporate Activity – Protection of Personal Rights from Invasion through Economic Power', *University of Pennsylvania Law Review*, c (1952); Arthur S. Miller, 'The Constitutional Law of the "Security State" ', *Stanford Law Review*, x (July 1958).

29 Berle, 'Constitutional Limitations', p. 943.

30 See, e.g., *Burton* v. *Wilmington Parking Authority*, 365 U.S. 715 (1961) (privately-owned restaurant leasing space in city-owned garage building); *Hampton* v. *City of Jacksonville*, 304 F. 2d 320 (CA 5, 1962), *cert. den.* 371 U.S. 911 (1962) (city-owned golf courses sold to private parties with reversionary clause insuring continued use as golf courses); *Derrington* v. *Plummer*, 240 F. 2d 922 (CA 5, 1956) (privately-owned cafeteria leasing space in county courthouse).

31 See, e.g., *Marsh* v. *Alabama*, 326 U.S. 501 (1946) (first amendment held applicable to company town); *Steele* v. *Louisville & N.R.R.*, 323 U.S. 192 (1944) (fourteenth amendment held applicable to trade union which is 'statutory representative of a craft'); and cases cited in note 30.

32 Henry Simons, *Economic Policy for a Free Society* (1948), quoted in Michael Oakeshott, 'The Political Economy of Freedom', *Rationalism in Politics* (New York: Basic Books, 1962), p. 57.

33 Even contemporary Marxists are discovering the importance of the market. See, e.g., Svetozar Stojanovic, *Between Ideals and Reality* (tr. by Gerson S. Sher; New York, London, and Toronto: Oxford University Press, 1973), chap. 6, esp. pp. 130–4.

34 Wolff, *In Defense of Anarchism*, p. 81.

35 Theodore J. Lowi, *The End of Liberalism* (New York: Norton, 1969), pp. 297–310.

36   Lowi is hardly alone in deploring the breadth and vagueness of recent delegations. See, e.g., Kenneth C. Davis, *Administrative Law Treatise* (St Paul: West Publishing Co., 1958), pp. 87–101, 148–58, and *Supplement* (1970), pp. 62–6, 76–8; Henry J. Friendly, *The Federal Administrative Agencies* (Cambridge: Harvard University Press, 1962), pp. 7, 21–2.
37   Lowi, *The End of Liberalism*, p. 298.
38   *Ibid.* p. 299.
39   Norton E. Long, 'Public Policy and Administration', *Public Administration Review*, XIV (Winter 1954), 29–31.
40   See *Selected References: Decentralization and Neighborhood Government* (New York: Urban Analysis Center, CUNY, 1972).

Chapter 5: The right to disobey, pages 145–168

1   H. A. Bedau lists eight definitions of civil disobedience which are all, in some way, inconsistent with each other or otherwise unsatisfactory. Bedau (ed.), *Civil Disobedience* (New York: Pegasus, 1969), pp. 217–28.
2   The rights I refer to are those outlined in chapter 4.
3   Lewis S. Feuer, 'We Should Distinguish between Disobedience and Resistance', in Bedau, *Civil Disobedience*, p. 204 (originally part of a symposium on civil disobedience published in *The New York Times Magazine*, 26 Nov. 1967).
4   A somewhat similar argument – that potential draft resisters should do nothing until they are personally ordered to do an immoral act – was presented by Judge Charles Wyzanski, Jr, in 'On Civil Disobedience', *The Atlantic Monthly*, CCXXI (Feb. 1968).
5   Michael Walzer, 'The Obligation to Disobey', *Ethics* LXXVII (1967), 171.
6   John Rawls, 'The Justification of Civil Disobedience', Bedau, *Civil Disobedience*, pp. 240–55. A similar argument is made by Rawls in *A Theory of Justice*, pp. 371–7.
7   Franz Neumann, 'On the Limits of Justifiable Disobedience', *The Democratic and the Authoritarian State* (Glencoe: Free Press, 1964), p. 156.

Chapter 6: The varieties of disobedience, pages 169–200

1   Abe Fortas, *Concerning Dissent and Civil Disobedience* (New York: New American Library, 1968), p. 63.
2   James Harvey Robinson, *The Mind in the Making* (New York: Harper, 1950; first published 1921), pp. 179–93.
3   Bedau, *Civil Disobedience*, p. 22.

Chapter 7: Stability revisited, pages 201–219

1 Richard Wasserstrom, 'The Obligation to Obey the Law', *U.C.L.A. Law Review*, X (May 1963), quoted in Bedau, *Civil Disobedience*, p. 258.
2 See, e.g., Marcus Singer, *Generalization in Ethics* (New York: Knopf, 1961), pp. 149–50.
3 Although this argument is rarely made in such absolute form, it is made occasionally with regard to democratic government. See, e.g., Louis Waldman, 'Civil Rights – Yes: Civil Disobedience – No', *New York State Bar Journal*, XXXVII (Aug. 1965), 331.
4 Fortas, *Concerning Dissent and Civil Disobedience*, p. 30 (emphasis in original).
5 Robert Paul Wolff, 'On Violence', *Journal of Philosophy*, LXVI (Oct. 1969), 601.
6 Hobbes, *Leviathan* (Oxford: Blackwell, 1957), p. 82.
7 Ortega, *Revolt of the Masses*, pp. 74–5.

Chapter 8: Permissiveness and restraint, pages 220–229

1 Oakeshott, 'The Political Economy of Freedom', pp. 54–8.
2 *Repouille* v. *United States*, 165 F. 2d 152 (CA 2, 1947).
3 Benjamin Cardozo, *The Paradoxes of Legal Science* (New York: Columbia University Press, 1928), p. 37.

Index

accountability: administrative policy controllers as mode of promoting, 138; as condition of obligation, 127-41; decentralization of industry as mode of promoting, 134-7; and disobedience, 130; imposed by market system, 135-6; imposition on bureaucracy, 137-41; imposition on corporation, 131-7; and law of delegation, 137; meaning of, 127-8; and participation, 129, 138-40; senses of, 128-9

Acton, H. B., 35, 230

administrative process: formality in, 137-8; public participation in, 138-40; values and expertise in, 139

Almond, Gabriel, 90

apathy: causes of, 88-90, 92; as limit on freedom, 105ff; and work environment, 89-90, 92

Arendt, Hannah, 120, 121, 233

Argyris, C., 232

Augustine, 23-4, 66, 98

autonomy, 100-4

barbarism, 66, 67-8, 81

Barker, Ernest, 76

Barry, Brian, 230

Bedau, H. A., 190, 234, 235

Bentham, Jeremy, 31, 33

Berelson, Bernard, 231

Berle, A. A., 133, 233

Berlin, Isaiah, 102-3, 110, 232

Blake, William, 95

Blauner, R., 232

bureaucracy: decentralization of, 141; imposing accountability on, 137-41; see also administrative process

Burke, Edmund, 77-8

Burton v. Wilmington Parking Authority, 233

Cardozo, Benjamin, 235

Christianity, 23-4

citizenship: and common life, 84-5,

93; as condition of obligation, 84-97; and integrative rights, 121-2; and participation, 87; as public office, 87; requiring presumption of rationality, 95-7; and self-government, 85;

civility: as attempt to conquer violence, 213-14, 215; and common life, 69; and culture, 65-9; in Hobbes and Locke, 4-6; and liberalism, 3-4; meaning for group politics, 15; and new public authority, 15; and social disintegration, 65; see also culture of civility

Cohen, Morris, 18, 230

Cole, Margaret I., 232

common life: as basis of obligation, 70-4; citizenship as element of, 84-5; and civility, 69; defined, 83; equality of participation in, 72; and juridical man, 73-4, 93-4; and mass society, 83; nature of claims on individual, 80-2; and political education, 81; and presumption of rationality, 96-7; relation to culture of civility, 69, 70, 74, 81-2; relation of equality to, 117-23; relation to self-government, 86-7; as requiring accountability, 127; as requiring equality, 112, 113, 115-16; as requiring freedom, 70, 72-3, 74, 98-9

community: authoritative concept of, 78; in Burke, 77-8; convivial concept of, 79-80; in Rousseau, 78-80

consent: as account of obligation, 37-62; and civic religion, 55-6; commonsense basis of, 37-8; to democratic procedures as limiting right to disobey, 165-6; distinguished from self-government, 85-7; and egoism, 58; and equality, 61; exclusivity of consenting population, 60-2; and liberty, 60-2; limits on, in Locke, 41-3; and natural law, 42-3; reasons for, as

237